C000176693

Tom McCarthy
Critical Essays

GYLPHI CONTEMPORARY WRITERS: CRITICAL ESSAYS

SERIES EDITOR: SARAH DILLON

Gylphi Contemporary Writers: Critical Essays presents a new approach to the academic study of living authors. The titles in this series are devoted to contemporary British, Irish and American authors whose work is popularly and critically valued but on whom a significant body of academic work has yet to be established. Each of the titles in this series is developed out of the best contributions to an international conference on its author; represents the most intelligent and provocative material in current thinking about that author's work; and, suggests future avenues of thought, comparison and analysis. With each title prefaced by an author foreword, this series embraces the challenges of writing on living authors and provides the foundation stones for future critical work on significant contemporary writers.

Series Titles

David Mitchell: Critical Essays (2011)
Edited by Sarah Dillon. Foreword by David Mitchell.

Maggie Gee: Critical Essays (2015)
Edited by Sarah Dillon and Caroline Edwards. Foreword by Maggie Gee.

China Miéville: Critical Essays (2015)
Edited by Caroline Edwards and Tony Venezia. Foreword by China Miéville.

Adam Roberts: Critical Essays (2016)
Edited by Christos Callow Jr. and Anna McFarlane. Foreword by Adam Roberts.

Rupert Thomson: Critical Essays (2016)
Edited by Rebecca Pohl and Christopher Vardy. Foreword by Rupert Thomson.

Tom McCarthy: Critical Essays (2016)
Edited by Dennis Duncan. Foreword by Tom McCarthy.

Tom McCarthy
Critical Essays

edited by
Dennis Duncan

Gylphi

A *Gylphi Limited* Book

First published in Great Britain in 2016
by Gylphi Limited

Copyright © Gylphi Limited, 2016

A CIP catalogue record for this book is available from the British Library.

ISBN 978-1-78024-060-2 (pbk)
ISBN 978-1-78024-061-9 (Kindle)
ISBN 978-1-78024-062-6 (EPUB)

Design and typesetting by Gylphi Limited. Printed in the UK by ImprintDigital. com, Exeter.

Gylphi Limited
PO Box 993
Canterbury CT1 9EP, UK

For Claire

Contents

Acknowledgements

I would like to thank Anthony Levings at Gylphi and the Department of English and Humanities at Birkbeck, University of London, for their support in running the Tom McCarthy symposium back in 2011. In addition, I would like to thank Sarah Dillon, the Series Editor at Gylphi for her patience and advice in putting this book together.

Since this collection grew out of a public event at which many people not represented here shared their thoughts, both from the stage and in casual conversation, it is important to acknowledge their contribution in informing many of these chapters, in particular my own.

Finally, I would like to thank Tom McCarthy for his ongoing support and enthusiasm for this collection, and for providing the material which has provoked and inspired the discussions contained here.

List of Abbreviations

Abbreviations of cited works by Tom McCarthy:

R   McCarthy, Tom (2006) *Remainder*. London: Alma.*

T   McCarthy, Tom (2006) *Tintin and the Secret of Literature*. London: Granta.

MIS   McCarthy, Tom (2007) *Men in Space*. London: Alma.

C   McCarthy, Tom (2010) *C*. London: Jonathan Cape.

SI   McCarthy, Tom (2015) *Satin Island*. London: Jonathan Cape.

* As has been well-documented, *Remainder*'s original edition was published in a small run by the Paris-based Metronome Press in 2005. However, for ease of reference, the more accessible Alma text has been chosen for all citations here.

FOREWORD
ON BEING THE SUBJECT OF A CONFERENCE OR, WHAT DO I KNOW?

Tom McCarthy

Dennis Duncan asks me to write a few words about 'being the subject of a conference'. And it's true: I was. But 'subject' is a loaded term. It suggests some kind of psychoanalytical relation, and invites a grammatical query: subject *of*? Or subject *to*? And who's the *I* in this construction anyway? A body of work was being discussed, for sure – a set of relations, borrowings, re-activations or re-workings: *that* was the subject of the conference. But as the author (signatory, countersignatory, whatever) of that body, I was implicitly cast in the role of Lacan's 'subject supposed to know'. At the same time, the exact opposite was true: the speakers, scholars, authors of the papers, were the analysts in this session, while the work itself was on the couch. And, as every good Lacanian knows, the analysand knows nothing – or if they do know something, they don't know they know it. Montaigne wore a medallion bearing the words *Que sais-je*? I thought of turning up in a t-shirt with the same catchphrase ironed onto it, or at least its contemporary t-shirt-text equivalent: *What The Fuck Do I Know...* ?

   A writer, once the work is written (if not long before), becomes just another reader of the work – not necessarily a good one, and certainly not a reliable one. They can regale you with anecdotes about the work's production (the stuff they were going through or reading

1

at the time, the world-events that caught their imagination), but even if these anecdotes are true, their value is pretty limited. I finished the manuscript of *Remainder*, with its airline-hijack ending, weeks before September the 11th 2001; on the book's publication in 2005, several critics described it as a 'post 9/11 novel'. Were they wrong? I'm not sure. Maybe the *Aeneid*'s a post 9/11 novel too, with its accounts (already mediated) of a vehicle full of terrorists, or at least enemies of Troy, driving straight into the city, of people leaping from the tops of burning towers before the towers themselves collapse. I hadn't read Paul de Man's 'The Rhetoric of Temporality' when I wrote the book – but does that mean that his brilliant analysis of inauthenticity and repetition has no part to play in thinking about the hero's quandary? Of course not. But then I'm probably not the best person to do that thinking.

In a way, it's tempting to write that I felt like a ghost, or maybe zombie, at the conference. But even that would be romantic, not to mention self-aggrandising: ghosts, returning to the place that's been laid for them but in which they're not meant to actually sit, play a dramatic and subversive role. An author, though, is more like a by- or waste-product of the work, and of literature in general. There are probably author-clusters, author-patches, floating idly around the Pacific Ocean. If I were to get really Lacanian about it, I'd have to put both 'Subject' and 'Being' under erasure, or render them as struck-through symbols in some crazy algebraic sequence. But even that's a side-show. The psychoanalytic phenomenon that was actually, palpably in play for me at the *Calling All Agents* conference was pleasure – pleasure that these excellent papers had been written, that they intersected, however tangentially, with my name. Pleasure, and anxiety too – both a personal one and an exhilarating awareness of participating in the collective anxiety towards meaning that all earnest thinking, all committed cultural production, represents. And, as we've all known since even earlier than Lacan (if we can imagine such a time), anxiety and pleasure are not that far apart.

London 2015

1

INTRODUCTION
CALLING ALL AGENTS

Dennis Duncan

'To proclaim a manifesto you have to want: A. B. C., thunder against
1, 2, 3, lose your patience and sharpen your wings to conquer and
spread a's, b's c's little and big, sign, scream, swear, arrange the prose in
a form of absolute and irrefutable evidence'
— Tristan Tzara, 'Dada Manifesto'

Just under half of the essays in this collection have developed out of
papers given at a symposium, held at Birkbeck, University of London,
in 2011, while several others come from scholars who attended but
did not speak that day. Sitting at the back, quietly scribbling notes on
the conference programme, was Tom McCarthy. At the end of the
day, he took the stage to be grilled by the other attendees. In his subsequent novel, *Satin Island*, the narrator, a figure not unlike McCarthy
himself, experiences both a conference disaster – the tumbleweed
moment of the speech that evokes utter indifference in its audience –
and a rapturous fantasy of the conference paper as Orphic rite: 'The
atmosphere inside the auditorium was, by now – each time – ecstatic.
[...] The cheering would be so clamorous that I'd be forced to come
back time and again, to take another bow' (*SI*, 108–10). It is therefore

tempting to wonder whether McCarthy, always a voracious assimilator of literary criticism, might not now be ironically reflecting his own
commentators, shining back at us two versions of ourselves, of the way
we treat the writers we consider: the post-Barthesian author, a ghost
at the banquet, embarrassingly surplus to requirements, and getting
in the way of the real work of the critics; and the author-as-Messiah,
the reason we have all come together, treating the faithful to exclusive
wisdom from the pulpit of the conference stage. In his Foreword to
this collection, McCarthy describes his experience as the former; yet
from discussions with other attendees, and on the evidence of some
of the chapters collected here, it is clear that the author's presence,
and clarifying insights, were a valuable aspect of the symposium.

The event title, *Calling All Agents*, was intended as a reference to the
fact that in the five years between the publication of McCarthy's first
novel, *Remainder*, and his third, *C*, a scattered collection of academics
had begun to incorporate McCarthy's work into their teaching and research. The novels were starting to appear on university courses, both
undergraduate and postgraduate, in a variety of contexts: predictably
perhaps as an exemplar of contemporary British fiction, but also, for
example, as a figure in trauma writing. *Calling All Agents*, then, was an
attempt to bring these disparate voices together and into dialogue, to
see if a critical community could be formed from the scholars who
felt that there was something worth saying about McCarthy's work;
whether there were common strands in our approaches, whether we
were beating a path, an emergent discourse, together; or whether instead there was merely an explosion of unrelated tangents, each charting its own course. As this collection, I hope, shows, what emerged
was a body of scholarship which is both diverse and coherent: a pattern of threads which are varied but interwoven, or of different ways
into McCarthy's work which nevertheless cross each other continually.

At the same time, the conference drew its title from one of
McCarthy's early publications for the International Necronautical
Society (hereafter INS), the organization – part art project, part
secret society – which he founded with Simon Critchley in 1999.
Calling All Agents, then, was intended as a reminder of McCarthy's

parallel existence as a conceptual artist, and the relationship between this aspect of his work and his better-known life as a novelist.

The Novels

There will be more to say about the INS shortly. First, it will be useful to recap McCarthy's literary career so far. *Remainder*, now published by Alma in the UK and Vintage in the US, first appeared with the Paris-based Metronome Press in 2005. The publisher is important. *Metronome*, the brainchild of curator and anthropologist Clémentine Deliss, was an art magazine established in the mid-1990s. As a spin-off from its ninth issue, the magazine released a series of four paperback novels – *Remainder* being one – printed in small runs and sold via *Metronome*'s usual outlets – galleries and art bookshops. *Remainder*'s first edition then was limited to 750 copies, and the novel's roots were firmly in the art world. In spite of this, the work was seized upon by the literary press. The *London Review of Books*, an early adopter, devoted a full-length review essay to it, describing it as 'a very good novel indeed' (Soar, 2006: 27). The review also drew a link between *Remainder* and Georges Perec's masterpiece, *Life A User's Manual*, a novel whose action is set not over time, but across space: its chapters describe, in turn, what is happening – at a single moment – in each of the hundred rooms in a Parisian apartment building. The comparison is an astute one, and several of the contributors in this collection (in particular, Partington and Blacklock) explore in more depth the way that McCarthy's writing privileges the spatial over the realist novel's traditional concerns of character and motive.

In fact, concerning character, let us make a stronger claim: from *Remainder* onwards, novelistic character, in the form of an explicit and recognizable connection between situation and emotion, has been McCarthy's principal *bête noir*. In an interview with Lee Rourke, he argues,

> I don't necessarily want to be contrarian, it's just that in order to do what needs to be done you need to reject a certain set of assumptions, certain models of subjectivity – for example, the contemporary cult

5

of the individual, the absolute authentic self who is measured through his or her absolutely authentic feeling. (Rourke, 2010)

McCarthy's protagonists offer no emotional traction for the reader; rather, it is a cornerstone of his philosophical project that relatability must be scrupulously avoided. Anything less would be to betray the legacy of modernist experimentation: 'it's an ethical thing: to brush all this aside and to regress to sentimental humanism is almost like revisionism: it's the cultural analogue to historical revisionism, it's just ethically wrong' (Rourke, 2010). There is, of course, a veiled criticism here of the current state of literary fiction – that it has sold out its modernist forebears and failed to incorporate the intellectual developments of the last century. Thus, Zadie Smith's influential essay, 'Two Paths for the Novel', draws a contrast between McCarthy's knowing, theoretical resistance to character and the dominant mode of 'lyrical Realism' or 'what we have been taught to value in fiction' (Smith, 2008: 89).

McCarthy's second novel, *Men in Space*, occasionally seems like less of a new path than *Remainder*: less alien, less explicitly conceptual, the syntax of its interwoven plotlines more familiar. If it has the feel of a formative work, this is understandable – it was written in large part prior to *Remainder*, though published in the wake of that novel's success. Nevertheless, certain McCarthy touchstones are already in place – for example, in the affectlessness of the following passage, as Nick awaits his death on an Amsterdam rooftop:

> Nick looks down. The table at which Sasha and Han are sitting is on a tangent that's set off the diameter's plumb line by an angle of perhaps thirty degrees. It, too, seems slightly elongated. (*MIS*, 274)

Nick's narrated monologue is fixated purely on the external, purely on the present: a geometric description of the way his surroundings appear to him. In this instance, we might read it as a psychological effect: Nick's shock response to the enormity of his situation. In McCarthy's third novel, *C*, however, this planar, emotionally-blank way of seeing the world is expanded to become the protagonist's default psychological mode.

The first novel written entirely after McCarthy's literary break-through, *C* is significantly grander – longer, broader in scope – than either *Remainder* or *Men in Space*. It returns to and develops the themes of the earlier novels – the fixation with the spatial, the abandonment of novelistic character, but also the fascination with psychoanalysts Abraham and Torok, carried over from McCarthy's non-fiction *Tintin and the Secret of Literature*.

Like this work too, *C* is intimately concerned with the physical transmission of information – with code and telegraphy – and with communication's potential for distortion and failure. A mysterious echo of this theme accompanied *C*'s appearance on the Man Booker shortlist in 2010, when, on 6 October – a week before the winner was due to be announced – the bookmaker Ladbrokes suspended betting on the prize. Most of the British press covered the story, the *Guardian* reporting why the sudden rush to back McCarthy's novel had drawn the bookies' attention: '£15,000-worth of bets were placed on *C* on Wednesday morning, completely outstripping all earlier betting on the prize, which had previously totalled just £10,000 since the announcement of the longlist in July' (Page, 2010). The *Telegraph* meanwhile gave us the detail of the bets' suspicious uniformity: 'almost 1,000 bets at just under £20, all within a 24-hour period' (Ward, 2010). And yet the panel of judges insisted that they still had not yet reached a decision on the winner: this could not, apparently, be insider dealing. What then was its purpose? To influence the judges? To use the context of the prize, regardless of its eventual outcome, to buy some column inches for the novel, presenting it as something subversive? Even so, as an advertising ruse designed to shift hardback literary fiction, it would be unlikely to recoup the outlay involved. Was it then a conceptual art stunt, relegating both book and prize to epiphenomena, reducing them to simply the materials of a larger work, one which, like *C*, takes the operations of media and capital as its subjects, but which operates in far wider communication mechanisms – bigger narratives – than the narrow world of literary fiction usually can? It reminds us perhaps of the jolt we feel when Gatsby casually describes Meyer Wolfsheim as 'the man who fixed the World's Series back in 1919' (Fitzgerald, 1925/1953: 48). Yet, by this comparison, it brings us up against how small the world of high literature is, how little it takes to constitute a suspicious activity: a thousand twenty-pound bets. The model is not Wolfsheim after all, but rather the distributed denial of service attack: communication as destructive agent, a hack taken offline and onto the highstreet.

Last year, McCarthy published his fourth novel, *Satin Island*. Like *Remainder*, it is both shorter and more intellectually compact than *C* – an essay on the information age and the novelist's role in an era where our activity is already exhaustively logged and recorded. Because of its recent publication, *Satin Island* is only slimly represented in this collection. It is my expectation, however, that in the coming years it will be this novel, rather than the more self-consciously literary *C*, that will receive the kind of critical attention that *Remainder* has so far.

McCarthy's Project

The INS, both in its structure and its pronouncements, is both backward- and forward-facing. Its motto, *cras ingens iterabimus aequor* ['tomorrow we shall set out upon the vast ocean'], looks to tomorrow even as it recalls Horace. There is undeniably something deeply nostalgic about the INS: an homage to the avant-garde movements, the *-isms*, of the early twentieth century: Futurism, Dada, Surrealism, etc. And yet in its pronouncements the INS also consistently exhibits a mindfulness of the futility of this nostalgia. A press release from 2003, for example, announces the expulsion of certain members from INS First Committee:

> ----- ----- and ---- ------ are expelled as they have become complicit with a publishing industry whereby the 'writer' becomes merely the executor of a brief dictated by corporate market research, reasserting the certainties of middle-brow aesthetics ('issues' of 'contemporary culture', 'post-colonial identity' etc.) under the guise of genuine creative speculation. The INS Executive Council expresses some sympathy towards both ----- and ------, and recognizes that they had to write 'to order' in this way in order to be published by the corporate presses in the first place. However, their decision to do so renders them useless to the INS. (McCarthy, 2003)

Expulsions like this draw consciously on a model of Bretonian authoritarianism, but replayed here as rose-tinted pastiche: ironic, humorous, without either Surrealism's political urgency or Breton's autocratic paranoia. Although the expulsions were real, and the expelled necronauts genuinely surprised and hurt, the re-enactment of the modernist collective has a clubby mildness, a lack of cruelty, which marks it as different from the original. In the same press release, McCarthy jokingly refers to himself as 'Founder and surviving General Secretary', as though the 'purges' were a game, like reality show evictions: a regular round of culls where anyone's number might be up. This necessary gap – the awareness of the incapacity of the reconstruction to match the supposed authenticity of its idealized model – is a keynote of McCarthy's project as a whole, something which can be traced to his very earliest publications.

The necronauts' Founding Manifesto first appeared in 1999, a photocopied sheet which McCarthy would hand out at art fairs. At the height of the pre-millennial panic over the Y2K bug, it calmly declared that '[o]ur very bodies are no more than vehicles carrying us towards death. We are all necronauts, always, already.' *Always already*, these days the beyond-parody shibboleth of intellectual imposture, is knowingly, mercifully broken up here. The wink to Derrida is still in place, but the comma invites us to pause. It lets us know that this is more than mere imitative ticcing; it is a genuine statement about time, something for us to dwell on. The necronauts' project *is* both forwards- and backwards-looking, and yet that 'always, already' suggests an inherent futility in thinking of time in these terms at all. Rather it implies a rejection of both, a shuffling of Eliot's opening to 'Burnt Norton' so that, for the necronaut, time past and time future are both perhaps contained in time present.

The INS manifesto, on the one hand, is of course a nostalgic document. A reproduction, to mark its tenth anniversary, photoshops the document onto the front page of *The Times*, recalling Marinetti's 'Founding and Manifesto of Futurism' and its appearances in *La Gazetta dell'Emilia* and *Le Figaro* in February 1909. But as Mary Ann Caws (2001: xix) points out, a manifesto is 'a document of an ideology, crafted to convince and convert'. It has aims, intentions, and is thus intrinsically future-oriented. Zadie Smith's (2008: 94) comment, that the INS manifesto is 'intellectually agile, pompous, faintly absurd, invigorating, and not at all new' simply won't do to distinguish it from its early twentieth-century antecedents. These themselves only harked back to nineteenth-century models – to Whistler's 'Ten O'Clock' (1885) or Jean Moréas's 'Symbolist Manifesto' (1886) – and for all their bracing impetuosity, were nevertheless pompous, and faintly absurd. The Modernist manifestos were spoofs from the beginning – always, already – and yet, for the most invigorating manifestos, the trick, as Caws (2001: xxi) puts it, is to '[take] itself and its own spoof seriously'. The double-take of simultaneous parody and future-facing earnestness is not a new problem for McCarthy's re-enactments; it is inherent in the form of the manifesto.

The points at which the statements of the INS take themselves most seriously – where the ironic surplus becomes almost negligible – are the moments when it sets out to critique contemporary aesthetics. The 'Joint Statement on Inauthenticity' for example, demands that those narrative staples – 'cults of authenticity' – in which 'the lonely hero, in death, is rewarded with authentic being' must be abandoned (McCarthy and Critchley, 2007). The nostalgia here is for an idealized era of both aesthetic and political rigour, and for an urgency in reconciling the two. More broadly, it is thus a nostalgia for an age of ideology – a belief that both the political and the aesthetic might proceed from the same theoretical first principles.

It is this sense of a *project*, expressed from the very outset and grander than any individual piece, which is most exciting about McCarthy's work – the idea that a coherent design connects his oeuvre as a whole, developing from that first statement of intent in the founding document of the INS, and anticipating McCarthy's work still to come. Drawing its power from manifesto culture, McCarthy's oeuvre is both serious enough to be ambitious – to want to be influential, to impact and change the work of others in its wake – and canny enough to remember how the avant-gardes of the last century fizzled into co-option and commodification. It is no surprise that the true hero of the INS is Wile E. Coyote 'who, like a true necronaut, dies almost without noticing, again and again' (McCarthy and Critchley, 2007).

Engaging with a Pre-Theorized Literature

In an interview in the early 1950s, long after Surrealism's heyday, Breton was invited to look back on the relationship between Surrealism and psychoanalysis. Becoming agitated he responded:

> Psychoanalysis had no secrets for the Surrealist painters and poets from the beginning, so that on many occasions they consciously played with the sexual symbolism attached to it. Thus it was a ridiculous business when that psychiatrist recently gave a series of public lectures at the Sorbonne attempting to submit the works of Max Ernst, Dalí and Brauner to the same investigations, and draw the same conclusions about their creators, as if they had never heard of Freud before executing them. (Breton, 1952: 258)

They had read Freud; they knew his symbolic vocabulary; they drew on it on purpose: therefore, identifying these symbols does not constitute a critique. One thinks of this when we consider what a critical work on McCarthy might look like and what it might accomplish. McCarthy's writing abounds in references to a tight canon of literary and critical touchstones, such that even the shortest work will contain, almost as a rule, an allusion to one or more of the following: Blanchot, Tintin, Cocteau's *Orphée*, the psychoanalysts Abraham and Torok, and a handful of others. Sometimes these references are explicit, but often they take the form of buried homage, as in the following scene from *Remainder*. Here the narrator is aghast to discover that the pianist he has hired to practise the same piece, day after day, deliberately making mistakes, has been using a recording in order to slip away unnoticed:

> The piano music was still spilling from his flat into the sunlit stairwell.
> 'I had an audition,' he stammered.
> 'Then who…' I asked.
> 'Recording,' he said, his eyes still moping at the floor.
> 'But there are mistakes in it!' I said. 'And loopbacks, and…'

11

'A recording of me. I made it myself, especially. It's the same thing, more or less. Isn't it?' (*R*, 147)

The scene is a re-enactment of the moment in Hergé's *The Castafiore Emerald* (1961–2) when Igor Wagner, accompanist to the opera singer Bianca Castafiore, is rumbled for being absent from his piano while the music plays on:

Tintin: Great snakes! A battery tape-recorder! It's a playback of his own scales! But what's it in aid of?…

Wagner: Oh, yes, the tape-recorder… Look, you must promise not to tell Signora Castafiore. I worked out a plan so I could get some fresh air from time to time. She keeps me at the piano all day long, you know, and… (Hergé, 1963: 54)

But what does this tell us, other than that McCarthy likes Tintin and that McCarthy likes restagings, both of which barely warrant a mention? Eric Langley's *tour de force* presentation at the conference was encyclopedic in showing the extraordinary frequency with which McCarthy revisits the Tintin series, using it a seedbed for everything from plot devices to the names of ships. In its exhaustiveness, however, it demonstrated that this avenue is now closed, that McCarthy's debt to Hergé must simply be taken as a given; his use of the Tintin books incessant, everyday. There is little real critical traction to be gained from identifying McCarthy's influences when these influences are so clearly and consistently telegraphed. These allusions function rather like dinosaur bones in the Creationist cosmogony: references planted, in the upper layers of the text, to test us by their illusion of depth. We must resist.

A more productive analytical approach then might be to look, not to the works' obvious intertexts from psychoanalysis and continental theory, but instead to consider their apparent moments of slippage. At the conference, McCarthy was asked about the illegal chess move which occurs at the end of *C*. What did it mean? He laughed; he didn't know about it; it must have been a mistake. Now it becomes interesting. With this denial of authorial intentionality – the refusal to serve up a readymade interpretation – the text now leaves space for the critic: the sheen of lyrical performance is momentarily ruptured, offering a glimpse of its underlying machinery. Andrew Gibson, in his chapter here, considers McCarthy's work as a mode of formalism – an examination of systems, replacing the Novel's classical concerns of plot, character, psychology, event. For Gibson, errata are thus an integral part of McCarthy's project: 'in his cunning [he] is aware that any given formalism may be subject to a glitch, like the uncorrected spelling errors that appear in the book [C] itself'.

Gibson also considers how we might situate McCarthy's work in relation to his contemporaries. Arguing that the tradition into which he best fits is 'a recent, European, intellectual tradition perhaps not best defined as strictly a tradition of the novel at all', Gibson tentatively allies McCarthy – if not quite aligning him – with the philosophers of the Speculative Realist current, coining the provocative term New Inhumanisms (reclaiming the inhuman from James Wood's notably pejorative usage) to encompass their common philosophical and aesthetic endeavours (Wood, 2000). This phrase echoes in Nick Lavery's chapter on representations of the 'post-human' in *Remainder*, yet in Lavery's analysis the *human* can be read more simply as the 'autonomous, rational subject' existing in a material world which is distinct from it. Lavery's essay, which traces 'the breakdown of the human' in the 'instability and incoherence' of *Remainder*'s protagonist, thus serves as something of a case history alongside Gibson's chapter, filling in the detail on one aspect of the more broadly-conceived humanistic world-view that Gibson articulates.

Similarly, Arne De Boever's chapter here offers a close reading of an affinity also suggested by Gibson, that of McCarthy's fiction with the thought of the Speculative Realist philosopher Quentin Meillassoux. Musing on literature, Meillassoux proposes the concept of 'extroscience fiction' which, as distinct from science fiction, presents its fictional world as one where 'experimental science is impossible in principle'. In De Boever's reading, *Remainder* fits this template – not a genre, but a mode – in which 'the real crumbles gradually, from one day to the next ceasing to be familiar to us'.

Returning to the notion of the slip – the glitch which punctures the text's mimetic performance, Sam Slote examines the problem of the remainder, the ineluctable gap between an event and its re-en-actment. In his discussion of the residual – the *recidual*, to borrow a slip of the ear from *Remainder*'s narrator – Slote outlines the novel's theme of the always-doomed attempt to capture authenticity (or the 'failure of transcendence', as McCarthy and Simon Critchley term it in the 'Joint Statement on Inauthenticity'). For Slote, the residual or *surplus* in a written work can be identified with irony: the excess of interpretive potential, the ineradicable additional possibility that the text means something other than what it says.

As with his fondness for Tintin, McCarthy makes no secret of his interest in the modes and experiments of modernism, and modern-ism's relevance to his work goes far beyond the manifestos and cod-expulsions of the INS. Justus Nieland's article 'Dirty Media: Tom McCarthy and the Afterlife of Modernism' (not collected here), is effective at examining McCarthy's 'modernist necrophilia' (Nieland, 2012: 570). Yet as Martin Eve's chapter argues, McCarthy's work can be productively analysed not in terms of its modernist characteristics, but in its stylistic debt to postmodernism. Eve places McCarthy with-in a genealogy of postmodernist novelists which includes Pynchon, Ballard and DeLillo, suggesting that despite its modernist archaeolo-gies, *C* exhibits a series of postmodern tropes which lead to the con-clusion that it is a novel about the history of genre.

For Sebastian Groes, however, postmodernism is 'the cultural period that [McCarthy] is trying to break free from'. Groes looks at *Remainder*'s representations of memory, seeing in these a 'tussle with postmodernism' and a return to 'an experimental, late modern-ist critical mode'. Noting the deluge of amnesiac narratives in post-modern culture – Amis's *Other People* (1981) and *Yellow Dog* (2003), Ondaatje's *The English Patient* (1992), Steven Hall's *The Raw Shark Texts* (2007), William Gibson's *Johnny Mnemonic* (1981), plus films such as *Total Recall* (1990), *Run, Lola, Run* (1998) *Memento* (2000) and the Bourne series (from 2002) – Groes considers *Remainder*'s amnesiac protagonist as representing 'a deliberate shift away from postmodernism's idealistic, utopian faith in textuality towards a re-valuation of materiality'. This is a line shared by Milly Weaver, who considers *Satin Island* as an attempt to navigate modernism's legacy

– specifically that of Mallarmé – by investigating 'the limited representational possibilities of literary language'. McCarthy's novel, she argues, apes non-textual forms of media – the visual, the material – as a response to the threat posed to writing by digital culture's ever-tightening web of data.

For Mark Blacklock and Gill Partington it is not quite materiality, but rather spatiality, which is key to understanding the turn which McCarthy represents in relation to his literary contemporaries. Blacklock, like Eve, proposes a genealogy in which to situate McCarthy, and the inclusion of Ballard in this family tree comes as no surprise. Yet Blacklock looks not to the categories of modernism or postmodernism, but instead posits a new canon of 'geometric fiction', aligning McCarthy and Ballard with Edwin Abbott's late nineteenth-century novella *Flatland*. (To this triumvirate we might add certain other McCarthy touchstones: the pure surface of Alain Robbe-Grillet's novels, perhaps, or the Viconian spiral of recirculation that underlies *Finnegans Wake*.) Blacklock considers McCarthy's first three novels, drawing on Michel Serres's work on the pre-Socratic origins of geometry and its roots in sacred violence. Through this reading, Blacklock's chapter mirrors those of Gibson and Laverty, finding in McCarthy's spatial depictions the same violent subversion of the humanistic worldview that the classic realist novel encodes.

Returning to *Remainder*, Partington sees that novel's fictional topography as wilfully paradoxical – a challenge to the notion, expressed by the narratologist Thomas Pavel, that fiction operates within 'a discrete, parallel imaginary realm'. Instead, in *Remainder*, 'it is the very nature of fictional space that the novel wants to question'. (There are shades of Meillasoux's extro-science fiction in this argument: the depiction of an Escher-world which rejects the principles of topographic realism.) Partington draws a parallel between *Remainder*'s fictional space and the extraordinary *Haus u r* project of the German artist Gregor Schneider. Schneider lives and works in a house which he has dismembered and reconstructed, filled with false walls, windows and ceilings, and populated with human enactors. For Partington, the model which can best help us to understand the spaces we find in McCarthy's and Schneider's work – 'where movement

and trajectory, surface and angle acquire such charged significance'
– is the crime scene.

The chapter which opens this collection, Henderson Downing's
'Crypt, Craft, Crackle', is devoted specifically to McCarthy's work
with the INS, and not least to the original *Calling All Agents* report. In
some ways, Downing's chapter serves a primer for McCarthy, laying
out, from his earliest works, the staples – *Orphée*, Abraham and Torok
– which return in the novels. But it is a bookend that might equally
have served at the collection's close: an essay which faces both forwards and backward, both an introduction to McCarthy and a charter
by which we might look back on his project so far and assess the extent to which it has deviated, or remained true, to its original course.
After all, as the Bellman of the Snark hunt so memorably reminds us,
'navigation was always a difficult art'.

Works Cited

Breton, André (1952) *Entretiens*. Paris: Gallimard.

Caws, Mary Ann (2001) 'The Poetics of the Manifesto: Nowness and Newness', in Mary Ann Caws (ed.), *Manifesto: A Century of Isms*, pp. xix–xxxi.
Lincoln, NE: University of Nebraska Press.

Fitzgerald, F. Scott (1925/1953) *The Great Gatsby*. New York: Scribner.

Hergé (1963) *The Castafiore Emerald*, trans. by Leslie Lonsdale-Cooper and
Michael Turner. London: Methuen.

McCarthy, Tom (1999) 'INS Founding Manifesto', URL (consulted 18 January 2015): http://www.necronauts.org/manifesto1.htm

McCarthy, Tom (2003) 'First Committee Purges', URL (consulted 18 January 2015): http://vargas.org.uk/press/ins/purge_first_committee.html

McCarthy, Tom, and Simon Critchley (2007) 'Joint Statement on Inauthenticity', URL (consulted 18 January 2015): http://necronauts.net/declara-
tions/ins_inauthenticity_new_york/inauthenticity_release.html

Nieland, Justus (2012) 'Dirty Media: Tom McCarthy and the Afterlife of
Modernism', *Modern Fiction Studies* 58(3): 569–99.

Page, Benedicte (2010) 'Booker Prize betting suspended after "inexplica-
ble" run on McCarthy', *Guardian*, 7 October, URL (consulted 29 January 2016): http://www.theguardian.com/books/2010/oct/07/booker-
prize-betting-suspended-tom-mccarthy

Rourke, Lee (2010) 'In Conversation: Lee Rourke and Tom McCarthy',
Guardian, 18 September, URL (consulted January 2016): http://www.

guardian.co.uk/books/2010/sep/18/tom-mccarthy-lee-rourke-conver-sation

Smith, Zadie (2008) 'Two Paths for the Novel', *New York Review of Books* 55(18), 20 November: 89–95.

Soar, Daniel (2006) 'The Smell of Frying Liver Drifting up from Downstairs', *London Review of Books* 28(5), 9 March: 27.

Tzara, Tristan (1973 [1918]) 'Dada Manifesto 1918', in *Approximate Man and Other Writings*, trans. by Mary Ann Caws, pp. 146–57. Detroit: Wayne State University Press.

Ward, Victoria (2010) 'Bookmaker suspends betting on Booker prize after frenzied backing of McCarthy', *The Telegraph*, 7 October, URL (consulted January 2016): http://www.telegraph.co.uk/culture/books/booker-prize/8046977/Bookmaker-suspends-betting-on-Booker-Prize-after-frenzied-backing-of-McCarthy.html

Wood, James (2000) 'Human, All Too Inhuman', *New Republic* 223(3), 24 July: 41–5.

2

CRYPT, CRAFT, CRACKLE
THE INS AT THE ICA. TWO TIMES.

Henderson Downing

Crypt, craft, crackle. Listen and repeat. Two events held at London's Institute of Contemporary Arts provide useful ports of entry for exploring the interrelated ways in which these three terms – *crypt, craft, crackle* – have been deciphered and disinterred by Tom McCarthy in his capacity as the General Secretary of the International Necronautical Society (hereafter INS). In December 2003, in the grand but grey surroundings of the Nash Room at the ICA, McCarthy delivered *Calling All Agents*, his second General Secretary's Report to the INS. The following April, a Transmission Room for the INS Broadcasting Unit was installed in the ICA's gallery in accordance with the findings of the report. The structure and content of both events indicate how the INS is saturated by processes of repetition and modification that function as integral components within various INS projects as well as in McCarthy's work more generally.[1] These interconnected processes can themselves be layered over the duplicate coordinates of reception and transmission through which McCarthy's reports (amongst other INS pronouncements and writings) attempt to filter the turbulent stream of information pumped into the dispersed systems that frame the theory and practice of this 'semi-fictitious avant-garde net-work'. As a phrase repeated in the biographical details accompany-ing McCarthy's first two novels, the capsule summary of the INS as a 'semi-fictitious avant-garde network' has become a default descrip-tion that simplifies the complex status of the organization as both fictional and real at the same time. Additionally, the somewhat disin-genuous use of the tag 'avant-garde' fails to elucidate how the INS si-multaneously operates as a pastiche of twentieth-century movements such as Futurism and Surrealism (with their manifestos, committees, denunciations, splits, etc.) and an experimental re-iteration of the cul-tural history of that avant-garde (including more recent formations such as the Situationist International, Neue Slovenische Kunst, and the Association of Autonomous Astronauts). Unsurprisingly, given the specific context of the INS Broadcasting Unit, the expanded field of cultural and technological production filtered through McCarthy's second report emphasizes the interpretive role of audibility: *listen-ing* to the repetitions and modifications of language; *listening* to the transmission of sense and nonsense across a multiplex spectrum of frequencies (including those that are coded or illicit); *listening* to the silence beyond the signal and noise of communications. The first General Secretary's Report (McCarthy, 2002), titled *Navigation was Always a Difficult Art*, featured McCarthy's repetition and modifica-tion of various themes generated by a series of hearings conducted as part of a two-week residency by the INS at the Office of Anti-Matter in the Austrian Cultural Forum in London. As the hearings formed the foundation of the findings of the first report, they also framed the investigations of the second set of hearings that resulted in *Calling All Agents*. Consequently, *Calling All Agents* repeats and modifies much of the thematic material already imbricated within *Navigation was Always a Difficult Art*. By using his second report to map the testi-monies from this second set of hearings onto the territory already charted by the INS, McCarthy derived a set of preoccupations and processes around which the ICA events were to be subsequently structured. Attentive to the associative patterns submerged within the data disclosed by ongoing INS investigations, in both reports McCarthy navigates the unstable boundaries between delirium and detection while also problematizing categorical distinctions between reality and fiction, seriousness and play. At the ICA, sensitized to the ways in which these associative patterns are received and transmitted, McCarthy incorporated them as part of a project designed to test their potential significance within the aims extravagantly formulated in the organization's founding manifesto: to compile a necronautical atlas of all forms of death in culture and science in order to construct a craft (or craft a construct) capable of entering, colonizing, and eventually inhabiting the space of death. As with the processes of repetition and modification, many of the themes and motifs located within the associative patterns that emerged at the ICA are repeated in variant forms throughout McCarthy's work. Revisiting the INS at the ICA allows me to clarify these introductory abstractions with specific examples (that will also be the source of several digressions and diversions propelled by the momentum of McCarthy's compulsive associationism) before concluding by turning to a seemingly unrelated event held every five years in my home town of St Ives in Cornwall that also resonates with the themes of *crypt, craft, crackle.*

The INS at the ICA

Embodying an image of repetition, McCarthy appears twice in an official INS photograph documenting the presentation of his second General Secretary's Report. He stands at the ICA lectern in the dimly lit Nash Room watched by members of the INS Communications and Encodings Subcommittee, but also appears on a background screen as the central figure seated behind a desk as part of another INS delegation.

This secondary image documents the INS hearings convened at London's Cubitt Gallery in November 2002.[3] On yet another screen, projected behind the INS delegation at the Cubitt Gallery, is an image of Ken Hollings, one of the expert witnesses invited to the hearings to be 'interrogated'. These witnesses were artists and writers with expertise in the fields of sound, communications technology, encryption, and broadcasting. As each witness took their turn to testify, a video

Figure 1. Calling All Agents: INS Report, ICA, London, 2003

of their recorded image was projected live on the screen. The design of the Hearings Chamber was a specially commissioned work by Laura Hopkins, a set designer appointed as the INS Environmental Engineer who also orchestrated the look of the ICA Transmission Room at the ICA. (*At the Calling All Agents symposium the image of Ken Hollings appeared on the screen within the screen within the screen in the room within which the symposium was held so that a refracted series of events and rooms were given a momentary simultaneity, all containing Tom McCarthy.*) The Hearings Chamber deliberately recalled the structure of the House Un-American Activities Committee Hearings, often erroneously associated with McCarthy's anti-communist namesake Senator Joseph McCarthy. Its form also echoed the interrogation scene from Jean Cocteau's 1950 film *Orphée,* an influential work within the research undertaken by the INS during this period. (*At the time of the Calling All Agents symposium in July 2011 another set of hearings dominated the daily radar. The 'phone hacking' saga that led to the closure of the News of the World earlier that same month had infiltrated my thoughts. A few days before the symposium I had watched the televised parliamentary hearings at Portcullis House that featured Rupert Murdoch gravely deflecting questions and a plate full of shaving foam. At the same time I had been reading McCarthy's Sonic Youth story 'Kool Thing; or Why I Want to Fuck Patty Hearst' – a title that repeats and modifies J. G. Ballard's 'Why I Want to Fuck Ronald Reagan' – and I briefly considered sub-titling my paper 'Why I Want to Fuck Rupert Murdoch'. But the critical conjunction between the phone hacking story and the INS occurred at a deeper level than the repressed and repressive undercurrents that bubbled to the bureaucratic surface of the kind of official hearings and committees whose structure the INS playfully and pointedly appropriate.)* As the next iteration of a model productively deployed in earlier INS investigations, the hearings generated the source code for McCarthy's viral voyages in *Calling All Agents* across the recurring themes of transmission, death, and technology in art, literature, and culture. The classification of these cultural interrogations as 'hearings' indicates the centrality of audibility to McCarthy's subsequent report. For example, *Calling All Agents* includes McCarthy's psychobiographical analysis of the intimate relationship between death and telecommunications located in the invention of the telephone by Alexander Graham Bell. McCarthy describes how, as children, Bell and his brother Melville built an automaton that could say the word 'Ma-ma', a word that their deaf mother could not hear. Attempting to make a more realistic speech-machine, the brothers killed the family cat and stripped its larynx. Persisting in these macabre medico-technological experiments, Bell also 'borrowed' a dead ear from a morgue. Haunted by a sequence of deaths in the family, Bell had made a pact with his brother Melville that should one of them die the other would construct a device capable of communicating with the dead. After Melville's death, Bell attempted to keep his side of the pact by building the telephone.[4] 'The prosthetic ear that we carry in our pockets is a family vault crammed full of absences, echoing with repeated, semi-repeated and mutated names of ghosts', writes McCarthy (McCarthy, 2003b: 7). Both McCarthy's report and the subsequent installation of a Transmission Room at the ICA also resembled vaults replete with absences and echoes, haunted by names that were decoded and encrypted, repeated and modified, received and transmitted.

The INS at the ICA. Two Times.

A key source for McCarthy's use of *Calling All Agents* as a title is an audio cut-up produced by William Burroughs and Brion Gysin in 1960. The short piece is composed of multiple tape loops of Gysin repeating permutations of the phrase 'Recalling all active agents' (Burroughs, 1986). It is an appropriate phrase to re-appropriate. The Nash Room at the ICA is Burroughs territory: a Grey Room aesthetic spliced with Regency icing (the INS photograph shows cream-coloured Corinthian pilasters simultaneously emerging and receding through the darkened walls). Imperialized, institutionalized, the entire building resembles a ghost embassy reconstructed as a cultural hub where every attempt at modernity is haunted by a cloyingly majestic past. Named after the architect John Nash who initially designed the building as part of the stables and coach houses for the adjacent Carlton House Terrace, McCarthy's presentation of the report temporarily realigned the name with that of the Situationist Jørgen Nash. Indeed, the phrase 'Calling all agents' suggests that the pool of active agents recalled by McCarthy could incorporate a number of notable predecessors referenced in the report and elsewhere. McCarthy has been repeatedly candid in naming his formative literary influences. Like Borges giving Kafka a series of apparently heterogeneous precursors that only harmonize through different octaves of the Kafkaesque, the dissonant genealogies that echo and entwine through McCarthy's work encompass Burroughs and Ballard as well as the canon of high modernism, Hergé alongside Barthes, Bataille, Blanchot, and Derrida. Indeed, Kafka and Burroughs, two of the twentieth century's greatest satirists of proliferating bureaucracies, can be glimpsed behind the logistical care that the INS take when replicating the structure of control.

The central focus of the *Calling All Agents* report proves to be a set of moments from Cocteau's *Orphée* in which the eponymous hero listens to a car radio broadcast of short lines of poetry such as '*Le silence va plus vite à reculons. Trois fois.*' ['Silence goes more quickly when played backwards. Three times.'] These cryptic lines are transmitted by Jacques Cégeste – a young poet, whose recent death Orphée had witnessed (in several senses). Believing that each of these lyrical fragments is more valuable than his entire poetic output, Orphée proceeds to copy the lines and publish them under his own name. As McCarthy notes in his report, these messages 'seem to be held together in some mathematical formation, led into by lists of numbers, counted off and repeated'. McCarthy then offers the following explanation:

> What Cocteau is doing, both through Cégeste and through the Cégeste-Orphée set-up – the transmission between and beyond the two men – is establishing an aesthetic of *repetition*. Orphée, the official author of the fragments, is not their originator but rather their repeater whose composing consists first and foremost of *listening*. Cégeste (who we never see composing, only repeating, again and again) is also a listener, even when what he is listening to is himself. (McCarthy, 2003b: 2)

Cocteau's inspiration for the lines that Cégeste transmits were the coded poem-messages known as *en claires* broadcast into occupied France by the BBC during the Second World War. In his report, McCarthy discusses the wartime memoirs of the cryptographer Leo Marks. By the time he was twenty-four, Marks was in charge of an entire section of the Special Operations Executive that dealt with training secret agents and receiving their coded messages from occupied Europe. During this period Marks sensitized himself to the setting and breaking of code, understanding that the key to code-breaking involved listening for frequencies of repetition that could then be deciphered to reveal the patterns of mutation and transposition around which the code had been generated. Duly sensitized, Marks began listening for repetition-frequencies everywhere, even deducing the menstrual cycles of female colleagues from periodic slippages in the usual high standard of their work (Marks, 1998). In his report, McCarthy aligns Marks's 'sense of a coded world' with the work of the artist Cerith Wyn Evans, one of the invited experts to the Second First Committee Hearings. McCarthy describes a work by Wyn Evans in which lines from William Blake are translated into Morse code so that they can be projected in light pulses across the Thames from Tate Britain onto the headquarters of MI6, the military intelligence descendants of the wartime SOE. McCarthy (2003b: 6) summarizes this work as 'a dead poet's words brought back to life only to be buried again in code. And make no mistake: all code is burial'. If all code is burial, perhaps the code-breaker's art lies in a form of subterranean piracy that patrols the shifting borderlands between grave-robbing and archaeology, plagiarism and psychoanalysis. From this perspective, Orphée's reception of the pirate frequencies transmitted via his car radio (and his subsequent repetition and modification of those transmissions) becomes a model for all creative endeavour including the combined signifying practices of reading and writing (or listening and speaking). If this points to McCarthy's suspicions regarding a liberal-humanist model of the originality of individual artists and authors (and his preference for tuning in to a galaxy of signifiers produced by a vast echo-chamber in which all texts and voices resonate), it also points towards important poststructuralist precursors, notably, in relation to codes, the work of Roland Barthes. Barthes (1974: 10) offers a version of 'all code is burial' when he writes that this '"I" which approaches the text is already itself a plurality of other texts, of codes which are infinite or, more precisely, lost (whose origin is lost)'. Elsewhere, Barthes (1977: 160) wryly notes that to locate 'sources' or 'influences' when engaging in a language consisting of 'quotations without inverted commas' is 'to fall in with the myth of filiation'. As with the seeming paradox of placing inverted commas around such comments, the identification of the different ratios of connectivity generated between these 'influences' – all the agents called by McCarthy – gestures towards a dynamic revision and expansion of static conceptions of authorship and authority rather than an unintentional reproduction of the ideology of such myths. As Jonathan Lethem wittily demonstrates in his essay 'The Ecstasy of Influence: A Plagiarism' (2007), these ideas emerge in different forms throughout the culture but occasionally need to have their absent commas re-inverted so that we can decode their (buried) presence. Intriguingly, Lethem's epigraph is from John Donne: 'All mankind is one author, and is one volume; when one man dies, one chapter is not torn out of the book, but translated into a better language; and every chapter must be so translated ... ', a quotation that

Lethem confesses to knowing from 'the movie version of 84, *Charing Cross Road*'. In his key to the essay, a catalogue that names the sources of the lines that he 'stole, warped, and cobbled together', Lethem (2007: 69) makes another confession, that he had never seen *84, Charing Cross Road*, but had cribbed the anecdote 'with an elision to avoid appropriating a dead grandmother, from Jonathan Rosen's *The Talmud and the Internet*'.[5] One correspondence that remains buried within this relay of transmissions enables an excavation of a formative influence on Leo Marks's interest in codes. As a child, Marks had been brought up in 84 Charing Cross Road. The antiquarian bookshop celebrated in the book and film of that name was co-owned and run by his father. Marks became fascinated by the coded prices that appeared on each of the books and quickly learnt how to decipher their meaning (Marks et al., 1998).[6] Another example of a code picked up by McCarthy has a more obvious correlation to burial:

> Consider the *Egyptian Book of the Dead*. One might say: 'This is truly a book concerned only with the afterlife.' But what is it actually? It is a set of more than a hundred spells – cipher-sequences that were learnt and reapplied tens of thousands of times by scribes sitting in rows in Microsoft-like corporations. The sequences were repeatedly inscribed and uploaded into coffins, like a kind of software. So the reality, the actual mechanics of the *Egyptian Book of the Dead*, is all to do with craft, writing, repetition. (McCarthy cited in Pilkington, 2002)

By making a link between textual codes and the digital codes used by computer technology, McCarthy touches upon another form of burial in which online authors produce electronic texts via proprietary software and operating systems that screen the user from the coded performance of their digital tools. But in such a digital context it is important to try to differentiate between the discrete specificities of code and text (and the ways in which discussions of computer code are attracted and subverted into being aligned with linguistic codes). Spun into a series of abstracted patterns through a simplifying web of medial ideology, cultural representations of digital code are often diverted through an overly textual critical framework that fails to capture fundamental aspects of the complex relationship between medium and materiality (that as a 'language' computer code exists only in finite bursts of site-specific activity that we cannot read or even decode).[7]

Crypt

The phrase 'all code is burial' is repeated several times throughout McCarthy's (2003b: 6) report, along with the observation that 'to operate or dwell within the space of code is to be already dead'. McCarthy eventually replaces these phrases with a single word used by Wyn Evans during the hearings: *crypt*. Wyn Evans had used the word *crypt* in relation to *encryption*; the two words share the Greek root *kryptos*, meaning *hidden*. Like a morbid hybrid of Leo Marks and Cocteau's Orphée, McCarthy is sensitized to those repetition-frequencies transmitting code on a necronautical wavelength. The *crypt* that Wyn Evans partially opened during the hearings referred to the work of the psychoanalytical writers Nicolas Abraham and Maria Torok.

As with the relay of screens located in the image of the INS at the ICA, and with the staggered transfer of the source quotation from Donne in Lethem's essay, it is important to maintain the momentum of the three 'R's – 'repetition, repetition, repetition' – by addressing the concept of the *crypt* through a *reading* of McCarthy's *reading* of Abraham and Torok's *reading* of Freud's analysis of the patient known as the Wolf Man. The main feature of the crypt is the failure to mourn. Crudely abridged and corrosively simplified, for Freud (*SE XIV*: 237–60), melancholia was caused by an inability to mourn that mutated the painful process of working through the affects of trauma and loss. Scrutinizing Freud's essay, Abraham and Torok (1994: 134) are struck by the 'recurrent image of an open wound'. For them, this image precisely represents 'the wound the melancholic attempts to hide, wall in, and encrypt'. For Abraham and Torok (1986), Freud's analysis of the Wolf Man provides the exemplary case history that reveals and conceals the absent presence of this encrypted wound that they call a *crypt*.

In his report, McCarthy positions the Wolf Man's neurosis as coalescing around two sites of 'enmeshing'. The first site is the Wolf Man's dream in which six or seven wolves sit in a tree watching him while he sleeps. All code is burial. For Freud, the dream of the wolves encodes a primal scene that he proceeds to unearth: aged eighteen months, the Wolf Man saw his parents copulating, the father behind the mother, upright like a wolf in a picture that he was later shown by his sister. For Freud, the repetition and modification of the sight of the copulating father in the image of the upright wolf triggers the Wolf Man's fear of wolves. In addition, Freud also unearths a scene of seduction in which the Wolf Man's sister played with her three year old brother's penis 'while telling him lewd stories about the nanny and the gardener' (*T*, 77). The Wolf Man's sister was a gifted linguist and an accomplished naturalist who studied the mutations of insects. While in her twenties she poisoned herself and died. Instead of working through the trauma and the loss, the Wolf Man failed to mourn her death. The second site of enmeshing involves a memory of a yellow-striped butterfly that the Wolf Man had suddenly developed a fear of while chasing. Again, Freud unearths a scene of attempted seduction involving an old nursery maid whose name was Grusha, the Russian name for a particular yellow-striped pear. This prompts the Wolf Man to recall coming upon Grusha scrubbing the floor in the same position as his mother in the primal scene. McCarthy observes that as an adult, the Wolf Man has 'a compulsive predilection for copulating with women from behind' (*T*, 77). Listening to the repetition-frequencies, tracing the patterns of mutation, Freud makes a breakthrough when the Wolf Man is recounting a dream in which he is torturing a yellow-striped wasp and suddenly mispronounces the German word for 'wasp', *Wespe*, as *Espe*, which Freud recognizes as the Wolf Man's own initials, SP, Sergei Pankajev. McCarthy writes that:

> Freud now has the key, and links all the screens together to show how a raft of incestuous desires (for his father, mother and sister) and fears (of castration and death) have coalesced around this elaborate network of transformations and repetitions – transformations and repe-

titions which the Wolf Man in turn re-transposes and repeats through his compulsive behaviour. The Wolf Man's neurosis is manifest, but in code. (McCarthy, 2003b: 8–9)

Another frequency of repetition can be detected here via McCarthy's novel *C*. Several details of the Wolf Man's case history are reconfigured within the fictional life of the novel's main character Serge Carrefax, particularly in relation to Serge's failure to mourn his sister Sophie, who also poisons herself and dies. Sophie is then buried in the crypt of the Carrefax country estate. The estate also operates as a day school for the deaf: McCarthy enmeshing the childhood of the Wolf Man with that of Alexander Graham Bell.

Reading Freud's case history six decades later, Abraham and Torok begin to listen to Freud listening to his patient. Discovering that English runs alongside Russian as the Wolf Man's childhood language, they tune in to 'a polyglottal zone of words' which crackle with significance. Behind these 'crackling words' they chart buried 'source-words' that have been excluded from the circuit of speech. Abraham and Torok call these *words that hide* 'cryptonyms' and add that 'the presence of the cryptonym signals the existence of a crypt'. In *Tintin and the Secret of Literature*, McCarthy provides a concise account of Abraham and Torok's *crypt* as:

> a loaded term that binds the architecture of burial to the language of secrets. Their crypt encrypts. [...] It buries and, in doing so, generates noise, coded speech. The crypt is resonant. It is also porous: its secret words can travel [...] through the partitions between the conscious and the unconscious – provided they are encrypted. They can also travel onwards, hidden on the underside of speech or via actions which perform them while still leaving them encrypted (such as, for example, torturing an insect), out into the world. The crypt's walls are broken; it oozes; it *transmits*. (*T*, 83)

McCarthy observes that 'whether or not Abraham or Torok are "right" [...] is irrelevant' (*T*, 83). What interests him is the model that they construct. Back at the ICA, McCarthy (2003b: 10) proposed to the Communications and Encodings Subcommittee that the volatile metaphor of the *crypt* will not only 'act as a screen for all the information in the scope of this report, but it will also furnish our organisation with a model, *the* model, for our current project'. What Abraham and Torok present is less a psychoanalytical therapy than a theory of readability and audibility.

Like Gysin enunciating the permutations of the phrase 'recalling all active agents', the Wolf Man's cryptonymy runs through a spectrum of permutations that Abraham and Torok describe as being 'like a textbook on poetics'. However, among the crackling words, there is one magic word that does not speak, a silent word so charged and seductive that the Wolf Man buries it inside the crypt, repeatedly saying it without saying it, especially to his analyst: 'Here is nothing, hold it tight' (Abraham and Torok, 1986: 22). For McCarthy (2003b: 16), the INS Broadcasting Unit must do that too. McCarthy suggests that the crypt's double-move of marking and erasure maps onto the movements of writing and reading. By tracing and repeating chains of crackling words, by reading the source code of the encrypted 'nothing' broadcast on illicit mental frequencies, and by transmitting the coded message outwards, he speculates that the INS may find 'that our culture also has a secret, silent word'. In the final part of his report, McCarthy explains that we, the public, will be placed in the role of Orphée by the INS Broadcasting Unit, because the INS love us and we love them too. In Cocteau's film, the dead poet Cégeste was directed to transmit his code-poems to Orphée by the character of the Princess. Cocteau (1994: 155) describes the Princess as 'not death represented symbolically' but specifically the 'Death of Orphée', the personalized death that 'takes charge of us from the moment of birth'. The Princess has fallen in love with her charge, an attachment that prompts her to call him through poetry and technology. Ultimately, to save him from his own death, she erases his knowledge of ever having reciprocated that love. Repeating and modifying the last words of Shakespeare's dying Hamlet, the last lines of the report explain that 'The rest, like the man says, is silence'.

SILENCE

LANGUAGE

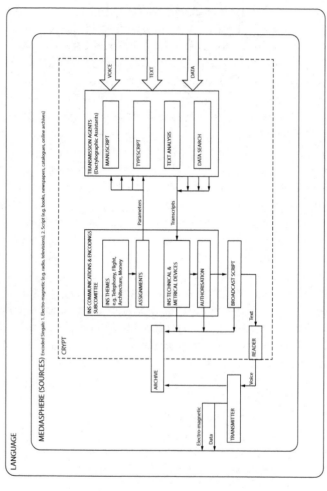

MEDIASPHERE (SOURCES) Encoded Singals: 1. Electro-magnetic (e.g. radio, televisions), 2. Script (e.g. books, newspapers, catalogues, online archives)

CRYPT

INS COMMUNICATIONS & ENCODINGS SUBCOMITTEE

INS THEMES
e.g. Telephony, Flight,
Architecture, Money

ASSIGNMENTS

INS TECHNICAL &
METRICAL DEVICES

AUTHORISATION

BROADCAST SCRIPT

Parameters

Transcripts

TRANSMISSION AGENTS
(Dactylographic Assistants)

MANUSCRIPT

TYPESCRIPT

TEXT ANALYSIS

DATA SEARCH

VOICE

TEXT

DATA

ARCHIVE

READER

Text

TRANSMITTER

Voice

Electro-magnetic

Data

Note: Art does not justify this process

CALLING ALL AGENTS: International Necronautical Society Broadcasting Unit
Type 1/2004, Communications and Encodings Subcommittee Document 100404

Figure 2. Calling All Agents: INS Transmission Room (diagram), ICA, London, 2004

The INS at the ICA. Two Times. I Repeat.

In April 2004, the INS returned to the ICA and installed their Transmission Room. The INS *crypt* became a variant of the radio broadcasts in which Orphée had been literally targeted by the agents of death. Dactylographic assistants generated texts culled from various media. These texts were then stamped and authorized at a central table by other INS officials and then recoded for an INS reader to broadcast punctuated by short bursts of crackle. The crypt leaked into the surrounding mediasphere, a zone itself surrounded by language, with language surrounded by silence (as in the diagram of the INS Transmission Unit).

As the first in a series of INS 'black boxes' broadcasting such coded transmissions, McCarthy's repetition and modification of this scene from Cocteau's film amplifies and reiterates the theme of re-enactment found within his work. Before returning to this point in relation to the potentially disruptive presence of *crackle*, a brief detour is necessary through the second term contained within the title of this text: *craft*.

Craft

The final section of the INS manifesto that McCarthy had started to circulate in 1999 declares that the 'ultimate aim' of the organization shall be 'the construction of a craft that will convey us into death in such a way that we may, if not live, then at least persist' (McCarthy, 1999). An asterisk after the word *craft* points to a supplementary note explaining that the 'term must be understood in the most versatile way possible', from designating 'a set of practices' to 'the building of an actual craft'. Craft is a key theme of McCarthy's first report, *Navigation was Always a Difficult Art*. The report begins with a consideration of the figure of Queequeg, the Polynesian harpoonist in Herman Melville's *Moby Dick*. In the grip of a deadly fever, Queequeg asks the ship's carpenter to build him a coffin. When the coffin is ready, Queequeg makes a sudden recovery. He turns the coffin into a clothes chest that he proceeds to decorate with what Melville describes as 'all manner of grotesque figures and drawings' as if he was striving 'to copy parts of the twisted tattooing on his body' (Melville, 1892: 451). Resembling the kind of 'software' coded into *The Egyptian Book of the Dead*, the re-styled coffin becomes the site of Queequeg's attempt to craft, to make legible, the hieroglyphic marks on his body that are said to comprise 'a complete theory of the heavens and the earth, and a mystical treatise on attaining the truth' (Melville, 1892: 451). McCarthy (2002: 2) explains that 'this little episode has everything. It cuts right to the heart of what this organisation is about and contains, revealing or concealing them, each line of enquiry'. Rather than copying a version of himself onto the coffin lid, Queequeg is *projecting* himself onto a screen, he is crafting a form of *mapping* in which self and space merge. McCarthy (2002: 8) argues that like Ahab, Queequeg is 'projecting himself *toward* death, not seeing himself *in* death'. In the novel, Queequeg's coffin also becomes a craft in the sense of a vehicle when Ishmael floats upon it after surviving the wreck of the Pequod.[8] An equally significant craft to consider in relation to *Navigation was Always a Difficult Art* is the ship captained by the Bellman in Lewis Carroll's *The Hunting of the Snark* from which McCarthy's first report derives its name. McCarthy (2002: 11) claims that Carroll's 'Agony in Eight Fits' is 'a major codex' for the INS. Artfully navigating between philosophy and nonsense, McCarthy steers this seemingly mischievous declaration of the necronautical relevance of Carroll's poem into a crafty decoding of its status as a treatise on materiality. Rather than disappearing into the purity of what appears to be a perfect and absolute blank, McCarthy argues that those on board Carroll's craft are forced to confront the full horror of matter, a reminder of the remainder of their failed transcendence.

Crackle

Similar matters cluster around crackle, a term that like crypt and craft, carries multiple meanings in its wake. To repeat, the poetic *en claires* that the INS broadcast from the ICA were punctuated by bursts of crackling static. Mark Fisher, channelling Derrida, has analysed 'the metaphysics of crackle', arguing that crackle 'disrupts presence in multiple ways: first by reminding us of the material processes of recording and playback, second by connoting a broken sense of time, and third by veiling the official "signal" in noise' (Fisher, 2010). Although the INS Transmission Room was officially sanctioned as an art installation with a temporary broadcasting licence, the audible static between *en claires* emphasized the ways in which those coded messages also crackled with significance, veiling the official signal of standard radio transmissions with the noise of encrypted language. Through the related process of re-enactment – the reconfiguring of the radio broadcasts in Cocteau's *Orphée* as a Transmission Room that functioned like a crypt – the INS used the disruptive materiality of crackle in other ways that correlate with Fisher's analysis. Visitors to the ICA were taken on guided tours of the Transmission Room by INS agents. As a crypt, the space became a model reminder of the material processes of recording and playback that also connoted fractured temporalities. Transmission Agents received thematic assignments from the INS Communications and Encodings Subcommittee and then recorded the relevant data from the multiple media sources (television, radio, newspapers – including obituary columns) that were being transmitted live into the crypt. Transcripts of data were then submitted back to the subcommittee for authorization as a broadcast script to be passed to the reader whose voice leaked out through the wall of the crypt via the radio transmitter.

The materiality of crackle not only punctuates the INS black box broadcasts but also disrupts presence in the duplication of counter-narratives that loop around the theme of repetition throughout McCarthy's art projects, essays, and novels. In *C*, Serge is carried away by the 'crackling waves' of static as he nudges the dial of his radio (*C*, 63). On Pageant Day at the Day-School for the Deaf in the same novel, 'an electric crackle whips the assembled crowd into attentiveness' (*C*, 51). The crackle is generated by a temperamental early model of an amplified public address system. Another crackle from the system interrupts a Pageant Day speech. The disruptive presence of crackle at these moments in the narrative, silencing listeners and speakers alike, connects to the audible crackle of the INS broadcasts. The term repeatedly resurfaces in his work, reminding us of that which resists representation, that which refuses to be absorbed back into the official signal of the pure space of the page or screen or brain. On the day of the first re-enactment in *Remainder*, the radio crackle of the back-up crew is accompanied by the 'static crackle' of wet liver landing in hot oil, a noise that McCarthy describes as breaking 'across the orphaned signals cast adrift from radios and television sets' (*R*, 126, 128). *Crackle* also incorporates the word crack, returning us to the crack in the bathroom wall that prompts the protagonist of *Remainder* to remember the details of a particular building that he then recreates in a block that crackles with the Proustian name Madlyn Mansions. For the protagonist, this is an attempt at reclaiming those spaces where his 'movements had been fluent and unforced', natural rather than 'awkward, acquired, second hand', spaces where he remembered being real 'without first understanding how to try to be' (*R*, 62). A space that could be defined as one in which his actions did not resemble re-enactments. Among the escalating sites of re-enactment in *Remainder* there are scenes that repeat and modify earlier INS reconstructions of other events. At the start of October 2001, the INS took up residence at the DasArts Foundation in Amsterdam. Working with choreographers, dancers, and physicists, the INS coordinated the re-enactment of certain sequences from a gun battle that had occurred three years earlier on an Amsterdam street that resulted in the death of a gangster's bodyguard. These sequences included the movement of the bodyguard into the line of fire and the moment when a witness fleeing the scene toppled over his friend's bicycle. Relocated to the Brixton of *Remainder*, this project is repeated and modified through the gangland murders re-enacted in the novel. 'After running through the shooting for the fifth time I was satisfied we'd got the action right: the movement, the positions. Now we could begin working on what lay beneath the surfaces of these – on what was inside, intimate', explains the narrator who re-enacts the part of the victim (*R*, 197). Slowing down the speed at which the sixth re-enactment unfolds, the narrator heads 'over the handlebars this time serenely, calmly, taking

time to greet the now-familiar moments of landscape that came at me'
(*R*, 194).

Coupling a desire for authenticity with transparent simulation,
in recent times the dialectical battlefield of re-enactment has proved
fertile territory for contemporary artists. Whether it is the INS meticulously plotting the trajectories of action sequences from a gun
battle, Jeremy Dellar restaging ferocious clashes between police and
workers during the 1984 miners' strike, or Rod Dickinson resurrect-
ing the ambient ghosts of Jonestown and Waco, re-enactments often
retain a focus on violence. If the compulsion to repeat is the psychological hallmark of traumatic experience, then perhaps these re-enactments offer a strangely vicarious form of catharsis that resonates
with the concept of the crypt. As Derrida (1986: xv) remarks in his
foreword to Abraham and Torok's *The Wolf Man's Magic Word*, 'we
have to know that the crypt itself is *built* by violence'. Of particular
relevance is McCarthy's collaboration with Dickinson on the installation Greenwich Degree Zero, an art work that consists of a reading
room containing an archive of purportedly late-nineteenth century
material in which extant reports of the actual attempted bombing of the Greenwich Observatory by Martial Bourdin in 1894 are
rewritten. These mutated reports include newspapers, pamphlets,
photographs, a map, and even a short piece of early film footage that
again crackles with a disruptive material reminder of its status as a
recording (on a hand-cranked camera). While Bourdin accidentally
blew himself up on the slopes beneath the undamaged Observatory
– the place from which time is measured, an emblematic reminder
of the British Empire's former imperial mastery – all of the items in
the reading room reimagine the failed original bombing as if it had
been successful. This project usefully illustrates the intertextual dimension of re-enactments, principally referencing Conrad's appropriation of Bourdin's bombing attempt in his novel *The Secret Agent*.
Ever attentive to such intertextual associations, in an article on the
history of the bombing McCarthy plugs another significant literary
precursor into the grid that surrounds *Greenwich Degree Zero*, connecting Bourdin and Conrad to the fragment of the first V2 bomb
that comes screaming across the sky at the start of Pynchon's *Gravity's*

Rainbow (McCarthy, 2004a). This bomb fragment is 'salvaged from Earth's prime meridian' at Greenwich and is found to contain a message from an SOE agent written in 'Kryptosam', a substance whose coded contents only achieve legibility when mixed with seminal fluid (Pynchon, 1975: 71, 72). Collapsing the spatial and temporal gaps between distance and intimacy, the coded messages borne by such technologies of transmission reveal kaleidoscopic interpenetrations of love, sex, violence, and death that share distinct correspondences with the code work carried out at the SOE by Marks and his team.

However, there is a crackling exception to these re-articulations of violence that intersects in intriguing ways with other preoccupations exhibited by the INS at the ICA. Threading a marginally more playful route through the ontological maze of re-enactment, the work of the artists Iain Forsyth and Jane Pollard has rejuvenated the fatigued concept of the cover version by remaking iconic gigs from rock 'n' roll's back pages. At the ICA in March 2003, a year before the INS took over the same space for their Transmission Room, Forsyth and Pollard coordinated *File Under Sacred Music*, a re-enactment of The Cramps's legendary performance at California's Napa State Mental Institute. Demonstrating their microscopic attention to detail, the artists painstakingly choreographed a reconstruction of a bootleg recording of the gig (including a replication of the lo-fi crackles that disrupt the pirated footage). The space of the re-enactment was supposedly divided between the mental health patients and their carers who formed the main audience and a second audience further back consisting of the film crew, the ICA staff, and invited art journalists such as McCarthy. Reflecting on this division, McCarthy wrote:

> Two different events, two different event-zones, might have been taking place simultaneously, superimposed over one another in the kind of quantum-logic way the real Cramps, fans of trashy sci-fi, would have loved – but the raw power of Zone One, the Orphic gig-zone, made it impossible to remain safely enclosed within Zone Two, the conceptual art zone. At the same time, the very process within which Zone One was framed made Orphic abandonment impossible, for me at least. I felt exhilarated and uneasy at the same time – which is more or less how I felt the first few times I went to gigs aged sixteen or

seventeen. This kind of split – in a less loaded context you might call it 'schizophrenic' – seemed to have found its way into each moment, every gesture. (McCarthy, 2004b)

The musician re-enacting the role of Lux Interior, the lead singer of The Cramps, embodied the rock critic cliché that the words he sang seemed to flow through him from somewhere else. Making (or re-making) this stock observation into a literal performance, Forsyth and Pollard position their band of re-enactors as another set of representatives of a mode or model of communication central to McCarthy's oeuvre, where the creative locus becomes both a receiver and transmitter. The Orphic resonance communicated in the passage from McCarthy's article on *File Under Sacred Music* connects this model back to Cocteau's *Orphée* and the more freewheeling approach to re-enactment that the INS developed through the construction of a Transmission Room.

The Transmission Room at the ICA functioned like a multiplex Burroughs cut-up. Operation Rewrite attempting to rupture the pre-recorded universe from a base close to Buckingham Palace and the Admiralty, intensifying paranoia in a culture of fear (see Burroughs, 2010: 38–42, 159–68). The transmission theme of each session – telephony, flight, architecture, etc. – was accompanied by a series of wall-high mind-maps that registered the intertextual repetition-frequencies and patterns of mutation detected by the Transmission Agents. Combined with a sensitive setting in terms of security, the interrogation of key themes and preoccupations resembles the methodology of Iain Sinclair in what can be tentatively labelled as London psychogeography, where a facility for pattern recognition is transposed into a paranoid-critical register to produce counter-narratives to the dominant versions of history and heritage associated with specific sites. Generated by a 'compulsive associationism' (Sinclair, 1991: 184) that encompasses the highest and the lowest of cultural references, such encyclopaedic eclecticism forms a fundamental part of Sinclair's psychogeographical repertoire, veiling official 'signals' with the crackling noise of his labyrinthine texts. Synthesizing the material gathered by hearings and Transmission Agents, McCarthy's INS writings (including the many transcripts of the interviews he has conducted with expert witnesses from across the cultural spectrum) demonstrate a comparable associative restlessness in their tracking and testing of potential necronautical connections. Death rather than London is McCarthy's domain. Given that the first declaration of the INS manifesto wryly concludes that 'death is a type of space, which we intend to map, enter, colonise and, eventually, inhabit', could McCarthy be reconsidered as a psychogeographer of death? There is a counter-precedent for this formulation. Almost a decade before McCarthy published the manifesto that launched the INS, Alan Moore had already labelled Sinclair a 'Necronaut' engaged in a 'pioneering and visionary' mapping of London's occulted histories (Moore, 1991). In spite of the manifest differences in the style and content of their work, McCarthy and Sinclair share uncannily similar operating systems. In *Hackney, that Rose-Red Empire*, Sinclair discusses McCarthy in relation to Stewart Home. Noting that the filmmaker and author Chris Petit, a regular psychogeographical collaborator, had recently moved to the Golden Lane Estate in London, Sinclair (2009: 384) declares that the neighbourhood could be called 'the golden section of the psychogeographers'. Petit had bumped into Home at the security gate and realized that they were now neighbours. Another local was McCarthy:

> McCarthy also lived in Golden Lane, in a different block, looking west. When Stewart was kicked out by his lover, he stayed from time to time with McCarthy. And he repaid the favour by granting McCarthy a pseudonym in his novel *Memphis Underground*. He called him 'Rob McGlynn'. (Sinclair, 2009: 385)

Following the crackling lines of association opened up by this correspondence, Sinclair picks up a paperback of *Remainder* and reads the much-repeated biographical blurb that states that McCarthy is 'General Secretary of the International Necronautical Society (INS), a semi-fictitious avant-garde network', a description that prompts him to consider a specific variation on the question of authenticity that is central to the novel in his hands (that presumably he has not yet read): 'Which was the pseudonym, McGlynn or McCarthy? Didn't

McCarthy sound more like Home's invention? An obvious nod in the direction of sweaty Joe, the red-baiting senator from Wisconsin?' (Sinclair, 2009: 393). Although McCarthy's sustained questioning of authenticity outstrips Sinclair's either/or musings (while reportedly scanning the blurb for *Remainder*), Sinclair's densely intratextual work is also marked by at least two of McCarthy's interrelated preoccupations: the author as a medium for reception and transmission; and a recurring recognition of the exhilaration and unease induced by the splitting of the self that renders any idealized individual authenticity both comically and traumatically unstable.

There is a seductive quality to McCarthy's reports and to the INS projects that makes it tempting when examining their composition and their execution to adopt a reciprocal interpretive delirium. For example, those who recognized the Mark E. Smith quote about the three 'R's' smugly embedded earlier in this text will probably remember that the song by The Fall from which the lines were stolen is called 'Repetition'. Several years ago, I listened to a radio interview featuring McCarthy. During the programme, he selected 'Repetition' as a suitable musical accompaniment to the themes and theories found in *Remainder* and *Tintin and the Secret of Literature*. Over a repetitive guitar loop, Mark E. Smith relays the information that 'we dig repetition'.[10] All code is burial. We dig repetition. In 2007, in an online interview with McCarthy in which he discusses another song by The Fall, 'W. B.', McCarthy speculates that because 'The Fall are super-literary' the title probably references W. B. Yeats (Battaglia, 2007). Given the contents of the lyrics, a more likely candidate with those same initials is William Blake, whose lines of poetry were being recoded for transmission across the chartered Thames by Cerith Wyn Evans around the same time. While the most appropriate W. B. re-appropriated for this paper would have been William Burroughs, if we heed the words of Walter Benjamin (another W. B.), whoever or whatever the W. B. signifies, it is the fleeting mention of those initials that requires an initial acknowledgment (see Benjamin, 1999: 470 [N7.4]). Other associative chains can then be clustered around the node, such as the crypt-like title of the album from which the track 'W. B.' is taken: *The Unutterable*. Ostensibly lacking the rational rigour of an academic argument, do such elective affinities produce too speculative a leap back into the realm of the *crypt*? In the interview discussing 'W. B.', McCarthy makes the following observation about The Fall's front man:

> Mark E. Smith is like the original classical figure of the poet – he's like Orpheus, you know, who's just halfway dead. He's got one foot in the underworld. He's just picking up some transmission on the threshold between sense and complete nonsense that might contain all these incredible words of wisdom, or might just be complete garbled rubbish. (Battaglia, 2007)

As should by now be apparent, the INS also tune in to this Orphic threshold between sense and nonsense, communication and communication failure. By crafting a crypt at the ICA, the INS contaminated the airwaves with the crackle of repetition, transmitting coded messages whose fleeting mention of necronautical themes might have also contained something incredibly wise or might just have been garbled rubbish as the language of death looped around the unutterable ... Calling All Agents. Two times. I repeat. Calling All Agents.

Knill's Crypt

To conclude, I would like to turn from Queequeg's craft and the crackle of re-enactments back to the cryptic quinquennial celebrations mentioned in my opening paragraph. These celebrations unfold high on a hill above St Ives from where, far below, the local surfers become coded dots paddling their craft through the incoming waves of the Atlantic Ocean. The focus of the event is a pyramidal structure intended as a crypt for John Knill. For much of the late-eighteenth century, Knill served as both the St Ives customs officer and the town mayor. He commissioned the construction of the pyramid to house his sarcophagus and also included detailed instructions in his will for a corresponding ceremony to take place every five years on the feast day of St James. Led by a fiddler, ten daughters of fishermen or tin miners, all aged under ten, are paid to ascend from the town and dance around the crypt while accompanied by two widows of fishermen or tin miners, the local vicar, and the town's customs officer. (*This conclusion was prompted by the fact that two days after the 'Calling All Agents' symposium the celebrations were to be repeated once more with a new set of participants dancing around the crypt*). To ensure that everything ran smoothly, Knill himself attended the first ceremony in 1801. However, when he died in 1811, bureaucratic issues relating to consecration meant that his remains could not be interred in the pyramid. The crypt remains empty. Designed to convey him into death in such a way that he might persist, could Knill's crypt be another model for an INS craft? Carved high into the granite surface of the pyramid are a series of texts that include the phrase 'nil desperandum', a pun on Knill's name that visually as well as verbally elides the silent K. This famous comment about there being nothing to despair can be found in the seventh ode of the first book of Horace. The words are spoken by a man flushed with wine, exiled from home, and are intended to reassure his comrades that they will eventually find fresh soil on which to re-enact the city to which they can no longer return. It is a short speech that concludes with the words 'cras ingens iterabimus aequor', a phrase repeated by McCarthy as the INS motto: 'tomorrow we'll sail the wide seas again'.

Notes

1 As a revised version of a paper first given at *Calling All Agents: A Symposium on the Work of Tom McCarthy*, this essay is marked by similar processes of repetition and modification. Italicized parentheses within this essay contextualize these processes as they intersect and overlap with the INS at the ICA.

2 The Office of Anti-Matter was a residency programme run by the artist Roman Vasseur at the Cultural Institute during March and April 2001.

3 Comprising the hearings that resulted in *Calling All Agents*, this event is classified by the INS as the 'Second First Committee Hearings: Transmission, Death, Technology'.

4 See also the John Cussans Transcript Testimony from the Second First Committee Hearings in which he discusses 'The Mother Code' devised by Harry Houdini. If Houdini's mother was able to transmit a coded mes-

sage to her son after her death he would be able to verify that there was an afterlife (Cussans, 2002).

5 Lethem immediately moves on to plagiarizing William Gibson's response to the plundering of literature by William Burroughs.

6 Another early influence on Marks's interest in codes had been his reading of the methodology deployed by Freud when listening to his patients. At the end of the 1950s, Marks was invited by the director Michael Powell to write a screenplay for a Freud biopic only to discover that John Huston was already working on a similar project. As a replacement, Marks proposed his code-obsessed script for *Peeping Tom*. For more on Marks, codes, and repetition, see Downing (2009).

7 I am deeply indebted to Zara Dinnen for her insightful comments on codes in general and on computer code in particular. On 'medial ideology', see Kirschenbaum (2008: 36).

8 This point was first raised at the Office of Anti-Matter in a deposition by Melissa McCarthy, the INS Obituary Reviewer, who also drew attention to the surfboard as a potential necronautical craft that would repay further investigation.

9 As the note at the foot of the INS Broadcasting Unit diagram states: 'Art does not justify this process'.

10 The track is also cited in McCarthy and Critchley (2007), a joint statement delivered at The Drawing Center, New York, 25 September 2007.

Works Cited

Abraham, Nicolas and Maria Torok (1986) *The Wolf Man's Magic Word: A Cryptonomy*, trans. by Nicholas Rand. Minneapolis: University of Minnesota Press.

Abraham, Nicolas and Maria Torok (1994) 'Mourning *or* Melancholia: Introjection *versus* Incorporation', in *The Shell and the Kernel: Renewals of Psychoanalysis, Volume 1*, ed. and trans. Nicholas Rand, pp. 125–38. Chicago and London: University of Chicago Press.

Barthes, Roland (1974) *S/Z*, trans. Richard Miller. New York: Farrar, Straus, and Giroux.

Barthes, Roland (1977) 'From Work to Text', in *Image–Music-Text*, trans. Stephen Heath, pp. 155–64. London: Fontana.

Battaglia, Andy (2007) 'Random Rules: Tom McCarthy', URL (consulted 18 January 2015): http://www.avclub.com/articles/random-rules-tom-mccarthy,1853/

Benjamin, Walter (1999) *Arcades Project*, trans. Howard Eiland and Kevin McLaughlin. Cambridge, MA and London: Belknap Press of Harvard University Press.

Burroughs, William (1986) 'Recalling All Active Agents', *Breakthrough in Grey Room*. Brussels: Sub Rosa [LP].

Burroughs, William (2010) *The Ticket that Exploded*. London: Fourth Estate.

Cocteau, Jean (1994) *The Art of Cinema*. New York: Marion Boyars.

Cussans, John (2002) 'John Cussans Transcript Testimony', *Second First Committee Hearings*, URL (consulted 18 January 2015): http://www.necronauts.org/cubitt_john.htm

Derrida, Jacques (1986) 'Fors: The Anglish Words of Nicolas Abraham and Maria Torok', trans. Barbara Johnson, in Nicolas Abraham and Maria Torok (1986) *The Wolf Man's Magic Word: A Cryptonomy*, pp. xi–xlviii. Minneapolis: University of Minnesota Press.

Downing, Henderson (2009) 'Fitzrovia Phantasmagoria: Notes for a Newman Passagenwerk', *Spectre and Fog* 1: 23–39.

Fisher, Mark (K-Punk) (2010) 'The Metaphysics of Crackle', URL (consulted 18 January 2015): http://pontone.pl/pontones-special-guest-mix-k-punk-the-metaphysics-of-crackle/

Kirschenbaum, Matthew G. (2008) *Mechanisms: New Media and the Forensic Imagination*. Cambridge, MA: MIT Press.

Lethem, Jonathan (2007) 'The Ecstasy of Influence: A Plagiarism', *Harper's Magazine* 314(1881): 59–71.

McCarthy, Tom (1999) 'INS Founding Manifesto', URL (consulted 18 January 2015): http://www.necronauts.org/manifesto1.htm

McCarthy, Tom (2002) *Navigation was Always a Difficult Art*. London: Vargas Organisation.

McCarthy, Tom (2003a) 'International Necronautical Society Event Report', *Rhizomes: Cultural Studies in Emerging Knowledge* 6, URL (consulted 18 January 2015): http://www.rhizomes.net/issue6/ins.htm

McCarthy, Tom (2003b) *Calling All Agents*. London: Vargas Organisation.

McCarthy, Tom (2004a) 'In Search of Terror's Degree Zero', *Strange Attractor* 1: 197–206.

McCarthy, Tom (2004b) 'Nests, Puke, Frames and Baby Faces', URL (consulted 18 January 2015): http://www.fileundersacredmusic.com/reading/index.html

McCarthy, Tom (2008) 'Kool Thing; or Why I Want to Fuck Patty Hearst', in Peter Wild (ed.), *The Empty Page: Fiction Inspired by Sonic Youth*, pp. 143–8. London: Serpent's Tail.

McCarthy, Tom, and Simon Critchley (2007) 'Joint Statement on Inauthenticity', URL (consulted 18 January 2015): http://necronauts.net/declarations/ins_inauthenticity_new_york/inauthenticity_release.html

Marks, Leo (1998) *Between Silk and Cyanide: A Codemaker's War 1941–1945*. London: HarperCollins.

Marks, Leo, Michael Powell and Chris Rodley (1998) *Peeping Tom*. London: Faber.

Melville, Herman (1892) *Moby-Dick, or The White Whale*. Boston, MA: St Botolph Society.

Moore, Alan (1991) 'Appendix to Volume One', in Alan Moore and Eddie Campbell, *From Hell: Being a Melodrama in Sixteen Parts*. Northampton: Mad Love.

Pilkington, Mark (2002) 'Roads Less Travelled', *Fortean Times* 159, URL (consulted 18 January 2015): http://www.necronauts.org/press_ft.htm

Pynchon, Thomas (1975) *Gravity's Rainbow*. London: Picador.

Sinclair, Iain (1991) *Downriver*. London: Grafton.

Sinclair, Iain (2002) *London Orbital*. London: Granta.

Sinclair, Iain (2009) *Hackney, that Rose-Red Empire: A Confidential Report*. London: Hamish Hamilton.

Sinclair, Iain (2010) 'Sickening', in *Restless Cities*, ed. by Matthew Beaumont and Gregory Dart, pp. 257–76. London: Verso.

3

Dummy Chambers and Ur-Houses
How to Find your Way Around in *Remainder*

Gill Partington

Tom McCarthy briefly entertained the idea of being his own central character, or so he would have us believe:

> When I first had the idea for *Remainder* my initial thought wasn't a novel. I had this moment of déjà vu in a bathroom, exactly like the protagonist, and I thought, I want to do that. It could have been an art piece, then I thought, maybe that's not really that interesting. I'd need the whole building, I'd want the cats, then it gets interesting. In fact it's only really interesting if you expand into the street. You'd have to have the shoot out and even that's not enough. You would need to do the bank heist, then I realised it would have to be a novel. (Morgan, 2010: 171)

The moment of déjà vu that Tom McCarthy refers to here is the book's crucial episode – an encounter with a fissure in the bathroom wall – which produces a intensely vivid yet unlocatable recollection of another building: '[I]t was growing, minute by minute, as I stood there in the bathroom, this remembered building, spreading outwards from the crack' (*R*, 61). The passage echoes that most iconic piece of literary remembering, in which the narrator of Marcel Proust's *In Search of Lost Time*, prompted by the taste of a madeleine dipped in tea, suddenly perceives the dimensions and details of his childhood home. And in naming his fictional building 'Madlyn Mansions', McCarthy gives a sideways acknowledgement to Proust, whose buildings similarly grow and spread, 'stretch and shape themselves [...] assuming form and substance' like Japanese origami miraculously emerging from a single pellet of paper immersed in water (Proust, 2003: 50). More of Proust and sponge cakes later but, returning to McCarthy's statement, it seems that this reverie occurs firstly in the author's own experience, in a real bathroom, where it produces an impulse to construct a physical space rather than a novel. He wants to build, not write.

Yet the possibility is rejected almost as soon as it presents itself: as an 'art piece' or 'installation' the bathroom could conceivably be recreated, but this is too limited in scope. At the same time, the more compelling prospect of recreating the building itself, and of pursuing this chain of reconstructions outwards to its logical conclusion, quickly reveals itself to be a logistical impossibility. So instead, McCarthy's demiurgical impulse is displaced onto his fictional stand-in, who does what the author himself cannot. Commandeering an entire building, he modifies every detail to correspond to an architectural blueprint which exists only in his own memory or imagination (we are not sure which). He shapes reality to conform to specifications at once demanding and mysterious to even himself. He meticulously recreates not only the phantom bathroom with its cracked wall, but the apartments around it, the other apartments around that, and the floors above and below. He recreates the marbled floor, the kinked glass in the windows, the cats on the roof and the stains on the ground. His imaginary house and the real one coincide exactly, right down to the parts that are less clearly pictured: their haziness is rendered as blank, white non-space. And it is not just the building itself that must be recreated. The moment of déjà vu involves the smell of frying liver, the sound of piano playing, a neighbour putting out the rubbish. And so the building is populated with actors, or rather 're-enactors', to perform these momentary acts over and over again. Soon, such re-enactment zones proliferate outwards beyond the boundaries of his initial building project, into a warehouse, a crime scene and eventually a real bank, resulting in a disastrous bank robbery known to be a re-enactment only by its perpetrators, but not its victims.

According to McCarthy's account, *Remainder*, in its gestation, hovered uncertainly on the boundary between novelistic space and physical space, fiction and the real world. The uncertainty is resolved in one sense: this is a novel, not an art installation or a building. In another sense, however, the ambivalence remains, played out in *Remainder*'s preoccupation with the nature of spaces and locations, their borders and intersections. Probing and finally dissolving the thin membrane between reality and 're-enactment zone', the novel makes its readers 'preternaturally aware of space. [...] It forces us to recognise space as a non-neutral thing' (Smith, 2008: 94). It is a novel that creates spaces only in order to collapse them, in a way that questions and subverts its own novelistic boundaries. Exploring the spatial conventions and limits that circumscribe it, it threatens simultaneously to collapse onto the flat surface of the page, and to spill off it. 'One thing all fiction guarantees is that it will describe a place that doesn't exist', writes Daniel Soar (2006: 27), 'ideally a place that bears some relation to the world you think you know but is larger, stranger, bolder and more promising'. He praised *Remainder*'s ability to conjure just such a vividly realized world. This notion of fiction as a 'world' is familiar one, and, as in Soar's review, often the criteria by which the worth of a novel is judged: Does it create a fully realized and three-dimensional imaginary environment? Can we believe in it, and lose ourselves in it? The idea has spawned a branch of theory exemplified in the work of narratologist and philosopher Thomas Pavel, whose *Fictional Worlds* (2008) elaborates a theory of such places. Fictional worlds, according to Pavel, must be considered as having an ontology of sorts. They may not have a concrete existence in the same way as, say, Birmingham or the Bodleian Library, but nevertheless they must be considered as having a kind of existence, as worlds complete in themselves but occupying a parallel realm. They are worlds separate from, yet resembling, our own. The formulation encapsulates some of the most culturally prevalent assumptions about the workings of fiction, but while it might describe a particular kind of novel – falling broadly in the realist tradition – it does not get us far with *Remainder*. Pavel's notion of a discrete, parallel imaginary realm does not adequately describe the spatial dimensions of *Remainder*, which seem instead to operate according to different topographical principles, continually shifting and probing the border between the imaginary and the real. The novel's plot turns precisely on the proliferation and overlapping of different kinds of space, and in this sense Soar's review misses the mark: rather than describing a single, non-existent place, *Remainder* describes multiple places that do not exist, each in a different way. It seems concerned precisely with questions of artifice and demarcation, with plural and complex spaces that interrupt and contradict one another. Conventional notions of a fictional world fall short precisely because it is the very nature of fictional space that the novel wants to question, rendering it unfamiliar, paradoxical and claustrophobic.

If the disorienting spaces that *Remainder* conjures into existence are not those of an immersive fictional world, then mapping them requires a different set of coordinates. McCarthy's own statements invite us to locate his work not in the naturalistic spaces of realist narrative, but in a more francophone lineage of Modernism and self-conscious experimentation. He acknowledges a debt to Robbe-Grillet's work, *Jealousy* (1957), in which the interior of a house becomes the minute and maniacal focus of a story of marital paranoia (McCarthy, 2012). Obsessively rehearsed, the details of the rooms and their layout lose any sense of naturalism, and instead assume a claustrophobic intensity analogous with the narrator's own disintegrating internal world. McCarthy likewise expresses admiration for Jean-Philippe Toussaint's *The Bathroom*, about a surreal and self-enforced confinement in a bathtub (McCarthy, 2010). But perhaps in its fascination with the paradoxes and *mise en abyme* of representation, *Remainder* most readily calls to mind the work of Jorge Luis Borges, whose work continually circled conundrums of authenticity and artifice, fictional and real spaces, and whose enigmatic, ludic philosophical fables are not so much stories as thought experiments, in which narrators come face to face with their doubles, and the text of *Don Quixote* is rewritten, word for word, by a different author. Borges famous para-graph-long story, 'On Exactitude in Science', about a map so large it precisely overlays the territory it charts, acts as a kind of conceptual template for *Remainder*. This Borgesian trope of a life-sized represen-tation of the real is the compelling and paradoxical idea at the heart of McCarthy's novel, and is one that leads us away from the familiar and comforting spaces of fictional worlds and into a more unsettling realm of simulacra and simulation. It is also one that seems to have a particular resonance in contemporary culture, having more than one recent iteration. The publication of *Remainder* occurred just a couple of years before the release of Charlie Kaufmann's film *Synecdoche, New York* (2008), featuring Philip Seymour Hoffman as a frustrated dra-matist who suffers a head trauma and receives a large sum of money, which he then uses to construct a stage set the size of a city. He hires an army of actors to re-enact his own life, but the performance, which has no audience, is unfinished and unfinishable, since it keeps pace with, and bleeds into, his real life. The striking parallels between novel and film, both featuring a neurologically-damaged protagonist obses-sively constructing increasingly elaborate simulated environments, led to speculations about influence and even plagiarism. However, the provenance of these plot elements and the question of which came first is less interesting than the disorienting and counterintuitive pos-sibilities they jointly suggest. In a sense, they exist as remediated, al-ternative versions of one another, their shared thematic logic preclud-ing any claim to originality and precedence, since both concern the impossibility of locating authenticity in a world of simulations. Their re-enactments are less fictional worlds than Baudrillardian simulacra, eclipsing their originals rather than existing in parallel to them, a log-ic which raises the intriguing possibility that McCarthy's novel and Kaufmann's movie could both be copies of one another: the film of the book is simultaneously the book of the film.[1]

Twin narratives of doubling and re-enactment, each existing as doubles of one another: the scenario is certainly strange enough to be the premise of a Borges story. But the case is stranger still, since *Remainder*'s plot of life-sized simulations has yet another it-eration, existing not in film or literature, or in fiction at all, but in

Monchengladbach, Germany. Tom McCarthy may have abandoned early on the idea of being his own protagonist, but in any case the gesture would have been superfluous, since a flesh-and-blood version of his fictional character already existed in the shape of artist Gregor Schneider, who obsessively turns existing buildings into life-sized replicas and populates them with enactors. Schneider lives and works in a three-storey house in Rheydt, Germany. In fact, the house *is* his work, an ongoing project entitled *Haus u r*. In the mid-1980s, while still a teenager, he 'began to transform this house into the projection of his thoughts', and for over twenty years he has been ceaselessly dismembering and reconstructing it from the inside, building false walls, windows and ceilings in front of real ones, creating new openings and spaces, and concealing others (Hoffmann, 2001: 107). The house, although its exterior remains nondescript, has effectively been turned into something else. Exactly what this might be is unclear: existing terminology falls short when it comes to describing the nature and scale of Schneider's building projects. They have been described as 'architectural palimpsests', sculptures, environments, installations, but Schneider himself insists that he just builds 'rooms' (Zamudio, 2004: 110). These are rooms within rooms, however. A coffee room looks like one of the more innocuous and normal places in the house but, exiting through a gap in the wall, another view reveals that the whole room is a fabrication, rotating imperceptibly on wheels. The daylight and breeze through the window are provided by artificial light and a fan.

More often, the artifice is indistinguishable from reality. Observers cannot know that walls conceal other walls, that surfaces are movable, or that a door has disappeared from view. Even Schneider himself declares that he 'can't distinguish anymore between what has been added and what has been subtracted' (Loers et al., 1997: 23). The house at times resembles a normal domestic interior, but at the same time there is something unnatural and unsettling about it. Schneider gives each room a title consisting of a number and a designation that sometimes has a ring of comforting familiarity (e.g. the coffee room) but sometimes produces just the opposite effect ('the largest wank', 'the smallest wank', 'the disco', 'the brothel'). This is a real building in an ordinary street, but the rooms inside it are 'located outside all normality' (Bronfen, 2001: 44). The house, like the one reconstructed by *Remainder*'s protagonist, is no longer itself, but a simulation. And Schneider's rooms, like those in the novel, are also populated by re-enactors. *Haus u r* is occupied, or at least haunted, by a mysterious character called Hannalore Reuen, whose name appears on the front door in the conventional German fashion. Questioned about Reuen, Schneider is evasive. It is not clear if she is an artistic collaborator, a real person or Schneider's alter ego. Her face is never pictured, but she features in a series of photographs, apparently the victim of a violent crime, prostrate and face-down. In 2004, Schneider took over two adjacent houses in London's Whitechapel to create a work entitled *Die Familie Schneider*. The two houses, all but indistinguishable from one another internally, had the same dreary décor, the same food in the fridge, and the same stains on the wall. They also had an identical cast of inhabitants engaged in the same repeated actions: a woman stood at the sink washing up, while next door her twin did the same. More disturbing goings-on in the bathroom and bedrooms were also duplicated: a man in the shower, hunched over, seemed to be masturbating; and a child sat in the bedroom with its head covered by a dustbin bag (Tóibín and O'Hagan, 2006).

The same real-yet-fabricated buildings; the same eerie moving tableaux repeating endlessly. McCarthy's and Schneider's buildings might be mirror images of one another, one in the pages of a novel and the other in an actual street. Reading these spaces alongside one another brings us closer to an understanding of the kind of shared territory they inhabit. It is a territory whose boundaries are difficult to discern. Schneider's walls behind walls mean that, like Russian dolls, layers nestle within one another, each calling the artifice or authenticity of the others into question. 'When you open a window, you get no view of the street or the garden. Behind the window is a second window. There seems to be no outside. Everything leads back to the house' (Birnbaum, 2000: 144). In *Remainder*, too, there are continual questions about what is outside and what is inside the main character's artificial world. Having turned an entire building into an imaginary environment, he then constructs a miniature scale model of it, complete with miniature re-enactors inside, making their movements dictate those of their full-size counterparts. He sets in motion what is known as a 'Droste Effect', a never-ending recursive device in which, for example, a painting contains a representation of itself. But what lies at the edges of these multiple levels of artifice? We are in a fictionalized south London that seems like the real thing, complete with mundane detail and authentic bars and street names. But is this Brixton setting only a 'set'? Is it real or an imitation of the real? One of these authentic street names in particular, Plato Road, draws attention to the whole vexed question of artifice versus authenticity. The narrator's relentless reconstructions are a search for ideal Platonic form, the singular, transcendent incarnation of his vision rather than a mere debased material copy. *Haus u r* carries similar implications, its initials standing ostensibly for Schneider's address – Unterheydernerstrasse, Rheyt – while gesturing also towards the notion of an elusive original or the source. In both cases the search for the Platonic ideal – the 'Ur-house' – is built on an insurmountable paradox: the real world is inauthentic and in need of modification; it must be adapted, replicated and reconstructed in order to be authentic.

The distinction between inside and outside, between real and artifice, is complicated still further by a proliferation of copies. Schneider's *Haus u r* has been recreated in its entirety down to the smallest detail in galleries around the world. In 2001, its anonymous, sometimes cramped and scruffy domestic interior was reconstructed, incongruously, inside that monument to Nazi bombast, the German Pavilion at the Venice Biennale. The house in Rheydt – itself already a replica – is replicated again and again as an art exhibit. Schneider and *Remainder*'s protagonist produce spaces that are doubled: they are physically 'real' yet simultaneously artificial, they are 'here' and yet at the same time elsewhere. Schneider describes the sensation of being simultaneously in two places: '[W]hen I was in the finished room in Berlin, I was in Rheydt. Do you know the way people on spaceships beam themselves from one place to another?' (Loers et al., 1997: 26). These doubled spaces, the same but different, with their overlapping layers of reality and artifice, are instances of what Anthony Vidler calls an 'architectural uncanny'. Vidler (1994: 3) shows how, in the uncanny's play of doubling, the other is experienced as a replica of the self, 'all the more fearsome because apparently the same'. And the site where such disturbing ambiguities between self and other, real and unreal are most frequently enacted is domestic space. Tracing early cultural manifestations of the uncanny, Vidler (1994: 11) writes that 'its favourite motif was precisely the contrast between a secure and homely interior and the fearful invasion of an alien presence'. The spaces constructed in McCarthy's novel and Schneider's work enact, in the most literal sense, the slippage Freud describes between that which is *Heimlich* (homely) and that which is *Unheimlich* (uncanny). In the German, the two are not simply opposites, but rather the meanings of the former contain elements of the latter, so that the space of the familiar is haunted from the start by that which is unfamiliar and threatening. In the case of *Remainder* and *Haus u r*, a lived environment is a replica, a home which resembles but is no longer itself.

These building projects share the same kind of disturbing ambiguities, and generate the same kind of uncanny spatial frisson. These are very similar kinds of space, clearly, but what kind is that? What type of space might exist both in a novel and in a real street, criss-crossing the boundary between fiction and its other? The novel's protagonist gives us some clues as to the nature of the place we are in, musing on the connotations of the sports pitch and the stage set. Both are arbitrarily demarcated zones in which space becomes 'charged', so that the movement of bodies within it, their trajectories, the precise details of their relation to one another and to the space and surfaces around them acquires a special significance. Schneider and McCarthy create sites that are similarly charged: 'fired up, silently zinging with significance' (*R*, 133). They are the focus of a baffling but exhaustive series of investigations. 'I look at a wall and am interested in any unevennesses on its surface: the tiniest hole, the slightest protuberance', says Schneider (Loers et al., 1997: 43). *Remainder*'s narrator is similarly transfixed by cracks and oil stains, capturing them in diagrams. Schneider describes 'experiments', involving 'going into a room and leaving it again, hoping that the experience would linger there', while the novel's narrator obsessively scrutinizes his own actions, practising an accidental turn of the body and a brush against the kitchen worktop over and over until it become 'natural' (Loers et al., 1997: 45). Equally closely, he dissects the gestures of his re-enactors, analysing their precise geometrical patterns moment by moment: 'I'd break the sequence down to its constituent parts – the changing angle of her headscarf and her stooped back's inclination as she moved between two steps, the swivel of her neck as her head turned to face me – and lose myself in them' (R, 151).

Schneider and McCarthy's spaces most resemble neither the sports pitch nor the stage set, but the crime scene. The kind of location where such investigations are carried out, where movement and trajectory, surface and angle acquires such charged significance is the aftermath of death or violence, sealed off so that events can be recreated through forensic examination of their traces. The analogy has already been noted in the case of Schneider, whose rooms seem to bear the traces of violent or disturbing events.[2] As a teenager he describes photographing a particular murder scene, scrutinizing it for echoes of what took place there. His later work, too, is often an overt attempt to engage with death and its aftermath, sometimes through replica bodies grotesquely strewn across the gallery floor, their faces covered, and other times through more subtle yet chilling details which speak of the unspeakable. Sharp-eyed visitors may spot blood on the radiator pipes in his twin Whitechapel houses, for instance. But even when devoid of blood and bodies, his bare and anonymous white rooms suggest a type of clinical violence. In their sheer mundanity, they resemble precisely the kind of spaces depicted in police photographs. *Remainder*'s buildings might lack the macabre menace of Schneider's rooms, but the re-enactments of inconsequential movements nevertheless foreshadow the crime reconstructions that the narrator is inexorably drawn towards. Encountering the scene of shooting in Brixton, he seems to discover what he was looking for all along. His minute obsession with angles, surface and details, his repeated replaying of certain movements and actions – in fact, pretty much his entire repertoire of obsessive behaviours – he finds all of these encoded within the disciplinary procedures of forensics. He immerses himself rapturously in the literature and the diagrams of forensic analysis. 'Each line, each figure, every angle – the ink itself vibrates with an almost intolerable violence, darkly screaming from the silence of the white paper: something has happened here, someone has died' (*R*, 173). Forensic procedure exerts this powerful hold over the narrator 'because it's real' (*R*, 173): it seems to guarantee a route out of the realm of the second hand and the simulated, and provide a way, finally, to merge with the real.

But even – perhaps especially – the crime scene is second-hand and simulated: 'the road itself was like a grand master, one of those Dutch ones thick with rippling layers of oil paint' (*R*, 187). Transfixed as he is by the details, the narrator nevertheless reveals that this scene is still caught up in the system of representation he seeks to escape. As his re-enactments seek to come closer and closer to reality, so they force a crisis in this system. His final project involves 'lifting the re-enactment out of its demarcated zone and slotting it back into the real world' (*R*, 244). He enacts an imaginary bank robbery, but stages it inside an actual bank. The boundaries of the re-enactment zone dissolve, and the scripted staging of a crime is transformed, catastrophically, into an actual crime. What results is not a seamless merging with the real, but an irresolvable conflict between differently constructed kinds of space. The episode in the bank is the culmination of an escalating territorial dispute between the private and public, the imagined and the actual, artifice and reality. The phrase 'turf wars' is one that the narrator muses on, thinking of gangland shootings and squares of grass (*R*, 206), but the turf war in which he is caught up is one between the fictional world and real world. This is precisely the logic of the crime scene as described by theorist Mark Seltzer, less a specific location than a focal point in the contemporary cultural imaginary, it is a site overdetermined with anxieties and fantasies about authenticity, violence and representation. At the crime scene, states Seltzer (1998: 16), 'fact and fiction have a way of changing places'. In *Remainder*'s re-enactment-turned-crime, the two cross and collide, producing a volatile scene whose scripted moves explode into violence and death when one of the enactors accidentally shoots another. A fictional bank robbery produces a real shooting, which is then reincorporated into fiction, 're-enacted' by the protagonist.

The crime scene is the epicentre of a wider cultural domain that Seltzer calls the 'pathological public sphere', an overlit, technologically saturated, unstable domain in which conventional modes of subjectivity and distinctions between the real and the imaginary are radically reconfigured. Seltzer draws on Baudrillard, suggesting that the individual and authentic, becoming incorporated into a limitless series of technological reproductions and duplicates, loses its claim to primacy. Such hyper-mediation erodes conventional distinctions between public and private. This new kind of public sphere is no longer the counterpoint to an individual, domestic or psychological domain, but becomes instead a 'crossing point of private fantasy and public space' (Seltzer, 1998: 31). It is this zone that accounts for the warped dimensions of both *Remainder* and Schneider's constructions. *Remainder*'s 'world', if it has one, belongs not in the space of fiction as such, but in this new zone of the pathological public sphere, which criss-crosses the conventional boundaries of the imaginary or the fictional. It is this territory that Schneider's and McCarthy's built environments share, operating precisely according to its 'intersecting logics of seriality, prosthesis and primary mediation' (Seltzer, 1998: 33). To catalogue Schneider's modifications is to work through 'every possible repetition and duplication of basic architectural units: "wall in front of wall, ceiling under ceiling, section of wall in front of wall, room in room, lead in floor"' (Birnbaum, 2000: 144). These reiterations of what is already there have become indistinguishable from the real thing: 'The original dimensions and configuration of the various rooms is all but impossible to reconstruct' (Birnbaum, 2001: 73). In fact, the only way to perceive its complex layers is not to view the house itself, but Schneider's videos of his tortured navigations as he 'huffs and groans to gain access to the crawl spaces and interstices that no one else sees between the pre-existing structural walls and his additional false ones' (Ward, 2004: 103). In *Remainder*, too, mediations continually replace their originals. 'It's me. [...] The real me,' says the narrator, interrupting his own prosthetic answerphone voice (*R*, 170), but in truth he has no real self. Every movement and action in his repertoire has had to be painstakingly learned from scratch, following his accident. His memories have returned 'in moving images [...] like a film run in instalments', which appear less real than watching Robert De Niro on the cinema screen (*R*, 22). At least De Niro seems natural. Everything about the narrator is unnatural, second hand: '[J]erking back and forth like paused video images', he is already his own mediated double (*R*, 15). His re-enactments are a bid to be authentic, to merge seamlessly with reality, but only introduce yet more layers of mediation. He insists that no cameras are used, but he himself is a kind of recording device, a one-man Xerox machine, capturing every detail and producing more and more sketches, transcriptions, representations. And, even as they are acted out, these re-enactments are played on a loop, rewound, paused, and replayed at half speed. Filming is redundant when reality already behaves like a recording.

And if these (re)constructed spaces characterize the pathological public sphere, then so do their monomaniacal architects. The subject proper to this sphere is no ordinary person, or rather, it is someone so extra-ordinarily ordinary they become 'hyper-typical'. This is the figure of the serial killer, not an individual so much as a 'type' generated by the statistical analyses and information processing of modern, bureaucratic criminal profiling. The serial killer himself is driven by these same statistical, informational imperatives. His is a pathology, Seltzer argues, that emanates not from the depths of the psyche but conversely, from external factors. It is a perverse internalization of the logic of machine culture, an 'utter absorption in the technologies of reflection, reduplication, and simulation' (Seltzer, 1998: 20). Serial killers are often described in terms of their blankness, their abnormal normality, their absence of distinguishing characteristics. This is an individual defined precisely by a lack of individuality who, chameleon-like, assumes identities according to context and surroundings. The serial killer thus experiences themselves as inauthentic, as a 'simulated person' (Seltzer, 1998: 43). Moreover, this tendency to blend into the background goes beyond mere camouflage: it is an effective (and affective) merging with the environment. In other words sheer absence of intrinsic identity leads to an over-identification with place, and particularly those which the killer himself constructs. For this reason construction projects are a character trait of the serial killer,

Seltzer argues. There is 'an absorption in place and place-construction that becomes indistinguishable from programmes of self-making and self-construction' (Seltzer, 1998: 34).

It seems that exactly this 'reciprocal topography of subject and scene' (Seltzer, 1998: 49) is what is at work in the building projects of Gregor Schneider and *Remainder*'s protagonist. Both eerily blank and characterless, they seem to match the composite image of the serial killer that Seltzer maps out. McCarthy's narrator, recently emerged from a coma and suffering from neurological trauma, experiences himself as deeply inauthentic. His only sensation – a 'tingling' – is one that he experienced through the process of enactment. Schneider, questioned about his motives, appears similarly blank and compulsive, merely responding that 'there was nothing else I could do' (Loers et al., 1997: 44). Whether or not this blankness is authentic or merely a persona (and the question seems beside the point in this context of hyperartifice), he claims to have no understanding of his own work. Other statements suggest darkly that his building projects are driven not by conscious aesthetic choice but by a logic of obsessive compulsion. He recalls being exempted from military service in his teens on the grounds of mental health: 'I was registered as having a perceptual disorder and being mentally ill, but I only told them what I was doing at the time. [...] I told them that I build rooms' (Birnbaum, 2000: 146). In a TV documentary, asked about the appeal of the filthy Hamburg alleyway he is meticulously recreating in a gallery, he merely freezes, staring blankly at the interviewer. The question of motivation and agency produces a total shut down, an inability to formulate any response at all. Compulsive building and compulsive violence seem somehow inextricably linked. 'The view I had of her was like a murderer's view' (*R*, 140) says the *Remainder*'s protagonist, as he describes one of his re-enactors. Schneider too, is prone to taking a 'murderer's view' of some of his visitors. Talking of his isolated guestroom, in which visitors might become trapped, possibly fatally, he reflects wistfully: 'I'd love to stop someone getting away some time' (Birnbaum, 2000: 143). And if serial killing is about the 'terrifying pleasures of endless replication' (Seltzer, 1998: 52), then their room-building and re-enactments is driven by a similar impulse and a similar cultural logic. *Remainder's* re-enactments begin to follow a chain of gangland shootings, their seriality and escalation shadowing the serial violence itself. And when, finally, the main character becomes a killer, it is not through a violent impulse so much as a mimetic one. He is merely playing someone else, and rehearsing the moments when, in a disastrous bank robbery re-enactment, someone is accidentally shot: 'Essentially, it was the movements, the position and the tingling that made me do it, nothing more' (*R*, 276).

If *Remainder* makes little sense in terms of a fictional world, it corresponds much more closely to the dimensions of the pathological public sphere as outlined by Setlzer, whose logic of primary mediation refuses to recognize the boundary between fictional and real zones. The space McCarthy creates in his novel is no self-contained parallel imaginative realm, but part of a continuum of proliferating artifice, duplication and iteration. In one sense, then, its spaces extend counter-intuitively beyond circumscribed novelistic boundaries, spilling off the page to haunt and double those of Schneider's *Haus u r*, Kaufman's immense cinematic set and perhaps other places. In another sense, however, its emphasis on artifice and mediation pulls in an opposite but equally disruptive direction, confronting us with its own fundamental artifice. It disturbs three-dimensional novelistic space by calling attention to its own spatial confinement within the two-dimensional limits on the page. Returning, as promised, to Proust, albeit via the unlikely route of serial killing, we can explore this through the analogy between Madlyn Mansions and Proust's madeleine moment. As McCarthy's sly misspelling indicates, their relationship is as much about differences as similarities. While they both involve the unfolding and realizing of a remembered place, the nature of these places is quite different. For Diana Fuss (2004), Proust provides the most complex and elaborate illustration of what she terms the novel's 'architecture of the interior'. Novelistic space, she demonstrates, is associated from its inception with ideas of 'interiority' in two senses: in the first place, the domestic space of the house commonly functions as an analogy for the novel, as in Henry James' 'House of Fiction'; but beyond this, the domestic topography of fiction maps onto personal, individual interiority. The realist novel finds its most common settings in the newly private domestic interior, and its signature subject matter in the interior landscapes of its characters, their development and growth. *In Search of Lost Time* elevates this link between setting and identity into its central principle: domestic space is imbued with memory and psychological significance to such an extent that it acts not only as a location of the narrator's childhood memories but also as a setting for his introspective reveries and self discovery as an adult and a writer. Proust is the apotheosis of the already profound novelistic entanglements of domestic and psychological interiority. If the etymology of 'interior' brings together both physical and mental senses of the word, it is in fictional space where the two become indivisible.

Marie-Laure Ryan, too, makes a link between Proust, interiority and fictional space. She invokes this Proustian architecture of the interior in order to describe how novels 'transport' readers into their own space. Like the narrator of *In Search of Lost Time*, we can be in one place while mentally inhabiting another. Here is a subtly different approach to the notion of a fictional world, therefore; where Pavel posits their existence in a parallel ontological realm, Ryan suggests they are summoned into existence by a congruence between the reader's affective interior spaces and those of the novel. Fiction's trick of spatial immersion she terms the 'madeleine effect' (2000: 121), most powerful when the reader's memory is stimulated and a mental world opens up before us. In a similar way to Proust's narrator, readers of novels bring their own experience and memories to bear in the imaginative construction of a convincing and fully realised fictional world. Clearly, a different kind of space is at work in McCarthy's novel, which disrupts this three-dimensional imagining of domestic and psychological interiority. The 'madeleine effect' as described by Ryan is quite different to the 'Madlyn effect' produced by *Remainder*. Where the former produces an immersive, fully-realised fictional world, the latter produces an effect of vertiginous artificiality and two-dimensionality. If novelistic convention often invokes domestic space as an analogue for psychological interiority, then McCarthy's Madlyn Mansions, like Schneider's *Haus u r*, is all surface and no depth. Its interior is not a space that can be read in terms of psychological privacy, since it is not really an interior at all, but a continuous facade. Its surfaces, walls, floors and windows have all been scrupulously re-created at great expense to resemble some lost original. Its hyper-artifice gestures not toward authenticity and an uncovering/recovery of the real, unique self, but instead to the individual as an inauthentic, interchangeable, mediated copy. *Remainder* does not operate according to the spatial conventions of fictional worlds, but rather those of Seltzer's pathological public sphere, where the concept of interiority no longer carries the same currency. It produces both a protagonist and a domestic space which are all surface and no depth. The interior, where it exists, is not something private and hidden, but transformed into surface spectacle, most strikingly in a moment when the body's inner spaces are opened to public view. The narrator, having just inflicted a fatal gunshot wound on someone he knows only as 'Two', scrutinizes the injury. In an instance of what Seltzer calls 'stranger intimacy' – a type of anonymised interaction characteristic of the pathological public sphere – he probes the wound, fascinated: 'I poked at his exposed flesh with my finger. It was a lot like Four's flesh, it had the same sponge-like texture: soft and firm at the same time' (*R*, 277).

If *Remainder* subverts the notion of fictional worlds, it is because of its refusal and subversion of the kind of immersive, interior spaces that Ryan and Fuss associate with the novel. Its protagonist creates worlds as artificial, depthless and blank as himself. In this sense he is not merely an unreliable narrator but an impossible narrator; he is a character within a novel, yet does not subscribe to the paradigm of novelistic fiction, nor to the depth model of subjectivity and space that underlies it. He seems incapable of inhabiting the fictional world as convention demands. Instead, his presence is disruptive, constantly drawing attention to the paradoxes and conventions of fictional, illusionistic space. Like Schneider's coffee room on wheels, he exposes the workings that lie behind the scenes. In staging his re-enactments, he produces a peculiar kind of Beckettian theatre of anti-illusionism, one resistant to immersion and affective involvement. The participants in one re-enactment, speaking at a half-speed monotone recite the words 'I – am – real' over and over again, suggesting just the opposite. He creates fictional worlds only to expose their strangeness and arbitrariness. He populates them not with psychologically rounded characters but 're-enactors' who perform the same actions repeatedly and mechanically at varying speeds. These actions he then scrutinizes not for what they might reveal about their performers, but instead as isolated movements, a set of angles and patterns to be 'captured'. In *Tintin and the Secret of Literature*, McCarthy argues that the famous comic book sleuth succeeds because he is an adept reader, and can navigate the world of signs. *Remainder's* protagonist seems to illustrate the obverse point, coming to grief precisely because he cannot. Despite his obsession with words, and with their definitions, he does not penetrate language to find its meanings, but focuses at the level of patterns and similarities. He is not at home with depth reading, with immersion, seeing instead only surface. He reads everything as flat, seeing diagrams of his fluctuating shares as purely geometric lines, and the actions he has scripted for his own cast of characters in similar terms. This world he creates is one in which the normal currency of the novel plotline – human subjectivity and moral agency – is excised, replaced instead with the geometry of movements, surfaces and patterns.

As readers, seeing events through his narratorial point of view, we are forced to read in something like the same way. *Remainder* does not permit the kind of readerly engagement we might conventionally expect in a novel. The protagonist's flattened and blank mode of narration prohibits us from empathizing with him, since he himself is unable to empathize, to relate to other people as individuals. Even more disconcertingly, however, the 'space' of the novel is something we are not permitted to enter fully. Having spent several pages recounting the story of a meeting with a homeless man, complete with details of dogs, restaurant interiors and waitresses, the protagonist's narrative abruptly breaks down: 'the truth is, I've been making all this up' (R, 56). This moment brings us up short; no sooner has the spatial illusion been created than it is collapsed, prompting a series of other troubling questions about how much we can believe of this narrator's story. What is 'real' in this novel? Which events actually happened and which are the product of a traumatized and possibly delusional mind? Is the narrator still in a coma, his mind 'still asleep but […] inventing spaces and scenes for me to inhabit' (R, 51)? There are hints that this may be the case, but embarking on this chain of logic leads us ultimately to the disconcerting recognition that of course none of this is 'real'. None of these events actually took place, except in the novel we hold in our hands. Ultimately, we are left confronting the flat surface of the page, but also a question about what it means to conjure imaginary places and people from this surface. Fiction is a highly artificial way of conceptually organizing space. Interacting with it successfully involves a knowledge of its conventions, its rules and zones of demarcation. Such rules may be second nature to novel readers, but, as *Remainder* indicates, they are in fact highly un-natural. McCarthy's novel 'trains you out of a certain way of thinking,' as Zadie Smith (2008) argues. If 'all novels attempt to cut neural routes through the brain', then *Remainder* reroutes the novel. Smith picks up on *Remainder*'s own neurological vocabulary. 'To cut and lay new circuits in your brain' explains the narrator, 'they make you visualise things' (*R*, 19). Following his accident, he undergoes therapy to recalibrate his hand–eye coordination and so, as he knows only too well therefore, the imagining and visualizing of space is learned behaviour, a neurological function that can be unlearned and relearned. In a similar way, the novel seems to imply, reading fictional worlds – reading depth from flatness – is not natural. From its affectless, traumatized, disconnected vantage point, imagining fictional space is not just defamiliarized but even pathologized.

Remainder initially hovered between novel and physical space, and in its finished form still oscillates between the two. It is a fiction that refuses fictional conventions, or rather, it consistently explores and exposes these conventions and the spatial paradoxes underlying them. Its narrator unfolds his imagined world only in order to collapse it again. In one sense this means that the novel continually exceeds its own textual boundaries, setting up disruptive relays between the supposedly separate zones of the fictional and the real. It doubles and reiterates other, similarly disconcerting non-places, merging with the continuous mediated surfaces of a technologized culture of simulations. In another sense, its flatness only draws attention to its own tangible, textual boundaries. McCarthy's earlier novel, *Men in Space* (written prior to *Remainder*, though published later), has as its central motif a Byzantine icon which is on the one hand figurative, but whose pictorial conventions and severe geometry draw attention to the flatness of the picture plane. It refuses to be read in terms of illusionistic, three-dimensional space, and instead produces a different, disruptive set of spatial coordinates. This disruption is something *Remainder* enacts also, setting up a constant tension between the illusion of depth and flatness of the medium. Conventionally, the illusionistic space of fiction depends on the effective dematerialisation of the page, a strategic forgetting of the surface in order to read through it and enter an immersive fictional world. *Remainder's* insistent flatness, its refusal to sustain such immersive places brings us back over and over to the artifice of the illusion. Ultimately it brings us back its own fundamental *trompe-l'oeil*: its own two-dimensional pages. Such paper surfaces may promise depth, it reminds us, but the printed words nevertheless remain there as a troublesome, material reminder that this is an illusion. Its narrator battles with 'stuff' (*R*, 121) that interferes with the neatness, coherence and perfection he seeks in his re-enactments. Messy brake fluid spills onto his lap, the phone socket disgustingly emerges from the wall and, most tellingly, ink clings to his fingers from his tube ticket. Like the narrator, we are left with the messy, material residue, the inky remainder that stubbornly refuses to dematerialize.

Notes

1 Kaufman's protagonist in fact considers 'Simulacrum' as a title for his demented magnum opus.

2 They are, as Ben Lewis observes, 'a cross between unfurnished lets and crime scenes' (Lewis, 2003).

Works Cited

Birnbaum, Daniel (2000) 'Interiority Complex: Gregor Schneider's Dead House UR, 1985 – ', *Artforum International* 38(10): 143–7.

Birnbaum, Daniel (2001) 'Before and After Architecture: Unterheydener Strasse 12, Rheydt', in *Totes Haus ur*, ed. Udo Kittelmann and Gregor Schneider, pp. 63–87. Ostfilern-Ruit: Hatje Catnz.

Borges, Jorge Luis (1999) 'On Exactitude in Science', in *Collected Fictions*, trans. by Andrew Hurley, p. 341. London: Penguin.

Bronfen, Elisabeth, (2001) 'Chryptotopias. *Secret Sites/Transmittable Traces*', in *Totes Haus ur*, ed. Udo Kittelmann and Gregor Schneider, pp. 33–60. Ostfilern-Ruit: Hatje Catnz.

Fuss, Diana (2004) *The Sense of an Interior: Four Rooms and the Writers That Shaped Them*. London: Routledge.

Hoffmann, Jens (2001) 'Gregor Schneider', *Flash Art* 216: 107

Lewis, Ben (2003) 'Gregor Schneider: House of Horror', *Art Safari 1* [DVD].

Loers, Viet, Brigitte Kolle and Adam Szymcyk (1997) *Gregor Schneider: Totes Haus ur/Dead House Ur 1985–1997*. Frankfurt am Main: Kunsthalle.

McCarthy, Tom (2010) 'Stabbing the Olive', *London Review of Books*, 11 February, pp. 26–8.

McCarthy, Tom (2012) 'Introduction', in Alain Robbe-Grillet, *Jealousy*, trans. Richard Howard. London: Alma.

Morgan, Catrin (2010) *Phantom Settlements*. London: Ditto.

Pavel, T. G. (1986) *Fictional Worlds*. Cambridge, MA: Harvard University Press.

Proust, Marcel (2003) *The Way by Swann's*, trans. by Lydia Davis. London: Penguin.

Ryan, Marie-Laure (2000) *Narrative as Virtual Reality: Immersion and Interactivity in Literature and Electronic Media*. Baltimore, MD: Johns Hopkins University Press.

Seltzer, Mark (1998) *Serial Killers: Death and Life in America's Wound Culture*. New York: Routledge.

Smith, Zadie (2008) 'Two Paths for the Novel', *New York Review of Books* 55(18), 20 November: 89–95.

Soar, Daniel (2006) 'The Smell of Frying Liver Drifting up from Downstairs', *London Review of Books* 28(5): 27.

Tóibín, Colm, and Andrew O'Hagan (2006) *Gregor Schneider: Die Familie Schneider*. Göttingen: Steidl.

Vidler, Anthony (1994) *The Architectural Uncanny: Essays in the Modern Unhomely*. Cambridge, MA: MIT Press.

Ward, Ossian (2004) 'The feeling is Mutual', *Art Review* 54: 103.

Zamudio, Raul (2004) 'Gregor Schneider at Barbara Gladstone', *Flash Art* 234: 110.

4

'STRANGE DIAGONAL WHICH WAS THOUGHT TO BE SO PURE' CALCULATING THE SQUARE ROOT OF TOM MCCARTHY'S GEOMETRIC EXHORTATION

Mark Blacklock

In his essay 'Stabbing the Olive', Tom McCarthy smuggled into his fulsome appreciation of Jean-Philippe Toussaint an exhortation: 'we don't want plot, depth or content: we want angles, arcs and intervals; we want pattern. Structure is content, geometry is everything' (2010: 26). While a call to arms is no shock from a writer who opened his account with a manifesto, this directive demands attention. After all, most such statements are issued by the INS; this was Tom McCarthy as literary critic. His elaboration of these lines, in reference to Toussaint's deployment of a geometric logic in his first novel, *The Bathroom*, gives us some useful triangulation points:

> We exist and assume subjectivity to the extent that we occupy a spot on or traverse the grid: an implicit assertion that's part Descartes, part Deleuze. Geometry is not just an aesthetic: it is, to borrow a term from Deleuze, our 'habitus'. (McCarthy, 2010: 26)

Descartes gives us co-ordinate geometry, the grid itself, and instigates a way of visualising algebraic functions, of performing analytic geometry. Deleuzean *habitus* is a rather more difficult, but more immediately literary, concept. It incorporates space and time in a shifting present. 'Habit is the foundation of time, the moving soil of the passing present,' writes Deleuze (2004: 101). It is a ground for repetition, set against memory.

McCarthy (2003: 31) has written elsewhere that 'the event field of trauma is a space of substitution and displacement and encoding – but most of all it is a space of repetition'. His assessment of the greatest legacy of the *nouveau roman* returns to this reading of space and trauma. He writes that it gives us 'an understanding of what renders space meaningful. It is an understanding that Greek tragedy (with its houses, cities and whole states founded on primal murders) also displays' (McCarthy, 2010: 26). 'For the Greeks,' he has argued, 'knowledge and trauma are never far apart' (McCarthy, 2003: 18). In *The Bathroom,* the single meaningful act is the throwing of a dart into someone's head.

The aim of this chapter is to put some flesh on the bones of these geometric exhortations, to expand these equations. What would a fiction corresponding to McCarthy's claims be like? Does the author's own fiction display obedience to these principles? Do we read in his novels 'angles, arcs and intervals'? And if we do, what sort of geometry is at work? What does it do and why? My first way in to this question, then, is a geometric reading of *Remainder, Men in Space* and *C.* I would also like to situate these claims. If we are interested in a fiction that borrows from geometry we need to identify what it is that geometry might be able to lend to such fiction, how we might move between these two seemingly alien modes of representation. I would like to sketch certain aspects of the heritage of McCarthy's claim, with particular attention to how this heritage informed artistic Modernism. Primarily, I want to construct a provocatively narrow and absurdly biased canon for geometric fiction, determined by a desire to draw a triangle with a work of fiction on each of its sides. I have no interest in entertaining anything that might distort my construction of a three-sided figure and make no apologies for so doing. I want to create a bed for McCarthy's work by locating at side *b*, Edwin Abbott's *Flatland* (1884), and at side *c*, J. G. Ballard's *The Atrocity Exhibition* (1970). This reading leads us towards an interrogation of the subjectivity that we assume on the grid, the bull's eye of the target made by a geometrically conditioned fiction. Drawing from Michel Serres's essays on geometry I want to read back into geometry's pre-Socratic history to consider its own roots in trauma, violence and the sacred, and to reinforce the project of the sacrifice of the humanist subjects of contemporary fiction.

Side *a*

Remainder's narrator inhabits grids. Rather like the reader of the text, he needs to 'cut and lay the new circuits' in his brain (*R*, 19). Attending a party at Dave Simpson's house on Plato Road – it is round the corner from Kepler Road, by the way – he notes the incomplete decor: 'there were wires dangling from the ceilings and lines sketched out in pencil on the walls showing where shelves were going to go up, plus little diagrams scrawled beside switches showing the routes electric circuits were to follow' (*R*, 57). Uninterested in sport before his accident, he can now recall the details of games he has watched on TV: 'overviews of the field's layout with diagrams drawn over them showing which vectors were covered and which weren't' (*R*, 88). He meets Naz for the first-time in the Blueprint Cafe. As he and Naz's staff search Belgravia in a gridding pattern he imagines watching the process from above, taking a cartographer's view: 'I imagined looking down from even higher up, the edges of the stratosphere. [...] It was good' (*R*, 92). Rehearsing the text-book accounts of forensic searches he describes how a chief investigator might organize a search: 'or he might cut up the area by laying a grid across it and assigning each investigator one of the grid's zones' (*R*, 174).

The Brixton crime scene offers a distinct and visual example of the presiding geometry of the text. It is centred on the outline of a body, a cliché of the police crime scene recognizable from a thousand films and crime dramas. Read geometrically this outline is a flattened, or orthographically projected, three-dimensional corpse. It is also a remainder, a mark left behind by a traumatic event, and our narrator wants to unlock its meaning, to put flesh back on its bones and to repeat its final actions, the actions that resulted in its dimensional reduction. A two-dimensional or planar geometry presides over all *Remainder*'s maps, plans and circuit diagrams, and here, marked onto the ground, is the trauma at their axis.

Remainder's close – it is certainly not an ending – illustrates an additional level in the novel's deployment of geometry. Following the bank heist, in the air, the hijacked getaway plane banks and turns under orders from the narrator: 'Our trail would be visible from the ground: an eight, plus that first bit, where we'd first set off – fainter, drifted to the side by now, discarded, a remainder' (R, 283). This shape has been anticipated. The insurance settlement the narrator receives is eight million pounds (eight and a half, if we're to include *that* remainder). If he were a chief forensic investigator the narrator would

> plump for a figure of eight, and have each of my people crawl around the same area in an endlessly repeating circuit, unearthing the same evidence, the same prints, marks and tracings again and again and again, recording them as though afresh each time. (R, 175)

The figure of eight is important to this text, and not as a number – turn the figure of eight on its side and you have the lemniscate, symbol for infinity, a repeating loop. The narrative is launched by the figure of eight and ends held in it. We are not dealing with eight units of anything, but rather what you can do on an eight-shaped circuit: repeat, revolve, loop. When the novel leaves the reader in this suspension, with the observation that it cannot last, it foregrounds the gap between mimetic art and the lived world. In the closed system of the novel, we can be left in suspension, infinity can be sustained. In the entropic physical universe, however

> [e]ventually the sun would set forever – burn out, *pop*, extinguish – and the universe would run down like a Fisher Price toy whose spring has unwound to its very end. Then there'd be no more music, no more loops. Or maybe, before that, we'd just run out of fuel. For now,

though, the clouds tilted and the weightlessness set in once more as we banked, turning, heading back, again. (*R*, 284)

McCarthy's next novel, *Men in Space*, features a character held in such suspension throughout its course, another individual held in stasis in a geometric pattern. Hàjek declares:

'A soviet cosmonaut is stranded in his spaceship. [...] This guy went up as a Soviet, on a routine space mission, and then, while he was up there the Soviet Union disintegrated. Now, no one wants to bring him down'. (*MIS*, 42)

The cosmonaut orbits the earth, and the text, *ex machina*, a piece of cosmic surplus matter. As with the figure of eight in *Remainder*, orbits repeat throughout *Men in Space*. Anton figures the mechanisms of the crime organization for which he works in engineering terms:

The basic mechanical principle by which the turning effect of a force about a given axis, its leverage or 'moment', can be said to be directly relational to the distance from the pivot to the line of force – this principle, they were told, was universally applicable. All systems have pivotal points: identify these and the whole structure will leap into focus. (*MIS*, 17)

Anton's observation is a guide to reading. The pivotal figure of *Men in Space* is this orbit, or rather the shape it makes when obliquely projected onto a plane. Contemplating the religious icon that Anton must have duplicated, Klárá notes its unorthodoxies. Figures in the scene are axonometric – 'there's no variation in their distance from the viewer' (*MIS*, 107–8). The surface of representation is flat, does not conform to Cartesian perspectivalism:

But the strangest thing of all is this: God's represented not by a circle but by an ellipse around the saint's head. Very, very bizarre. The coding of these icons is rock-solid: God's *always* substituted by either a Christ figure or a perfect circle in ascensions. But an *ellipse*, a kind of oval which itself seems to retreat as though its top edge were being dragged back by some magnetic force? It's simply, well, just *wrong...* (*MIS*, 108)

As in *Remainder* we have projection, the representation of a three-dimensional figure in two-dimensional space, but here the projection is oblique rather than orthographic: the object to be reduced is not directly between the observer or light source and the plane or screen onto which we are projecting it, but to the side, above or below.

Oblique projection gives us more information than does orthographic: we represent more of the object's faces. Turn the process on its head and shift the position of the observer rather than the object, and we enter the realm of a favourite technique of renaissance painting: perspective anamorphosis is a form of oblique projection. In order to bring the text into focus we need to shift our position in front of it. We may call to mind the skull in the foreground of Holbein's *The Ambassadors* (1533). We *should* call it to mind. For the twenty-first century reader of cultural artefacts, anamorphosis is coded with that death's head.

The ellipse in this novel, like *Remainder*'s figures of eight, also highlights the symbolic function of language. The elliptical form of the halo in the icon signifies an unorthodox iconography: the geometric shape is put to use to symbolise something beyond geometry. In purely geometric terms we should consider the relationship between the descriptive geometry of drawing and the analytic geometry of algebra as instigated by Descartes. I shall return to this below but for now let us note that in McCarthy's novels geometric symbols are never just geometric symbols.

Ellipses make an appearance in the novel's penultimate scene, another mechanical system held in stasis. Nick Boardman finds himself lying on the roof of a house supporting a bundle of books – what else? – on a *touw en blok*. Nick's elevated position gives him an unusual perspective and he begins to process the scene in entirely geometric terms:

> The wheel, right by his head. From this strange angle it seems not round but slightly elongated, like the halo in that painting which must be down in the transit van right now. The wheel could be a halo to him, or a crown, proclaiming him king of this elevated, horizontal plane that he alone is occupying. The cross around it, viewed from

this close, doesn't seem like a cross any more – more like a set of geometric exercises, like the ones Manasek was doing when he started copying the thing. Its two intersecting lines demarcate radii and segments. Behind them, the wheel's spokes cut the sky behind them into smaller, secondary segments. That slice of lemon. Nick looks down. The table at which Sasha and Han are sitting is on a tangent that's set off the diameter's plumb line by an angle of perhaps thirty degrees. It, too, seems slightly elongated. (*MIS*, 273)

The description continues. Nick has become part of the mechanism of the *touw en blok*. He has an anamorphic relationship to the world around him: he is distorting it through a particular perspective. He is static, it continues to revolve. Nick has a privileged position. He 'feels close to the dead' (*MIS*, 275). He becomes increasingly delirious: 'the boat's spinning, or is it the wheel spinning or is it just the earth, in orbit, spinning?' (*MIS*, 276). Once again, the novel leaves the scene in suspension. His delirium is caused by a Copernican confusion. Has Nick truly transcended? Is he free from the delusion that he is the centre of the universe of thought? Has he realised that the orbits are circles when viewed from a sufficient distance?

Perhaps we should turn the ellipse on its side, as we did the figure of eight, and read zero. Infinity in *Remainder* and zero in *Men in Space*? Since we're dealing with mathematical semiotics we should not be surprised that the third element we encounter is to be termed C. C is, of course, a symbol in any number of equations. In Pythagoras's Theorem, c stands in for the length of the hypotenuse. Of the proliferating circuits we can construct from a single letter, there's the one that nods to Toussaint, who prefaced *The Bathroom* with Pythagoras's theorem and structured it in three parts: Paris, Hypotenuse, Paris.

We are informed early that Serge suffers from a bizarre perceptual shortcoming:

> He's a steady brushman, and has a good feel for line and movement, but he just can't do perspective: everything he paints is flat. [...] Serge just can't do it: his perceptual apparatuses refuse point-blank to be twisted into the requisite configuration. He sees things flat; he paints things flat. Objects, figures, landscapes: flat. [...] The scenes accordion down into two dimensions. (*C*, 39)

We should not be surprised to discover that Serge is another flattener, a grid-imposer, a projector. For Serge, as for the narrator of *Remainder*, there are gaps; he blanks out at the edges. Following a highly geometric training in aeronautics he has lunch with his godfather Widsun. As he relates his pleasure in the training, Widsun remarks that he didn't have Serge down as a mathematician: 'Oh, I don't think of it as mathematics,' Serge replies. 'I just see space: surfaces and lines... and the odd blind spot ... ' (C, 121). In Alexandria, Serge is tasked with something beyond him. Major Ferguson, the local head of the Ministry of Communication, tells him, 'What we want from you is a different angle on it all, a wider perspective' (C, 244). Serge begins to explain: 'Perspective was never my– ,' but he is cut off, his attempted communication interrupted.

This shortcoming becomes strength when Serge is given the right perspective as an observer in an RE8 for 104th Squadron. He can read the geometry of what he observes from his elevated vantage point: 'The shapes made when trails intersect, lines cutting across other lines at odd angles or bisecting puffballs' circles to form strange figures, remind Serge of the phonetic characters his father would draw across the schoolroom's whiteboard, the way the sentences would run and overlap' (C, 142). In fact, he *becomes* the geometry of what he observes:

> Within the reaches of this space become pure geometry, the shell's a pencil drawing a perfect arc across a sheet of graph paper; he's the clamp that holds the pencil to the compass, moving as one with the lead; he *is* the lead, smearing across the paper's surface to become geometry himself ... (C, 143)

Not just geometry, but geometry rendered in carbon, C, that base form of human matter.

It is no accident that Serge's story, and his life, ends in Egypt. He observes to his colleague Petrou that the tram system is 'very geometric'. Petrou replies:

> 'That started here as well. [...] Geometry. Euclid was Alexandrian: worked under Ptolemy Soter, the first one. Eratosthenes as well:

he calculated the diameter of earth from the sun's shadow as it fell across the city's streets at noon. And Sostratus, their contemporary, conceived Pharos, the great lighthouse, as an expression of shape and form and boundaries: dividing sea from land and light from dark, cutting the night up into cones and blocks and wedges...' (*C*, 245–6)

That lighthouse is a gnomon, a marker. Eratosthenes is using the same technique as Thales, to whom we will come soon enough. Alexandria makes quite an impression upon Serge.

In the city's pulses, in its interrupted flows, there lurks some kind of unrequited longing. [...] A longing for some kind of world, one either disappeared or yet to come, or perhaps even one that's always been there, although only in some other place, in a dimension Euclid never plotted, which is nonetheless reflecting off him at an asymptotic angle; and reflecting, it increasingly seems, straight towards Serge. (*C*, 251)

This is pushing beyond projection or anamorphosis; beyond, indeed, Euclid. We are not standing at an angle, aslant, to get more information. The unrequited longing is coming from without the three dimensions of traditional Euclidean geometry.

At the Central Station, Serge is briefed by Macauley on what will be the final stage of his assignment: travelling upriver, like Marlow, to assess, not Kurtz, but a suitable site for a transmitter in the Imperial Network Chain. The 'parallel erection' needs a certain type of landscape: 'flat, unencumbered plain.' Serge receives this information in an interstice: 'Serge watches his figure shrink beneath the station's geometric mesh, then turns away from this to face the utterly ungeometric desert' (*C*, 271). Arriving in Sedment he finds precisely the terrain he is looking for: 'To the north, the landscape flattens; to the south, it rises in ridges, plateaus, hillocks' (*C*, 288). The excavation taking place there is resolutely geometric, divided into triangular sectors by strings between pegs. In fact, it is another crime scene but one given depth. Serge wanders into the cross-hatched network of tombs and meets the archaeologist Laura working with sarcophagi, bones and corpses, to whom he remarks: 'Wow, you really are forensic' (*C*, 291). As Serge and Laura have sex, deep in the tombs, amid muck and slime, matter and remains, Serge receives the insect bite that proves fatal.

Returning downriver, and beginning to hallucinate, he experiences the exterior world as inverted: 'but since he's moving the wrong direction these fragments play themselves out backwards, words and gestures scrambled through reversal' (C, 298). The port of Boulaq is also 'not quite right', nor is Pollard, who meets Serge there, with his parting on the wrong side of his head. Such inversion can be achieved by rotation in a fourth dimension of space, assumed as the location for the communicating intelligences in séances by some late-nineteenth century theorists. H. G. Wells's Gottfried Plattner, hero of 'The Plattner Story' (1896), experiences corporeal inversion himself after a bizarre accident sends him to an optically inverted spirit world. Is Serge dead? Has he ever been alive?

For the purposes of the characters sharing his fiction, at least, Serge dies onboard the Borromeo, a steamer out of Port Said, his final tumult of hallucinations reuniting him with Sophie and giving us a churn of code to pick at. C does not close in stasis – the mechanisation of those around him occurred to Serge back in Alexandria – but it does end with marks equivalent to *Remainder*'s figure of eight:

> The moon's gone: only the ship's electric glow illuminates the wake, two white lines running backwards into darkness. When the stretch in which the scraps are bobbing fades from view, the steward turns away towards the staircase. The wake itself remains, etched out across the water's surface; then it fades as well, although no one is there to see it go. (C, 310)

Equivalent might well be *le mot juste*. If we are to read the figure of eight as infinity and the ellipse as zero, these two white lines might be an equals sign. They are certainly parallel lines, whose extension to infinity caused such problems for readers of Euclid in the nineteenth century that they threw out his fifth postulate and developed entirely consistent non-Euclidean geometries that supposed parallel lines *did* meet. When they fade, do the parallel lines of the wake re-stage the dissolution of the parallel postulate? It probably does not matter. No one is there to see it.

To recap, we have three repeated geometric strategies that warrant closer attention: (1) we have projectors, flatteners, reducers: characters performing geometric functions, engaging in the world in a geometric fashion but employing a very specific form of geometry; (2) we have mathematical, geometrical symbols; (3) we have stasis, mechanical and interlocked engagements from which narrative time has been removed, rendering them geometric.

To start with the last of these: as is typical, McCarthy has already published his account of stasis in the same *LRB* essay from which I have already quoted. Referring to Toussaint's essay *Le Melancholie de Zidane*, about the legendary French footballer, McCarthy writes:

> Toussaint ends, Zidane-like, by removing all possibility of endings in invoking yet another Z, Zeno: Zidane's head, he points out, cannot really have reached Materazzi's chest, since it would have had to travel half the distance there, then half the remaining distance, and so on to infinity – what Toussaint calls 'le paradoxe de Zidane'. Thus we're left, appropriately, in suspension: held, geometry-bound, in a space, or time, that has become pure interval. (McCarthy, 2010: 27)

The removal of narrative time is then a way of 'short-circuiting finitude', as he writes, and it is employed in both *Remainder* and *Men in Space*. Remove time and we are held 'geometry-bound'. Coming at the same question from a different tangent, Michel Serres (1982a: 87) writes: 'Thales stops time in order to measure space. [...] Hence it becomes necessary to freeze time in order to conceive of geometry'. Being held geometry-bound is also conceiving geometry: we have shifted the observing subject into the system.

Geometric function the second: projection; flattening and gridding. There are in fact two distinct actions here, the gridding a Cartesian move, the projection already present in perspective drawing but developed formally in the early nineteenth century. I think it is fair to treat the two together here because the texts with which we are working elide the practices. Given the modern period of the novel, an art historical approach is illuminating. Rosalind Krauss's canonical account of the use of grids in modern art is worth revisiting. Krauss (1979: 50) pushes beyond the reading of the grid as a Modernist ground zero that 'announces among other things, modern art's will to silence, its hostility to literature, to narrative, to discourse'. She uses the tools of structuralism to burrow deeper and to recuperate the hidden narrative of the grid:

> In the cultist space of modern art, the grid serves not only as emblem but also as myth. For like all myths, it deals with paradox or contradiction not by dissolving the paradox or resolving the contradiction, but by covering them over so that they seem (but only seem) to go away. The grid's mythic power is that it makes us able to think we are dealing with materialism (or sometimes science, or logic) while at the same time it provides us with a release into belief (or illusion, or fiction). (Krauss, 1979: 54)

The grids Serge imposes are in this tradition; as with McCarthy's deployment of geometry in his previous two novels, Serge's gridding conceals as it reveals, but it cannot conceal sufficiently: the repressed returns.

As an aside, it is interesting to note that the narrator of *The Bathroom* is a fan of grids and understands the Serresian removal of time from geometry. 'What I like about Mondrian's painting,' he states with no preamble,

> is its immobility. No other painter has come so close to immobility. Immobility is not absence of movement but absence of any prospect of movement, it is dead. Painting, as a rule, is never immobile. As with chess its immobility is dynamic. Every chessman, an immobile potential, is potential movement. In Mondrian, immobility is immobile. Maybe that's why Edmondsson thinks Mondrian is such a crushing bore. I find him reassuring. (Toussaint, 2008: 67–8)

This is as close to motive as we get for the narrator's next action, the hurling of a dart into Edmondsson's forehead: 'Dart in hand, I looked at the target hanging on the wardrobe door and wondered why the target made me think of Edmondsson and not Jasper Johns.' Everyone's a critic. To quote the *LRB* essay again: 'We exist and assume subjectivity to the extent that we occupy a spot on or traverse the grid.'

Again we encounter the dual joy and frustration of working with a rich, coherent and allusive project developed over at least twelve years. This all comes pre-theorised by the author. This, from 'Navigation Was Always a Difficult Art':

> If necronautism was initially conceived around two strategies toward space, a quick study of cartography unites both under the banner of one term: projection. As the first page of any introduction to the study of maps explains, our earth is spherical but paper is flat. As it is impossible to make a sheet of paper rest smoothly on a sphere, so it is impossible to make a correct map on a sheet of paper. It is for this reason that projections have become necessary (McCarthy, 2002: 3).

The essay goes on to describe how mapping distorts and mutates, how projection maps vanish into infinity as we reach their edges. This is anamorphosis at its furthest extremities, and it brings us back to the final element of the geometric analysis of McCarthy's novels. What about those symbols? The lemniscate holding pattern, the ellipse or zero, the equals sign of parallel lines. Figures.

These remind us that geometry can be practically worked through drawing and through algebra. In the eighteenth century, the techniques of descriptive geometry enabled three-dimensional spaces to be geometrically modelled in drawing as they were in the analytic mode of Cartesian geometry: descriptive and analytic geometry were briefly perfectly aligned. With the development of non-Euclidean and n-dimensional geometries through analytic methods in the nineteenth century, however, Euclidean descriptive techniques fell short: how could one draw a four-dimensional object that had never been seen on a two-dimensional piece of paper?

The fact that geometry itself is already a symbolic language becomes clear. Geometry is not a perfect mimesis of space, but a way of describing it. At first glance it signifies the ideal, pure rational thought, but such thought slips away, vanishes at the edges. Repressed irrationality returns. Stuff remains. We can see the evidence for this in McCarthy's geometric fiction forebears.

Side *b*

Geometric flattening in fiction has an ur-text. Edwin Abbott Abbott's 1884 novel *Flatland* is narrated by A Square, a citizen of a world of two dimensions inhabited by geometric figures whose social status ascends in lockstep with their increasing polygony – women are lines, the working class are triangles, professionals are squares and the ruling priesthood circles. A Square transcends this world when he is visited by a Sphere who grants him a vision of 'Spaceland', the world of three dimensions.

Abbott's little book provoked confusion on publication, although recent critical discourse has located it squarely in the midst of debates surrounding non-Euclidean and *n*-dimensional geometries contemporary to its composition, and has honed in on its use of the dimensional analogy, the rhetorical figure that asks us to conceive of higher dimensioned space by thinking of the difference between two-dimensional and three-dimensional space.[1]

Flatland is a particularly interesting text in the context of this discussion of McCarthy's geometric exhortation: after all, it provides angles, arcs and intervals in profusion; its characters are nothing but. It also highlights what is happening in geometry immediately before Modernism, the uncoupling of descriptive and analytical geometries in non-Euclidean and *n*-dimensional geometry. It flags up geometry's symbolic nature at precisely the moment in time that many are forgetting about it, although not without causing considerable consternation in the process.

From *Flatland*'s title illustration (see Abbott, 1992: Figure 1), however, it indicates that we need to expand the field of reference beyond geometry. Abbott quotes *Hamlet* and *Titus Andronicus*. When Horatio responds to Hamlet, 'O day and night, but this is wondrous strange', he responds to a man in the grip of hallucinations, a prince who has lost his mind and is conversing with ghosts. For a contemporary reader the reference to ghosts in the context of higher dimensionality would have been entirely appropriate: a spiritualist hypothesis locating séance phenomena in the fourth dimension was gaining considerable popularity by 1884. Experiments conducted with the

spirit medium Henry Slade by the German astrophysicist Johann Carl
Friedrich Zöllner had been widely reported in both spiritualist and
mainstream journals. Zöllner claimed to have experimentally demonstrated the fourth-dimensional origin of communicating intelligences
(Zöllner, 1901), and his status as a leading scientist leant his claims
considerable credence. The line from *Titus Andronicus* – 'Fie, fie, how
frantically I square my talk' – is taken from Shakespeare's bloodiest
tragedy, from a scene steeped in violent horror, and used as a straight
pun. If Abbott is having fun and playing games, this extreme irony is
his acknowledgement of the seriousness of his endeavour and of the
violence lurking beneath his humour.

Flatland's illustrations throughout are intriguing. The title page illustration and its closing partner (see Abbott, 1992: Figure 2) might
be characterized as maps, though evidently not planar. For the most
part the remaining illustrations are concerned with lines of sight and
perspective, subverted diagrams from a projective geometry text-
book, perhaps (see Abbott, 1992: Figure 3). These serve to indicate
that drawing is a geometric function itself. Two illustrations, however,
deal with Flatland's architecture: plan views of Flatland houses illustrate social segregation but also the perspective of the higher dimensional reader, the reader who can see 'inside' the two-dimensional
figure (see Abbott, 1992: Figure 4). Maps, plans, lines of sight and
perspective and architecture are never far from the scene in geometric
fiction.

It is also significant that *Flatland* arrives in the midst of an emergent theoretical squabble over the soul of the novel. Robert Louis
Stevenson's 'A Gossip on Romance' and Walter Besant's lecture 'The
Art of Fiction' had been published and delivered sufficiently in ad-
vance of *Flatland* to have allowed response, and Henry James's version
of 'The Art of Fiction' arrived as *Flatland* was beginning to circulate.
The psychological novel of interiority and the novel of incident and
adventure were the poles of the engagement; the Jamesian idea that
'the moral consciousness of a child' was as worthy a subject of fiction
as a quest for buried treasure was met with Stevenson's repudiation of
what he characterised as effete, continental nonsense.

Flatland perhaps most obviously responds to Stevenson's work. *Treasure Island*, published the year before *Flatland*, also featured a map on its inside front cover. Tellingly, as its subtitle announced, *Flatland* was 'a romance of many dimensions'. Readers expecting a swashbuckler were likely to be disappointed. So too would those interested in what was going on inside their characters, unless they were happy to read interiors as the section of surface area bounded by a geometric figure. At one stage, A Square becomes obsessed with seeing inside things, with accessing the intra-vision afforded by his raised dimensional status. Why, he asks the Sphere, can he not discern the Sphere's heart, lungs arteries and liver? The Sphere responds:

> It is not given to you, nor to any other Being to behold my internal parts. I am of a different order of Beings from those in Flatland. Were I a Circle, you could discern my intestines, but I am a Being, composed as I told you before, of many Circles, the Many in One, called in this country a Sphere. (Abbott, 1992: 70)

This might not quite amount to a critique of the Jamesian quest for interiority, but *Flatland* is certainly a novel that disdains the idea of the mimetic or the naturalistic mode, and it is doubly uncertain about locating the human subject at the centre of the universe. Elsewhere, the Sphere grants A Square a vision of Pointland, a land of no-dimensions, whose sole inhabitant is convinced of his 'omnipresence and omniscience' (Abbott, 1992: 76). A Square mocks him, but the monarch of Pointland is undisturbed: 'Ah, the joy, ah, the joy of Thought! What can It not achieve by thinking! Its own Thought coming to Itself, suggestive of Its disparagement, thereby to enhance its happiness!' (Abbott, 1992: 76).

Returned to Flatland, A Square attempts to convince his countrymen of the existence of higher dimensions and is imprisoned for his heresy. *Flatland*'s last line borrows from *The Tempest* a phrase repeated on the closing illustration: 'These very tablets on which I am writing, and all the substantial realities of Flatland itself, appear no better than the offspring of a diseased imagination, or the baseless fabric of a dream' (Abbott, 1992: 82). Abbott's insistence on the ideal nature of geometry should also be applied to fiction: his text is wrapped up between references to Hamlet and Prospero's speech. Abbott presents an anti-mimetic fiction but while it is 'such stuff as dreams are made on', does it really 'leave not a rack behind'?

Flatland is side *b* of my canonical triangle, then: a novel of modern sensibility that flags up geometry's symbolic nature. As is perhaps obscured by this brief account, it is a hybrid work: divided into two books, the first is an alternate world history, the second a description of a series of visions and a quixotic voyage. Abbott deploys illustrations freely and slips into dramatic dialogue for large passages in the second part. It is playful and resistant to being fixed, located between high and low culture and between the Victorian and the Modern. It remains a difficult text to classify and is frequently excluded from canonical fin de siècle literary history by dint of being considered a genre text, a children's book or a mathematical folly.

Side *c*

J. G. Ballard's *The Atrocity Exhibition*, which like *Flatland* refuses period or generic categorization, shares that work's obsessive concern with geometry. The word 'modulus' (Ballard, 2001: 31), a focal point for a number of critics, seems to act as a hinge for the entire project.[2] Meanwhile, the phrase 'the angle between two walls' taken from this novel's question 'does the angle between two walls have a happy ending?' has been used by Roger Luckhurst as the title of his study of Ballard (Luckhurst, 1997).

Ballard's multi-named protagonist, Traven, Tallis, 'the T-cell' in Luckhurst's phrase, is an exemplar of 'flat' psychology. He does not change (*pace* modulations of nomenclature). He repeatedly arranges his exhibits, like the author, organizing geometrically, to try to locate the 'modulus'. Arrangements of limbs are described in geometric terms, as are landscape and architecture. Abstraction sets in rapidly: 'a neural interval' (Ballard, 2001: 20), 'anxieties' (Ballard, 2001: 33), 'guilt' and 'an accusation' (Ballard, 2001: 88) are considered in terms of their geometries. Technical geometric terms outpace the non-scientific reader's understanding: we encounter 'Enneper's models'

(Ballard, 2001: 7), 'radial geometry' (Ballard, 2001: 51) and 'transfinite geometry' (Ballard, 2001: 119). So too do the scientific and the spiritual unite, in 'transcendental geometry' (Ballard, 2001: 59) and the geometric symbol of the 'yantra' (Ballard, 2001: 59) or the Hebrew script of the 'tetragrammaton' (Ballard, 2001: 136).

This is part surrealist collage, part surgical distillation of form: Ballard writes in his gloss to the section 'You: Coma: Marilyn Monroe' that geometry offers the 'simplest terms possible' (Ballard, 2001: 62) in which to understand the universe. When he notes in a later gloss that the central character in this chapter behaves 'like an element in a geometric equation' (Ballard, 2001: 138), we are drawing closer to McCarthy's invocation of geometry. In this chapter the characters experience a 'displacement of time' (Ballard, 2001: 56). They perceive each other as geometric operations. Tallis recognizes Karen Novotny as 'a modulus; by multiplying her into the space and time of the apartment he would obtain a valid unit of existence'. Novotny watches 'his tall figure interlocking with the dimensions and angles of the apartment' (Ballard, 2001: 57). By the end of the chapter, Novotny is 'confusing the perspectives of the room', an 'unbearable intrusion' that ends in one of her many deaths (Ballard, 2001: 60).

Repeated juxtaposition of these geometric tropes with anatomical descriptions of sexual organs and pornographic acts suggests a model for C's mechanical primal scene. Ballard describes 'a Kraft-Ebbing of geometry and posture', memories of erotic scenes: 'These mental Polaroids form a large part of our library of affections. [...] Turning their pages, we see what seems to be a ghostly and alternative version of our own past, filled with shadowy figures as formalized as Egyptian tomb-reliefs' (Ballard, 2001: 101). In a later section, describing a 'deformed marriage of Euclid and Freud', he returns to this process (Ballard, 2001: 118). *Atrocity* makes explicit the violence of geometry obscured beneath *Flatland*'s apparent lightness. Illustrations of dimensional perspectives have become in *Atrocity* the trajectories of the bullets that killed John F. Kennedy. The Commission into the Kennedy assassination established by Lyndon B. Johnson and chaired by Chief Justice Earl Warren, produced a mammoth 888-page report, whose detailed reconstructions of potential assassins' lines of sight, ballistic calculations of trajectories of fire and angles of entry – the intersections of hard matter and soft flesh – are *Atrocity*'s version of Euclid's axioms. Karen Novotny is repeatedly killed and placed into architectural geometry. *Atrocity*'s geometry is incantatory, looping and repeating throughout the text.

McCarthy has been vocal in his appreciation of Ballard recently, declaring him 'a genius' in interview in the *New Statesman* (Evers, 2010: 49). We might note the shared source in Marinetti, whose Futurist Manifesto McCarthy reprises in the car crash which ends the 'Crash' chapter of *C*, and in the figure of the Sudanese cook in the novel's final paragraph. For Ballard too, Marinetti informs his obsession with the car crash as 'a fertilizing rather than a destructive experience' throughout the distillation of *Atrocity*'s 'Crash!' and 'Tolerances of the Human Face' chapters. We read in *Atrocity* the seed of *Crash*. In fact, we might note that *Atrocity*, *Crash* and *C* are all 'dripping with spunk'.[3] We certainly should note that the T-Cell is a flat vessel of a character. He does indeed behave like an element in a geometric equation, running the routines, re-organizing the elements and running them again, plugging himself and others into his geometric surroundings. Geometry is poetry, logic and narrative in *Atrocity*. Where *Flatland*'s characters were no more than geometric figures, *Atrocity*'s participants are no more than algebraic terms.

The Set Square

In an effort to escape decryption of McCarthy's work as guided by authorial direction, a persistent obstacle with an author as theoretically astute as McCarthy, I would like to jink past Deleuze and into the writing on geometry of his friend Michel Serres. Serres has a number of essays that would yield useful insights here. In 'The Origin of Geometry', translated into English in the 1982 collection *Hermes*, he provides a brief summary of his thinking on geometry to date. Firstly, his consideration of the passage from geometry to rigorous mathematics, routed through a McCarthyite concern: information theory, communication networks, noise and code. He records the successes of this attempt:

> Mathematics presents itself as a successful dialogue or a communication which rigorously dominates its repertoire and is maximally purged of noise. Of course, it is not that simple. The irrational and the unspeakable lie in the details; listening always requires collating; there is always a leftover or a residue, indefinitely. (Serres, 1982b: 126)

That residue, that remainder, is noise as well as matter. Serres continues with the wonderful line: 'Strange diagonal which was thought to be so pure, and which is agonal and which remains an agony' (Serres, 1982b: 127). Here is a particularly intriguing reading of mathematical history routed through the science behind the McCarthyite concerns of encryption and broadcast. Mathematics presents itself as pure communication – it conceals its noise, its irrationality, but the channel is not pure communication: no channel is. Irrationality remains, repressed.

In his next pass, Serres records that he contemplated Thales standing in the shadow of the pyramids, the moment of intuition in which the Greek geometer discovered the abstract idea of the module, the ratio, realizing that he could calculate the height of the pyramids by freezing time and measuring their shadow. Serres adds here an afterthought:

> I had not taken into account the fact that the Pyramids are also tombs, that beneath the theorem of Thales, a corpse was buried, hidden. [...] I had seen the sacred above. [...] I had not seen it below, hidden beneath the tombstone, in the incestuous cadaver. (Serres, 1982b: 127)

The sacred; a crypt containing an incestuous cadaver; a realization achieved by removing time from a moving system. The resonances with C require little expansion: its final scenes as discussed above feature very similar elements, and we can begin to sketch the parallel reasoning here. Serge returns to the birthplace of geometry and disinters incestuous death. The idea that death itself is what is encrypted into geometry is a powerful reinforcement of the necronautical appropriation of the practice.

Serres's attention for the main part of this essay is devoted to the double writing of geometry: figures and drawings; algebra and descriptive geometry. The figure of eight as a holding pattern traced in the sky and as a symbol for infinity. Serres wants to glue back together the two writings of geometry, which he reads as the distinct writing systems of Egypt and Greece, ideograms and letters. He focuses on the crisis of irrational numbers as the locus of the rift, because what separates the Greeks from the Egyptians is the establishment of a proof, specifically the apagogic disproof, the first *reductio ad absurdum* – Serres's rehearsal of the disproof is included here as an appendix. By attempting to calculate the length of the side *b* of a triangle using the other two sides, it concludes: 'The situation is intolerable, the number *b is at the same time even and odd*, which, of course, is impossible' (Serres, 1982b: 130).

Serres reads this crisis in mathematical reasoning reflected across different types of texts – histories, geometric works and philosophical texts. The crisis of irrational numbers, he argues, can be read across all three in symbolic deaths: he reads these as sacrifices made in order to recast the *logos*, to produce a new theory that can deal with the crisis. The royal weaver of Plato's *Statesman* 'combines in an ordered web rational proportions and the irrationals' (Serres, 1982b: 132). Again, I think the resonances with *C* are worth highlighting: *C*'s grids are also webs; webs of communication or silk or Serge, with Carrefax at their junction. 'I observe,' says Serge, 'and navigate. I make everything fit together' (*C*, 128).

Serres concludes:

> The origin of geometry is immersed in sacrificial history and the two parallel lines are henceforth in connection. Legend, myth, history, philosophy, and pure science have common borders over which a unitary schema builds bridges. [...] The irrational is mimetic. The stone which we have read was the stone of the altar at Delos. And geometry begins in violence and in the sacred. (Serres, 1982b: 133)

A first pass through Serres's early essays, then, gives us some ways in which to read McCarthy's geometric injunction. We should acknowledge the 'angles, arcs and intervals', but fill out the death, violence and irrationality that are coded into them. This is already richly necronautical territory but it is worth following Serres yet further down this line of thought.

In 'Gnomon: The Beginnings of Geometry in Greece', Serres devotes his attention to the pyramid in the Thales myth, the 'intermediate object' casting a shadow on the sand:

> It was more of an observatory than a clock. We do not really know why the shaft or pin is called a gnomon, but we do know that this word designates that which understands, decides, judges, interprets or distinguishes, the rule which makes knowledge possible. The construction of the sundial brings natural light into play, intercepted by this ruler, a tool of knowledge. (Serres, 1995: 79).

The gnomon itself, the sundial, is a machine, argues Serres, producing automatic knowledge. It defines no position for an operator, inscribing its knowledge directly onto the sand. What does this mean for the human subject? Implicitly invoking the alternate versions of the Thales myth, in which Thales uses a peg rather than his own shadow to perform his observation of ratio, Serres explains:

> The world represents itself, is reflected in the face of the sundial and we take part in this event no more and no less than the post, for standing upright, we also cast shadows, or, as seated scribes, stylus in hand, we too leave lines. Modernity begins when this real world space is taken as a scene and this scene, controlled by the director, turns inside out – like the finger of a glove or a simple optical diagram – and plunges into the utopia of a knowing, inner, intimate subject. (Serres, 1995: 80)

The human subject is also a gnomon and its sublimation of the gnomon marks the emergence of the modern subject. Perhaps most significantly for the terms of the current essay, 'we take part in this event no more and no less than the post'. To put it another way: 'We exist and assume subjectivity to the extent that we occupy a spot on or traverse the grid.' The knowledge happens without us. Serres argues that

> in order that we moderns might gain access, once more informed by the gnomon, to this automatic science, to this artificial intelligence, we should forget the philosophical prejudices of the modern interlude: man at the centre of the world, in the place of the gnomon, the subject in the middle of knowledge. (Serres, 1995: 86)

It is from this analysis that we might most usefully draw an improved understanding of how geometry might be what 'we want' in fiction: a science that can guide us towards a fiction that has 'an anti-naturalist, anti-humanist bent [...] an encounter with structure' (McCarthy, 2010: 26). A fiction that by flattening, gridding, freezing time and recognizing noise and matter, shifts the subject from the centre of the universe, makes it into an element in the equation and sends it out into orbit, or beyond, *ad mortem*.

Appendix: The Apagogic Disproof

Given a square whose side AB = *b*, whose diagonal AC = *a*:

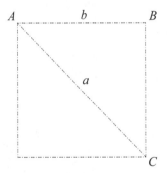

We wish to measure AC in terms of AB. If this is possible, it is because the two lengths are mutually commensurable. We can then write AC/AB = a/b. It is assumed that a/b is reduced to its simplest form, so that the integers a and b are mutually prime. Now, by the Pythagorean theorem: $a^2 = 2b^2$. Therefore a^2 is even, therefore a is even. And if a

and b are mutually prime, b is an odd number. If a is even, we may posit: $a = 2c$. Consequently, $a^2 = 4c^2$. Consequently $2b^2 = 4c^2$, that is, $b^2 = 2c^2$. Thus, b is an even number.

Notes

1 See Jann (1985) and Smith, et al. (1996).

2 This is the first of many repetitions of the term, but the idea of geometric models is introduced as early as the second page of the book.

3 McCarthy used this phrase in the Q&A session at the conference *Calling All Agents*, Birkbeck, University of London, 23 July 2011.

Works Cited

Abbott, Edwin A. (1992) *Flatland: A Romance of Many Dimensions*. New York: Dover.

Ballard, J. G. (1993) *Crash*. London: Flamingo.

Ballard, J. G. (2001) *The Atrocity Exhibition*. London: Flamingo.

Deleuze, Gilles (2004) *Difference and Repetition*, trans. Paul Patton. London: Continuum.

Evers, Stuart (2010) 'The Books Interview: Tom McCarthy', *New Statesman*, 9 August: 49.

Forster, E. M. (1927) *Aspects of the Novel*. London: Edward Arnold.

James, Henry (1884) 'The Art of Fiction', *Longman's Magazine* 4: 502–21.

Jann, Rosemary (1985) 'Abbott's "Flatland": Scientific Imagination and "Natural Christianity"', *Victorian Studies* 28: 473–90.

Krauss, Rosalind (1979) 'Grids', *October* 9: 50–6.

Luckhurst, Roger (1997) *The Angle Between Two Walls*. Liverpool: Liverpool University Press.

McCarthy, Tom (2002) *Navigation Was Always a Difficult Art*. London: Vargas Organisation.

McCarthy, Tom (2003) 'Between Pain and Nothing', in Steve Rushton (ed.) *The Milgram Re-enactment*, pp. 16–32. Maastricht: Jan van Eyck.

McCarthy, Tom (2010) 'Stabbing the Olive', *London Review of Books* 32(3): 26–8.

Serres, Michel (1982a) 'Mathematics & Philosophy: What Thales Saw…', in Josué V. Harari and David F. Bell, eds and trans. *Hermes: Literature, Science and Philosophy*, pp. 84–97. Baltimore and London: John Hopkins University Press.

Serres, Michel (1982b) 'The Origin of Geometry', in Josué V. Harari and David F. Bell, eds and trans. *Hermes: Literature, Science and Philosophy*, pp. 125–33. Baltimore, MD: John Hopkins University Press.

Serres, Michel (1995) 'Gnomon: The Beginnings of Geometry in Greece', in Michel Serres (ed.) *A History of Scientific Thought*, pp. 73–123. Oxford: Blackwell.

Smith, Jonathan, Lawrence I. Berkove, and Gerald A. Baker (1996) 'A Grammar of Dissent: "Flatland," Newman, and the Theology of Probability', *Victorian Studies* 39: 129–50.

Stevenson, Robert Louis (1882) 'A Gossip on Romance', *Longman's Magazine* 1: 69–79.

Toussaint, Jean-Philippe (2008) *The Bathroom,* trans. by Nancy Amphoux and Paul D'Angelis. Champaign, IL: Dalkey Archive.

Zöllner, Johann Carl Friedrich (1901) *Transcendental Physics*, 4th edn, trans. Charles Carleton Massey. Boston, MA: Banner of Light.

5

RESTRICTED ACTION
McCarthy's Modernist Legacy?

Milly Weaver

Satin Island opens with an extract from Stéphane Mallarmé's short 1886 essay, 'Restricted Action', an essay which, in its entirety, concerns the limits of literary writing conceived as action. Mallarmé begins by outlining a young colleague's expressed wish for 'success with words' and for action, with poetic action being understood as the capacity 'philosophically to effect motion on many' (Mallarmé, 2001: 21–2). Mallarmé's subsequent response is to state the futility and naivety of this aim. Poetry – 'lonely in its chaste crises' – is necessarily insubstantial, 'gifted only with a feeble outer power' (Mallarmé, 2001: 23–4). It is unable to produce the kind of event one might witness in the theatre, as the output of poetry or prose fiction is limited to 'a representation – the immediate disappearance of the written' (Mallarmé, 2001: 23). Essentially, writing's enactive capacity is a specific and restricted one; it concerns only the scene of writing, and the space on the page.

In this chapter, I read *Satin Island* as a working through, or response to, the sentiment of its own epigraph. The novel is troubled by literary expression's supposed limitations – its representational defi-

ciencies, its inability to stage an event – and reveals a sustained fascination with other, possibly more able, forms of representation. This
fascination plays out on a thematic and technical level, pivoting on
three aspects in particular: an interest in representation or information that expresses itself by recourse to materiality; the use of visual
media as an emulative model; and writing figured as a record of its
author's thought process.

To read McCarthy with Mallarmé in mind is, in many respects, an
obvious move. The contemporary author freely cites Mallarmé's work
as a point of interest and influence and conceives of his own work
as closely engaged with literary modernism in general.[1] 'The task for
contemporary literature', he is quoted as saying in interview, 'is to
deal with the legacy of modernism' (Purdon, 2010). McCarthy's stat-
ed motivation is therefore to 'navigate the wreckage of that project'
(Purdon, 2010), and *Satin Island* certainly participates in such a navigation. The novel's 'Great Report', for instance, finds its prototype in
Mallarmé's idea of the 'Book': 'the quintessence of all literature and all
reality – the Total Book' (Polieri, 1968: 180). Similar in their porten-
tous capitalization and their desired scope, both aspire towards being
absolute records of the state of things, but both remain unrealized.
McCarthy even makes explicit this link between U (*Satin Island*'s
anthropologist narrator) and Mallarmé in 'The Death of Writing', an
article apparently intended as a companion piece to the novel: the
thinking of 'Bronisław Malinowski, the father of modern anthropology', McCarthy writes, 'was remarkably close to that of the man many
would credit as the father of modern literature, Stéphane Mallarmé'
(McCarthy, 2015).

A matching up of equivalences between Mallarmé's thought and
the various thematic concerns of *Satin Island* could easily continue.
Indeed, the text's prefatory quotation apparently encourages such a
reading. This chapter argues that *Satin Island*'s principal way of navigating Modernism's legacy is to take up the challenge of its epigraph
by investigating the (limited) representational possibilities of literary
language.

On the one hand, *Satin Island* expresses a desire to do away with
literary expression in its traditional form. The figure of the novelist

has morphed into that of the anthropologist. It is now the latter who deals 'in narratives' (*SI*, 15): 'If I had', says U's boss, 'to sum up, in a word what we (the Company, that is) essentially do, I'd choose not *consultancy* or *design* or *urban planning*, but *fiction*' (*SI*, 48). And it is the latter that is called upon to pen the 'Great Report', to capture the zeitgeist: it is to be 'the Document ... the Book. The First and Last Word on our age' (*SI*, 61). Rather than being figured as a necessarily literary project – as the tags 'document', 'book', and 'word' imply – this report need not even take written form: 'What medium, or media, would it inhabit?' wonders U (*SI*, 78).

And if it is to be written, it is not a given that a human individual need be its author. Near the novel's end, U has this exact realization:

> the truly terrifying thought wasn't that the Great Report might be unwritable, but – quite the opposite – that it had *already been written*. Not by a person, nor even by some nefarious cabal, but simply by a neutral and indifferent binary system that had given rise to itself, moved by itself and would perpetuate itself: some auto-alphaing and auto-omegating script – that's what it *was*. (*SI*, 133–4)

McCarthy repeats the latter half of this passage verbatim in 'The Death of Writing'. The article questions 'what it means to write today – to write, that is, in the shadow of omnipresent and omniscient data that makes a mockery of any notion that the writer might have something to inform us' (McCarthy, 2015). The shared wording and sentiment of *Satin Island* and McCarthy's manifesto-like article positions the former as a knowing elaboration on the near impossibility of writing literature in an age of data overload. What used to be the task of the writer might as well freely be yielded over to software.

And yet, the internal workings and representational techniques of *Satin Island* itself actually offer up a part solution to the problem. The impasse that McCarthy expresses is similar to that of 'Restricted Action'. Both counterpose literature to action – '*events*! If you want those, you'd best stop reading now' is the metafictional aside at the beginning of *Satin Island* (*SI*, 14). But now the contemporary writer faces the added problem of technology's ever increasing superiority with regard to writing.

And yet, the thematic concerns and representational strategies of *Satin Island* itself may be read as responding to this impasse. The crux of this response is an aping of the mechanics of other, non-textual media forms. In particular this takes the form of a literary enlistment of visuality and of materiality that permits the literary text to question the kinds of production – digitality, real 'event' – that might otherwise displace it. And this, in turn, can also be parsed as part of *Satin Island*'s wider enterprise of questioning the validity of the sentiment – literature's limited representational capacity and sphere of action – invoked by its epigraph.

Representational Frameworks: Anthropology, Pattern, Data

At an elemental level, *Satin Island*'s subject matter prepares the ground for this kind of reading. The respective merits of different representational approaches are subject to sustained mediation throughout the novel. U repeatedly questions what form or genre most appropriately accounts for his Great Report:

> On the one side, scientific, evidence-based research; on the other, epic art. If my Report had come to be completed, which side of the paper would it have been written on? More to the point: to which side does this not-Report you're reading now, this offslew of the real, unwritten manuscript, belong? Perhaps to neither side, but to the middle: the damp, pulpy mass that forms the opaque body at whose outer limits, like two mirages, the others hover. (*SI*, 125)

I will return to the import of U's metafictional aside – which posits both the Great Report, and the novel itself as subject to the same representational ambiguities – in this chapter's final section. For now, what is important about the passage is how it places the workings of scientific investigation in opposition to those of artistic representation. The implication – supported by the strong chiastic structure of the extract's first sentence – is that final product must belong either to one or the other; the alternative is an unsatisfactory, indefinable 'middle'.

We might infer that *Satin Island*'s preference lies with the former, scientific category. Its promotion of anthropology as a representational paradigm figures as possible indication of this: the discipline – its history, methods and concerns – is a key point of interest for the novel. And U's overriding fascination is with one strand of the discipline in particular: the translation of human behaviour and culture into data. 'The base premise of all anthropology', U claims, is that 'behind all behaviour, issuing instructions, sending in the plays – just as in life itself, its endless sequencing of polymers – there lies a source-code' (*SI*, 112). Accordingly, anthropology's primary impulse is to 'capture it all, turn it *all* into data': secondary sources exist simply 'to be quantified, sucked dry' (*SI*, 79), and tribes to be 'decoded' (*SI* , 88). The lexicon is explicitly mathematical, and points up the narrator's privileging of quantitative analysis and empirical study as modes of comprehension: allusions to 'quantitative analysis, econometric modelling' (*SI*, 23), 'tangible undertakings that had measurable outcomes' (*SI*, 43) and 'concrete' results persist throughout the novel (*SI*, 89).

In line with this leaning towards the mathematical and the statistical, the detection or imposition of sweeping frameworks emerges as one of U's characteristic narratorial tics. The ideal is the seamless incorporation of information into 'a master-pattern' (*SI*, 33), or the 'joining of isolated dots into a constellation-pattern' (*SI*, 53). Pattern – both the word itself and the structure that it denotes – figures as a repeated trope in *Satin Island*. At a basic level, the trope evidences and reiterates U's preference for universals and connections over individual particularities: '[an] anthropologist's not interested in singularities, but in generics' (*SI*, 37). Lévi-Strauss, for instance, is described as having 'remade the globe into a collage of recurring colours, smells and patterns' (*SI*, 31). But for the purposes of this study, the figure is additionally interesting in terms of the visuality – as suggested by the above allusion to 'colours' – that it invokes.

Pattern is fundamentally a visual arrangement, as well as a figurative and structural one. And this primary visual aspect is something that McCarthy's frequent deployment of the term always keeps in mind:

> Sometimes these patterns took on visual forms, like those that so enchanted eighteenth-century scientists when they scattered salt on Chladni plates and, exposing these to various acoustic stimuli, observed the intricate designs that ensued – geometric and symmetrical and so generally perfect that they seemed to betray a universal structure lurking beneath nature's surface, only now beginning to seep through. (*SI*, 16–17)

This easy leap from hearing the acoustic patterns produced by an office ventilation system to a mental visualization of these sounds makes explicit the inherently visual nature of pattern as cognitive structure. Vocabulary to do with the outward expression of form – 'geometric and symmetrical' – reiterates this connection.

This figure of the Chladni plate suggests why pattern should be such a privileged form in the novel. It locates sound as essentially commensurate with its material realization: the arrangement of salt on a plate expresses the character of a particular sound. Pattern's representational system clearly permits a contiguity between object and mode of expression. And in this respect, it is an appropriate structure for an anthropologist wanting to map out, and make easily discernable, 'universal structure[s]'.

Ostensibly, pattern's communicative process is much closer to the workings of the 'omniscient and omnipresent data' that McCarthy denotes as a threat to fiction, than it is to the expressive modes of literary writing itself. The figure allows underlying meaning to be grasped from surface arrangement. It finds its analogue in raw data's closeness to its source, or in processed data's tendency towards visual expression by means of graph or image. This internal promotion of an empirical, mathematical and closely source-based approach towards registering and recording – as embodied by U's version of anthropological enquiry and its graphic, statistical rendering – is seemingly at odds with the novel's own outward form of literary fiction, and the associated ambiguities of verbal representation. A structuralist approach would bring literary criticism the closest to U's data privileging mode. But literary production itself, the narrator suggests, is superseded by machine code. '[T]he software that tabulates and cross-indexes' ably identifies and communicates 'the very *raison d'être*, of someone like me', rendering obsolete the human hand's own, vaguer attempts at similar expression (*SI*, 133).

The tension places *Satin Island*'s thematics firmly in dialogue with questions regarding the workings of literary expression in respect of other representational forms, apparently supposing the former to be at a disadvantage. A data-driven approach, especially when expressed visually, makes for easy and instant assimilation: the shape of an actual graph or the organization of a cognitive framework bears a visual relation to what it means. Such contiguity between means and meaning is less available to literature. Written expression is more mediated: words on the page must first be decoded before they are comprehended.

But at odds with its thematic promotion of data and technology, *Satin Island* does not wholly subscribe to any such counterpointing of statistical versus literary production. Rather, it seeks to push its own representational techniques closer to the purity of expression associated with other, non-literary and less-mediated approaches. There are three key strands to this enterprise: the novel's sustained thematic and technical interest in indexicality; its assimilation of features of visual perception into the fabric of the text; and, finally, its wish to make text itself reflective of the conditions of its creation.

The Index

The term 'index' as it applies to semiotic theory has its origins in a theory of signs devised by the pragmatist philosopher Charles Sanders Peirce. Peirce's sign system is composed of three elements: the icon, the index and the symbol. The first of these, the icon, bears a physical resemblance to what it denotes; 'a quality that it has *qua* thing renders it fit to be a representamen' (*Collected Papers*, 2.276). Examples include portraits or diagrams, and iconicity partly accounts for the function of *Satin Island*'s many patterns: the distribution, angle, repetition or density of a pattern's elements have a direct visual correspondence to what they convey. Iconicity plays a role in sign languages, logographic writing systems and the kind of typographic experimentation seen in Mallarmé's *Un Coup de Dés*, or in later concrete poetry.

Typographically ordinary prose written in the Roman alphabet, on the other hand, is rarely considered iconic. Instead, its dominant semiotic structure is typically that of Peirce's third category: the symbol. Peirce explains:

> All words, sentences, books, and other conventional signs are Symbols. We speak of writing or pronouncing the word 'man'; but it is only a *replica*, or embodiment of the word, that is pronounced or written. The word itself has no existence although it has a real being, *consisting in* the fact that existents *will* conform to it. (*CP*, 2.292)

On this reading, words figure as at one remove from the real, denoting it only by association. Thus mediation plays a strong role in both iconic and symbolic representation: the respective constructs of visual and verbal systems must be negotiated in order to infer meaning.

The index, by contrast, exhibits a closer – and specifically material – bearing on what it represents, and it is this sign that holds a particular sway over *Satin Island*'s narrative. In order to be considered as an index, a sign must be in 'dynamical (including spatial) connection' both with the object itself, and 'with the senses or memory of the person for whom it serves as a sign' (*CP*, 3.5.305). The indexical sign therefore holds an existential relation to the object that it represents – pointing fingers, smoke denoting a fire, a weathervane, footprints and the photographic image are all examples of the type. Like the salt on a Chladni plate – which the viewer recognizes as product of a recent sound pattern – all of these signs evidence that their referent was originally present; 'the concept of the index', as Mary Ann Doane (2002: 70) summarizes it in relation to cinematic representation, 'seems to acknowledge the invasion of semiotic systems by the real'.

This invasion is something that McCarthy's prose encourages. From the outset *Satin Island* discloses a fascination with representational systems that work according to Peirce's understanding of the index. The Turin Shroud, for instance, is the novel's opening image. The shroud's imprinted image is a product of the earlier physical presence of Christ's body. Accordingly, it is an object that Rosalind

Krauss, writing in relation to photography, locates as an archetypal index:

> For photography is an imprint or transfer off the real; it is a photo-chemically processed trace causally connected to that thing in the world to which it refers in a manner parallel to that of fingerprints or footprints or the rings of water that cold glasses leave on tables. The photograph is thus generically distinct from painting or sculpture or drawing. On the family tree of images it is closer to palm prints, death masks, the Shroud of Turin, or the tracks of gulls on beaches. For technically and semiologically speaking, drawings and paintings are icons, while photographs are indexes. (Krauss, 1981: 26)

In line with Krauss' designation, McCarthy's description draws attention to this materialization of meaning that the Shroud embodies, explicitly juxtaposing it with other ways of registering information that are less rooted in the material:

> People need foundation myths, some imprint of year zero, a bolt that secures the scaffolding that in turn holds fast the entire architecture of reality, of time: memory-chambers and oblivion-cellars, walls between eras, hallways that sweep us on towards the end-days and the coming whatever-it-is. We see things shroudedly, as through a veil, an over-pixellated screen. (*SI*, 3)

The anchoring structures of 'foundation' or 'imprint' figure as corrective to the vagaries of human knowledge, allegorized here – in a play on 1 Corinthians 13:12 and reference to the veil of Omar Khayyam's *Rubaiyat* – as screen viewing. And the allusion to memory palaces – a mnemonic technique that relies on architectural visualization – further reiterates the attraction and typicality of concretized, rooted ways of thinking and understanding.

Satin Island's extended opening mediation on the Shroud sets up a dichotomy that figures throughout the novel. While *Satin Island* on the one hand positions itself as product and exploration of a virtual age, its typical interest is in information that comes in physical form. U's version of sociocultural anthropology is ostensibly set against earlier, more archaeological forms of the discipline.

Claudia, curator of the Frankfurt anthropology museum, outlines this latter practice:

> The idea was that you needed to study the morphology of, say, a cooking pot: how the shape and decoration varies from one village or one family to the next... The prevailing wisdom was that you had to gather *everything*: a hammer or a pair of scissors might tell you as much about a culture as a sacred fetish – suddenly release its inner secrets, like some codex. (*SI*, 104)

Here, hammers or scissors carry an indexical status; they hold both a temporal and physical relation to their culture of origin. The choice of the term 'morphology' is important in this respect. Often used figuratively, here McCarthy teases out and reiterates its literal meaning; that is, the word's bearing on physical form and appearance, which the passage above stresses by reference to 'shape and decoration'. Thus knowledge figures as readily available in the shape of a tangible, visible object.

U's anthropological approach, on the other hand, is more abstracted: it involves studying 'patterns of behaviour and belief and so forth' (*SI*, 104). But, as already outlined, pattern as mode of comprehension in the novel *does* bear a strong visual and material orientation, apparently aiming at some variety of dynamic and sensual connection with its object of reference. Further, U's mode of thought and perception as a whole demonstrates a similar recourse to indexical structures. U describes how consequences, for instance, leave an 'imprint' (*SI*, 40), or how behavioural habits must be probed for 'blueprints' (*SI*, 23). Anthropology is parsed as soothsaying – 'cutting fish open to tease wisdom from their entrails' – in reiteration of this preference for matching up concept with its original, physical source (*SI*, 23).

The characteristic mode of U's phraseology is to figure the abstract in material terms. I outlined earlier McCarthy's readiness to stress the visual currency of pattern as structure, and a similar descriptive motivation – an interest the literal basis of particular words or thoughts – is discernable elsewhere in the novel. U, for instance, offers to 'shine a (no more than anecdotal) spotlight on specific moments of Koob-Sassen's early phases' (*SI*, 14). The parenthesis implies that U's offer might otherwise be taken literally. It is an unnecessary qualification in this written context and so essentially functions as a kind of preterition, obliquely drawing attention to what it professes to omit.

References to form or shape in the novel work similarly. Statements in relation to the Great Report's progress doubly assert the dossier's organizational and literal shape. The claim that the document is 'finding its form' is repeated, refrain-like, throughout the novel: 'I said: it's finding its form' (*SI*, 29); 'I answered: it's finding its form' (*SI*, 39); 'I said: it's coming along slowly; still finding its shape' (*SI*, 57); 'it will find its shape' (*SI*, 63). Primarily, the phrase functions as a platitude to imply general progress, and to dismiss further inquiry. But its significance can be expanded to encompass form's other, physical and technical, meanings: it denotes the material shape and look of the project – photography, collage, prose, poetry, etc.

And McCarthy's prose continually stresses this literal aspect, doing so primarily by means of sustained attentiveness to the occurrence and effect of different compositional choices: 'the collage-effect it created, was constant' (*SI*, 10); 'all in unison, the image's whole texture changed' (*SI*, 96); it 'was being shown in close-up, from the land and long-shot, from a plane – but the same effect could be seen in both views' (*SI*, 98). Artistic representation, on this reading, emerges as highly dependent on its outward expression: texture, collage, zooming in or panning out determine the image. It is clear, therefore, that *Satin Island*'s descriptive choices are interested in both drawing out the physical basis of language constructions and in asserting the importance of physical form for artistic expression. Furthermore, a priority is lent to those expressions that exhibit a pleasing symmetry between meaning and external form. Appropriateness is key: 'it struck me as the right effect to use, aesthetically speaking', U observes in relation an edited photo sequence (*SI*, 9). And although various 'frames, context, modes, tones, formats would suggest themselves' for the Great Report, none are considered appropriate vectors for its content (*SI*, 63).

How best to figure the Great Report continues to be the subject of extended mediation throughout the novel:

What if, rather than *it* finding its shape, the age itself, in all its shape-shifting and multi-channelled incarnations, were to find and mould *it*? What if the age, the era, were to do this from so close up, and with such immediacy and force, that the *it* would all but vanish, leaving just world-shape, era mould? I started to think thoughts like this. They excited me. Beneath their vagueness, I felt something forming – something important and beautiful and momentous. (*SI*, 76)

This passage's concern is with de-mediation, with achieving a complete coherence between object and mode of expression. The Great Report, on these terms, would look like, and constitute, a real material trace of what it represents. And McCarthy's repetition of words denoting physical form, placing them here into stressed, adjectival constructions – 'shape-shifting', 'world-shape' and 'era mould' – reiterates this. As with the relation between foot and footprint or body and shroud, here the relation between report and world is one of direct, physical connection. It is, in essence, an expression of how U's project might assume an indexical relation to its subject matter.

The above account, however, leaves little room for writing or literature's intervention in indexical expression. The omission is notable: U's speculation is, after all, inset in a novel. *Satin Island*'s descriptive interest in representational forms that function as an 'imprint or transfer off the real' is clear (Krauss, 1981: 26). Less immediately obvious is whether McCarthy's novel figures literary production itself as able to participate in such an approach. Whether, that is, its thematic content establishes a basis for a more rigorous and self-conscious examination of how literary writing represents.

Photography and the Afterimage

On account of the supposedly arbitrary nature of linguistic signs, we might expect writing to be closed off from indexicality. Language's representational mode generally functions at a level of abstraction, with its meaning being liable to contingency. In this respect, it is at a remove from the physical, one-to-one connection that the index displays towards its referent. But writing can approach this kind of close material connection, often by means of copying the representational modes of other media forms.

Pictorial emulation, for instance, might be productive. This is the kind of approach that concrete poetry takes, in which typographic arrangement aims to unite content and its expression. Pictorial emulation is, however, still an indirect and highly mediated representational approach, working only as an approximation of what it wants to represent. More iconic than indexical, it remains at a remove from the 'world shape, era mould' relation that U intends for his Great Report, and so precluded from a direct intervention in the real.

The graphic arts face the same restriction. John Berger outlines this difference between the more direct representational mode of traces, and that of drawing or painting. He writes of how 'every time a figuration is evoked in a drawing, everything about it has been mediated by consciousness, either intuitively or systematically' (Berger, 2013: 67). That is to say that while 'in a drawing an apple is *made* round and spherical; in a photograph, the roundness and light and shade of the apple are received as a given' (Berger, 2013: 67). The same distinction holds for (typo)graphic or linguistic representation – both of which have been subject to conscious mediation – versus the direct, indexical impressions that figure as such a dominant thematic trope in *Satin Island*.

However Berger's distinction does suggest one further model for literary production that aspires towards directness: the photograph. The photographic image acts as material trace of its origin. Its way of representing, as Rosalind Krauss outlines, is analogous to the object of *Satin Island*'s introductory description: the Turin Shroud. And the superficial impression of indexicality that the novel's opening image establishes – and which is continued by means of repeated reference to similar representational objects – finds further realization in *Satin Island*'s technical recourse to photography. That is, *Satin Island*'s prose description can be seen to imitate the manner and effects of viewing or taking photographs. And in so doing, it pushes its own representational mode closer to the more direct, non-literary media forms that so fascinate its narrator.

The use of photography as a more general literary trope initially hints at *Satin Island*'s technical interest in the medium. The novel's opening description of the shroud is keen to mention photography's instrumental role in the discovery of the image: 'when some amateur photographer looked at the negative of a shot he'd taken of the thing, and saw the figure – pale and faded, but there nonetheless' (*SI*, 3). And this surface level invocation of photography quickly expands into a more sustained technical model. In his description of screen viewing, U enlists photography to figure perception as rooted in the material:

> When the shapeless plasma takes on form and resolution, like a fish approaching us through murky waters or an image looming into view from noxious liquid in a darkroom, when it begins to coalesce into a figure that's discernable, if ciphered, we can say: *This is it, stirring, looming*, even if it isn't really, if it's all just ink-blots. (*SI*, 3–4)

'Darkroom' explicitly signals a photographic analogy at work here. Images are figured as developing in the mind as they do in a darkroom, with the continuous tense of 'approaching', 'looming' and 'stirring' stressing this gradual emergence. And further, the passage figures the image as a discrete physical unit: '*a* fish' or '*an* image'. This singularity of the mental percept is a fundamentally photographic conception of the image; it figures the image as a discrete object, capable of being sorted, stored, considered in sequence or individually. McCarthy deploys a similar analogy later in the novel, as his narrator describes 'the image of a severed parachute that floated, like some jellyfish or octopus, through the polluted waters of my mind' (*SI*, 83).

Important in all of these various examples is McCarthy's stress on the agentive, material nature of the thing perceived. The verbs that accompany these visual images all imply movement – physical action – in the narrator's mind: they loom, stir and float, fish-like, in the narrator's mind. The impression is one of imposition; the narrator's mind figures as a plate set up for the reception and recording of external phenomena. Thus as with the photograph that bears a material trace of its moment of conception, U narrates as if as his thoughts and visualizations were direct products of an earlier, physical encounter.

And these concretized, internalized images in turn invoke that earlier encounter. A 'vague image from a previous reverie', for instance, can be summoned to conjure the past memory of a parachute (*SI*, 62). This vague image is, then, demonstrative of that 'dynamical' or 'spatial' relation with an individual's 'senses or memory' characteristic of the indexical sign.

So *Satin Island*'s focus on physicality in its description of mental images maps onto its wider thematic interest in representational forms that want to bear a more direct material relation to their referent, or that want to do away with mediation altogether. In line with this, McCarthy's placement of his narrator's mind as a kind of photographic plate or film – a receptor and relater of direct physical images – continues throughout the novel. The repeated act of 'picturing' forms a particularly striking example of this. Constructions that pivot on the verb 'to picture' feature as a dominant expressive trope in the novel: 'I pictured them still running' (*SI*, 18); 'I pictured a giant über-server' (*SI*, 73); 'I tried to picture cells' (*SI*, 79). These examples are simply representative of a much larger collection.

What is notable about this construction, aside from its striking frequency, is the way in which it affords the novel's visual description some kind of material basis. That is to say, visual description in *Satin Island* does not occur in the abstract. Instead, it must be introduced as product of the narrator's mental picturing and, further, these are mental pictures that generally bear the imprint of what they visualize.

In this sense, *Satin Island*'s visual descriptions follow a pattern similar to that of the afterimage, and specifically the concept's relation to photography. The afterimage describes the image that persists on the retina, and correspondingly in the mind, after the disappearance of the original visual referent. It is the visual, internalized equivalent of the various actual imprints – shrouds, patterns, moulds – that U detects and delineates throughout the novel.

Jonathan Crary, in his study of the changes to visual culture in the nineteenth century, associates the retinal afterimage primarily with subjectivity. He stresses the image's ability to remain on the eye and in the mind after its actual disappearance, writing of how the nineteenth century's privileging of subjective phenomena such as the afterimage 'allowed the thought of sensory perception cut from any necessary link with an external referent' (Crary, 1988: 9). So by according sway to the perceiver rather than what is perceived, the afterimage posed a 'theoretical and empirical demonstration of an optical experience that was produced by and within the subject' (Crary, 1988: 9).

I want to keep this focus on the visual agency of the subject in mind during my reading of the phenomenon's relevance to *Satin Island*. It is a focus that does, after all, provide an interesting counterpoint to the emphatically impersonal, 'neutral and indifferent binary system' that *Satin Island* suggests as possible future scribe (*SI*, 133). More immediately important, however, is the afterimage's relation to materiality. As well as being rooted in the vagaries of an individual's perception, the phenomenon also, perhaps counter-intuitively, invokes mechanical modes of capturing and conveying information.

Doane (2002: 69) draws out the afterimage's bearing on the physical, by describing how the theory 'in one sense inscribes the indexical image within it by assuming the analogy between the eye and a camera, in which the retina acts as a kind of photographic plate, registering and retaining, if only momentarily, an image'. The index, the afterimage and the photograph are therefore united in forming part of a representational paradigm that privileges the physical imprinting of information. And I read certain descriptive tropes in *Satin Island* as coded by this particular paradigm, revealing how the novel's own representational techniques approach the various non-literary and less-mediated media forms that pepper its narrative.

Analysis of the following example demonstrates how exactly McCarthy incorporates this rhythm of the photographic afterimage into his prose's descriptive constructions:

> Looking at the chart, its directional arrows, I thought of those two boys, those brothers or not-brothers: I pictured them still running, sliding, plying their oval loop – not in the airport anymore, but on some other floor, a kitchen's or a school refectory's or playground's. Flipping onwards through the paper, I found my attention caught by a small item half way through. (*SI*, 18)

Firstly, we see a sequentiality at work. The image of directional arrows conjures a previous image of two boys running in Turin airport. And, in turn, the image of their oval running loop prompts a visualization of its continuation and expansion into other contexts. So, from the outset, the passage asserts the mental continuation of the visual image after the initial exposure. Primarily this sequentiality applies to the narrator's mental process, but it is also impressed upon the reader: these running boys have been described earlier in the novel. This particularly visual internal analepsis – image recalling previous image – allows the reader's assimilation of the narrative to take on some of U's picture-based modes of recall and reprisal.

Important too is the passage's invocation of visual or material trace as facilitative of memory. The detail of an 'oval loop' stresses how the airport incident achieved a visual – specifically oval – imprint on the narrator's mind. And McCarthy furthers this sense of direct correlation between perceived object and its mental reception or recall. The prominent position of 'looking' in the first sentence stresses how the chart's visual presentation is the crucial facilitator. There is a close material connection between what is *seen* – 'directional arrows' – and how this impacts on the mind: the evocation of analogous directional loops. Similarly, the use of the passive voice in the final sentence – 'I found my attention caught' – sites mental process as the unavoidable recipient of external phenomena.

So the descriptive structures of the above passage emerge, to a certain degree, as photographic in execution. U's mind is set up as a receptive surface upon which past sights and experiences leave their trace. The outcome of this is to locate representation as deriving immediately from its object. To return to Berger's analysis of the photographic image, the qualities and conditions of the representation 'are received as a given'. And U himself – his descriptive traits, the morphology of his brain – figures as direct transmitter of these external conditions. It is the descriptive equivalent of his continually expressed wish to collapse all distinction between himself, the age itself, and his Great Report:

What if just *coexisting* with these objects and this person, letting my own edges run among them, occupying this moment, or, more to the point allowing *it* to occupy *me*, to blot and soak me up, rather than treating it as feed-data for a later stock-taking what if all this, maybe *was* part of the Great Report? What if the Report might somehow, in some way, be lived, be *be*-d, rather than written? (*SI*, 77)

So we see that *Satin Island* does stage a direct conversation between its thematic content and its own technical choices. Both attempt to figure out the difference between representation that simply soaks up its object, and representation – specifically writing – that constitutes a more conscious and artificial medial intervention. McCarthy's deployment of particular constructions – for instance 'picturing' and its related description – pushes the text towards the former representational mode by emulating the structures of other, non-literary representational techniques that have a more direct, material relationship with the real.

The Writing Process

Satin Island's wider, and specifically meta-fictional, structures and concerns also enact a working through of literary writing's representational abilities: they demonstrate how McCarthy's text as a whole aims for a closeness to its origins reminiscent of the patterns, images and indexes that make up its internal descriptive landscape. Two features of McCarthy's novel in particular contribute to this working through: its promotion of writing as product of an author's thought process, and its use of metafictional allusion.

In the acknowledgements to *Satin Island*, McCarthy explains the novel's material origins:

> *Satin Island* gestated during a 2010 residency at the Internal Artists Studio Programme in Stockholm, which I spent projecting images of oil spills onto huge white walls and gazing at them for days on end. A year later I was the recipient of equally generous hospitality from the Center for Fiction in New York, who lent me a spacious office

in which to sit and think about the general impossibility of writing a
novel about the general impossibility of etc. (*SI*, 189)

The events described here bear a striking resemblance to the plot of
Satin Island itself – the 'general impossibility' of writing the Great
Report is one of the novel's driving tensions: 'I'd begun to suspect',
says U towards the end of the novel, 'that this Great Report was un-
plotable, un-frameable, un-realizable: in short, and in whatever cross-
bred form, whatever medium or media, *un-writable*' (*SI*, 126). We
also see a similarity between McCarthy's preparations for the novel,
and U's own creative process: analyses and manipulations of pictures
of oil spills make up a substantial share of U's activity. And further, as
with McCarthy, this consideration is predominantly wall-based: 'my
dossiers largely consisted of scraps of paper stuck around my walls,
with lines connecting them and annotations, legible only to me,
scrawled at their margins. Each one would stay up for a while, then be
replaced by the next one' (*SI*, 36).

Such correspondences mean that *Satin Island*'s narrator's creative
approach is reflective of how the novel itself was written: reading
through U's working practice therefore equates to a reading through
of the conditions of *Satin Island*'s own production. The upshot of this
effect is to establish two mutually reflective narrative strands – one
internal, one more literal – that promote creative output as highly re-
velatory of its author's thought process. In this sense, we can consider
the novel as a whole to bear on indexical forms of representation. That
is, its total form and content serve as the imprint of a particular process, actual locations – rooms in Stockholm or New York, for instance
– and specific images.

Many features of *Satin Island*'s narrative style support this reading.
McCarthy is keen to get the workings of his narrator's, and implicitly
his own, thought processes down on the page. This passage from the
beginning of the novel walks its reader through the exact form and
matter of one such process:

Hub-airports are predominantly transfer points, rather than destina-
tions in and of themselves. The webpage showed a diagram of a rim-
less wheel, with spokes of different lengths all leading to the centre,

such that communion between any two spots on the wheel's surface area was possible despite no direct line connecting these. It looked like Jesus' crown, with all its jutting prongs. A link took me to an external page that explained how the hub-model was used in fields ranging from freight to distributed computing. Soon I was reading about flanges, track sprockets and bearings in bicycle construction. Then I clicked on *freehub*. (*SI*, 5)

Here, the sequentiality of U's cognitive process is laid bare on the page. Each sentence functions as a single thought unit. The use of simple past tense to begin sentences – 'the webpage showed', 'it looked like', 'a link took me' – outlines how these thoughts occurred one after the other. And clear temporal markers further denote their linear progression: 'soon I was', 'then I'. McCarthy also clarifies the exact nature of these mental associations. He outlines how U might get from one idea to the next primarily by means of visual similarity. 'It looked like', for instance, explains U's cognitive leap from contemplation of an airport plan to an allusion to Jesus's crown. And this mental image of spokes and prongs in turn propels his reading onwards from the wheel-like structure of hub-airports, to the actual wheels of bicycles.

So this passage aims to illustrate the method, rather than just the content, of U's thought. McCarthy deploys this – almost didactic – illustrative mode throughout the novel. U does not just record his thoughts. Rather, he habitually explains both their origin, and where they might lead to next: 'considering the picture, I found my focus, my point of identification within it and my attendant sympathy, shifting from the diminutive man to his expanded, if detached, paraphernalia' (*SI*, 83). The effect of such repeated practice is to stress the impact of the originary creative thought process on narrative progression itself. The order of this process necessarily conditions the reader's own assimilation of the text. The reader is led from impression of 'diminutive man' to his 'paraphernalia', in reflection of U's – and correlatively McCarthy's – way of thinking.

While this may be characteristic of the reading experience in general it is also a feature that *Satin Island* emphatically highlights. Metafictional allusion figures as the most elemental indication of this: when not weaving the processes of literary inspiration into the very progression of the text, McCarthy simply invokes them by reference to paper, writing, typing – the material ephemera and conditions of the act of writing itself. I have already shown how one particular aside – 'this not-Report you're reading now' (*SI*, 125) – asserted a strong correlation between the fictional Great Report and the actual novel in hand. And instances throughout the novel carry a comparable impact. The narrative is shot through with similar allusions: 'lower-case letters' and 'distinctive font' (*SI*, 15); 'field-notes which I'd type up in the evening' (*SI*, 75); and 'this act of scrawling, this graffiti gesture' (*SI*, 84). And all the while these isolated instances are supported by *Satin Island*'s extended metaphor of anthropology as narrative, as fiction. But the effect of such references is less to invoke fiction in the abstract, more to call to mind the actual physical scene of literary production.

A particular set piece emphasizes the novel's wish to foreground the concrete scene of writing. U recounts:

> I installed myself at the desk. It was a good desk; it had cost me quite a bit of money. It had an elegant teak body on whose upper surface sat a leather desktop of a dark-blue tint; set in the leather was a large rectangular writing surface with a blotter backing. That Saturday, I cleared the desktop thoroughly and ruthlessly: every object had to go from it; each notebook, stapler, pencil-holder, scrap of paper; the telephone, the clock (especially the clock); rubbers and paperweights – everything. (*SI*, 93)

Far from being a casual metafictional aside, this passage represents an extended meditation on writing's physical basis. The focus is emphatically with physical stuff, illustrative of McCarthy's own sense of how a writer's tools impact on the final product: writing technologies colour 'not only the rhythm but the whole logic' of a work; and they 'become the subject, not just the medium, of the story' (Johncock, 2011).

Correspondingly, McCarthy stresses the material aspects of the desk in his above description. He details its composition (teak, leather) along with its size, shape and colour (dark-blue, large, rectangular). Even the financial conditions – the desk's expense – are up for consideration, recalling McCarthy's own acknowledgement of 'generous' grants and hospitality. And the final long list of writing equipment cements this impression of material conditions' formative impact on the final work – the novel is composed out of what physical paraphernalia are (or are not) enlisted in its production.

The effect of such passages is to bring the work continually back to the concrete scene of its creation. We can locate it as part of *Satin Island*'s interest in how different representational forms might more closely approach or reflect that which they figure. Metafictionality that draws attention to writing's physical aspects promotes the act as direct product – and accordingly a reflection – of a real, lived scene. The suggestion is that any supposed limitations for literary representation might be mitigated by the fact that writing is, at a base level, closely representative of this originary external event.

This impression is not limited to *Satin Island*'s various writing scenes. Rather, it works on the novel's compositional structure as a whole. The repeated imagery of oil spills figures as one particular example of how a novel might evidence its own material and creative origins. Commentary on such spills make up a substantial part of *Satin Island*'s narrative. U provides this initial description:

> aerial shots of a stricken offshore platform around which a large, dark water-flower was blooming; white-feathered sea birds, filmed from both air and ground, milling around on pristine, snowy shore-lines, unaware of the black tide inching its way towards them; and, villain of the piece, shot by an underwater robot, a broken pipe gushing its endless load into the ocean. (*SI*, 6–7)

Much of the above imagery serves a metafictional purpose. The passage pivots on two complementary semantic clusters: one fixing on darkness or blackness and implying tarnish, the other involving whiteness, snow and purity. This highly visual contrast invokes the look of black type on a white page. The figure of the dark, blooming flower is particularly reminiscent of ink seeping into, and marring, paper. And McCarthy's allusion to 'lines' also participates in this textual lexicon.

Aside from holding a metaphorical relation to writing, such descriptions also cite the workings of U's creativity. He returns, obsessively, to both this original spill and to other subsequent, similar spills as the novel progresses. In doing so, he deploys similar descriptive techniques and notices similar details to this original passage. The same kind of movement is continually evoked – a sense of slow encroachment. And so we read of oil 'blooming' (*SI*, 7) and 'creeping' (*SI*, 37), of oil that 'flowed and reflowed' (*SI*, 10). While the effect of such reiteration is primarily to stress what U sees as the 'generic' nature of oil spills (*SI*, 64), it also means that the reader's experience of these images is rooted in a familiarity with the same details that U finds so memorable and striking. U's perceptive processes filter through into the descriptive techniques of the novel. To read these descriptions is to follow how U assimilates and processes this visual information. In this way, the form and content of *Satin Island*'s description ably evokes the thought process of its narrator.

It also, crucially, looks back to the thought process of its author. These inset oil spills of course allude to McCarthy's artist's residency in Stockholm in a very straightforward manner. *Satin Island*'s acknowledgements figure its preceding mentions of oil spills as simple, metafictional nods to McCarthy's own working practice. But McCarthy takes this correspondence further by weaving the experience of his residency into the very structure of his novel. The novel's descriptive makeup is essentially a patchwork of certain repeated images – namely oil spills, but the trope of parachute accidents may be parsed similarly. These repeated, inspirational images denote their original recurrence in the author's mind and, further, evoke the material scene of his writing: the visual collage of McCarthy's office walls translates into the collage-effect of his novel's descriptive topography. And so, on this reading, we can surely conceive of a novel's internal makeup as stamped by its originary creative process.

Such an effect may not necessarily bring literary production all that much closer to the kind of action hoped for by Mallarmé's frustrated colleague in 'Restricted Action', namely, to move others intellectually or 'philosophically' (*SI*, 21). But, even if still unable to act outside of the literary sphere, fiction does now figure as expressive of a reciprocity between this – literary – sphere, and lived reality. We see a correlation, for instance, between the novel's descriptive makeup and the conditions of its production. And, further, the reader's own experience is lent a somatic, as well as cerebral, aspect: repeated images and details impress upon the reader in mimicry of the writer's own original attention. By contriving some kind of material correlation between the act of writing and its subsequent reception in the real world, the boundaries of literature's area of action push further towards the space of the latter.

In this way *Satin Island*'s own compositional techniques manage to negotiate the various representational impasses contemplated by its narrator. For U, the aim is to produce a report that is as de-mediated as possible, so that the sources are themselves the final product:

> How could I elevate the photos I had pinned about my walls, the sketches, doodles, musings, all the stuff cached on my hard-drive, the audio-files and diaries not my own – how could I elevate all these from secondary sources to be quantified, sucked dry, then cast away, to primary players in this story, or non-story? Above and beyond this, how could life *as lived* become transmogrified from field-work into work, *the* work? (*SI*, 78–9)

As this chapter has shown, *Satin Island* does manage to succeed on the terms given above. Its source images and the writing process can be understood as the basic content of this novel, evident in its collaging effects and its repeated invocation of both conceptual and material origins. On this reading, *Satin Island*'s structural and formal choices reflect its internal preoccupation with those signs and images that bear a strong – often visual or material – relation to that which they represent: patterns, shrouds, anthropological artefacts. And, further, by reprising its original event – the very act of being thought up and written – *Satin Island* queries the sentiment, invoked by its preface, that literary production need entail any such 'immediate disappearance of the written' (*SI*, 23).

Note

1 In relation to U's anthropological pursuits McCarthy says, 'But I think it's plugging into a deeper anxiety about contemporaneity. He goes to this sort of TED Talk and explains to everyone that the whole idea of the

contemporary is ridiculous, which I take straight from Mallarmé. He says exactly this' (Sturgeon, 2015).

Works Cited

Berger, John (2013) *Understanding A Photograph*, ed. Geoff Dyer. London: Penguin.

Crary, Jonathan (1988) 'Techniques of the Observer', *October* 45: 3–35.

Doane, Mary Ann (2002) *The Emergence of Cinematic Time: Modernity, Contingency, the Archive*. Cambridge, MA: Harvard University Press.

Johncock, Ben (2011) 'Tom McCarthy: My Desktop', *Guardian*, 24 November (consulted 8 January 2016): http://www.theguardian.com/books/2011/nov/24/tom-mccarthy-desktop

Krauss, Rosalind (1981) 'The Photographic Conditions of Surrealism', *October* 19: 3–34.

Mallarmé, Stéphane (2001) 'Restricted Action', in *Manifesto: A Century of Isms*, ed. Mary Ann Caws, pp. 21–4. Lincoln, NE: University of Nebraska Press.

Mallarmé, Stéphane (2010) *Un Coup de Dés Jamais N'Abolira le Hazard*. Paris: Ypsilon.

McCarthy, Tom (2015) 'The Death of Writing', *Guardian*, 7 March (consulted 17 December 2015): http://www.theguardian.com/books/2015/mar/07/tom-mccarthy-death-writing-james-joyce-working-google

Peirce, Charles Sanders (1932) *Collected Papers of Charles Sanders Peirce*, eds Charles Hartshorne and Paul Weiss. Vol. 2 of 8. *Elements of Logic*. Cambridge, MA: Harvard University Press.

Polieri, Jacques (1968) 'Le Livre de Mallarmé: A Mise en Scène', *The Drama Review: TDR* 12.3: 179–82.

Purdon, James (2010) 'Tom McCarthy', *Guardian*, 1 August (consulted 17 December 2015): http://www.theguardian.com/books/2010/aug/01/tom-mccarthy-c-james-purdon

Sturgeon Jonathon (2015) 'Kafka and the Crash of the System: An Interview with Tom McCarthy', *Flavorwire*, 26 February (consulted 17 December 2015): http://flavorwire.com/506844/kafka-and-the-crash-of-the-system-an-interview-with-tom-mccarthy

6

The Recidual Remainder

Sam Slote

Remainder, Tom McCarthy's first published novel, presents the problem of an ethics derived from ontological uncertainty. The unnamed narrator of the novel experiences an indefinable and ambiguous sensation of absence and, because of a large financial settlement in the wake of an unspecified accident, he enjoys the financial and logistical means to cope with this uncertainty. Specifically he finds himself compelled to stage painstakingly elaborate re-enactments of various scenes he remembers. This project of enstaging re-enactments is his chosen response to an uncertainty he cannot otherwise articulate. In this essay I will examine the implications and consonances between these re-enactments and allegory.

The narrator's project of re-enactment is a kind of inversion (or literalization) of Proustian recollection, an inversion made possible by wads of cash and the logistical acumen of his personal assistant Naz and his 'facilitation' organization, Time Control UK. In the *Recherche*, Proust learns that he cannot actually *control* time, and so the name of the corporation in *Remainder* immediately suggests a contrast with the Proustian project. In the *Recherche*, we see an articulation of this Proustian project of memory when Marcel returns to Balbec about a year after his grandmother has died. At the moment when he feels returned to his younger self in the presence of his doting grandmother, he finally realizes that she is dead. The moment he feels her presence is exactly when he knows she is forever gone:

> I had only just discovered this because I had only just, on feeling her for the first time alive, real, making my heart swell to breaking-point, on finding her at last, learned that I had lost her forever. Lost for ever; I could not understand, and I struggled to endure the anguish of this contradiction. (Proust, 1992: vol. 4, 182)

His remembrance of her is at once an experience of both a proximity never before felt ('feeling her for the first time alive') and an utter, abject absence. The remembrance is this 'anguish of contradiction' between memory and absence. The Proustian realization is that the urge to remember the past is actually a reminder of its pastness and apartness. To remember is to realize that the past is gone, and thus memory affirms separation. It does not and cannot overcome that gulf.

Memory is an act of negativity in that it testifies to some kind of absence. As the narrator of *Remainder* states on more than one occasion, 'Everything must leave some kind of mark' (*R*, 11, 94, 185). Thus, these remainders too testify to an absence, specifically the absence of coherent memories in the narrator's mind after the unspecified accident. However, another remainder of this accident is the huge cash settlement that he invests into creating a supplement for this negativity of memory. Likewise, the barely-perceptible scar is also a remainder from the accident, or more specifically from the plastic surgery he had had after the accident. Indeed, the narrator himself is a remainder from this event. However, even a Proust armed with a digital video camera, or the services of Time Control UK, would still experience the anguish of contradiction between presence and absence, and, for the most part, with the exception of a few isolated moments, the narrator of *Remainder* still finds himself confronted by absentation and negativity. As Beckett (1957: 72) writes in the conclusion to his monograph on Proust, the *Recherche* ultimately serves to reveal the meaning of the word 'defunctus': that which is left over, the remains of what was once vital but now is gone, finished, over. The remainder is a reminder of that which is beyond control, a reminder of the perseverance of the provisional. The narrator is haunted by the remainder he seeks to tame and control and transvalue (with Naz's technological assistance).

We see this problem with the conundrum of 'recidual', a word which the narrator believes his phantom councillor had used, although at first he mistakes it for 'residual': 'To attain – no, to *accede to* – a kind of authenticity through this strange, pointless residual' (*R*, 240). The idea of *remnant* does not seem quite right to him, even though this word is what remains in his mind after his encounter with the councillor, which presumably was the result of his delusion, itself the remainder of his accident. And so he thinks the word is 'recidual' (*R*, 249). Recidual, a nonce-word, is thus the residual of this encounter, a residual that suggests a variety of different possible meanings, no one of which can be properly tabulated or reckoned by those gurus at the other end of Naz's phone who have access to the *OED*. And so they suggest possible glosses for this word: '"Recision", he read; "the act of rescinding, taking away (limb, act of parliament etc). Recidivate: to fall back, relapse – into sickness, sin, debt ... "' (*R*, 251–2). Thus, instead of meaning that which is left over, it means (or might mean) that which is taken away, or that into which is relapsed, repeated, again and again. Not the remains, but the removal of the remains; which is, in a certain sense, exactly what the narrator is up to with his re-enactments. It is not just a task of re-presenting scenes or events from the past, it is also the annulment of the distance between the present moment and those past scenes. The whole apparatus of recreation which Naz is hired to organize involves the elimination of all traces of effort which go into the recreation. And, as with the windscreen fluid that appeared to mysteriously vanish when he took his car to have its flat tyre replaced, the narrator wants to 'Remove traces, all that stuff' (*R*, 250), or *dematerialize* since, as he puts it at the end of the first chapter, matter is his undoing (*R*, 17).

> They'd vaporised, evaporated, And do you know what? It felt wonderful. Don't ask why: it just did. It was as though I'd just witnessed a miracle: matter – these three litres of liquid – becoming un-matter –

not surplus matter, mess or clutter, but pure bodiless blueness. Transubstantiated. (*R*, 159–60)

That fluid might have temporarily vanished, but in terms of the re-enactment of that particular scene, a whole complex apparatus involving
tubes and tanks is installed into the narrator's car in order to simulate
and recreate that same scene. However, as he soon realizes, the miracle of the disappearing fluid did not happen after all:

This miracle, this triumph over matter, seemed to have occurred, then
turned out not to have done at all – to have failed utterly, spectacular-
ly, its watery debris crashing down to earth, turning the scene of a tri-
umphant launch into the scene of a disaster, a catastrophe. (*R*, 161–2)

The vanishing, then, did leave its trace after all and thus it did not vanish. Matter still matters and the remainder remains, despite all efforts
to the contrary.

So, the narrator is after a residual that is also recidual, that is, a residual that is annulled and repeated. But this nonce word has many
other possible connotations: it has a surplus of meaning. In other
words, there is always a remainder; just as each act of re-enactment
leaves its own traces, even if it's Naz's job to eliminate these. As he
tells Naz at one point, his job is to strip away the 'surplus matter' (*R*,
121); the problem is that that cannot be done, at least not absolutely.

In an interview with Radio Einz, McCarthy (2009) explained that
'there's always this material extra and, in a way, it is an allegory of art.
No matter with how much craft we simulate the world, the world itself will be too much'. Indeed, the phrase 'surplus matter' first occurs
in the book when the narrator remembers an instruction from his art
classes in school: "'Your task isn't to create the sculpture," he said, "it's
to strip all the other stuff away, get rid of it. The surplus matter"' (*R*,
87). The problem is that excision is never perfect, there is always a
material remainder, which works as a reminder of the craft involved.
The surplus marble of the block out of which Michelangelo sculpted
David remains *in absentia* precisely through the traces of Michelangelo's skill. The world is a world of excess and is thus immune to a
complete subservience to human understanding and control.

The idea of remainder and excess is linked with what Nietzsche, in *The Gay Science*, diagnoses as the failures of our aesthetic anthropomorphisms. Nature exceeds our understanding of it. Nietzsche writes:

> Let us beware of attributing to [nature] heartlessness or unreason or their opposites: it is neither perfect nor beautiful, nor noble, nor does it wish to become any of those things; it does not by any means strive to imitate man. None of our æsthetic or moral judgements apply to it. Nor does it have any instinct for self-preservation or any other instinct; and it does not observe any laws either. Let us beware of saying that there are laws in nature. (Nietzsche, 1974: 168, §109)

We may be able to come up with provisional laws that explain nature for our own delimited pragmatic purposes: we can squeeze some use-value out of these, and, in Nietzsche's analysis, that is what the sciences are able to do. But we should not mistake our provisional understanding for a complete understanding since there is always something left over, a remainder. For every $F=ma$ or $E=mc^2$, there is always a bit left over at the side. Each perspective, no matter how valuable and insightful, is always partial and delimited and cannot quite account for *everything*. The remainder is a reminder of the vanity of human wishes.

The narrator's project manifests an odd tension about this remainder: on the one hand it is entirely dependent upon remainders – the ineluctable remainder of memory, but on the other it tries to eliminate those remainders in the staging of the re-enactments. For someone so obsessed by paring away the remainders, it is a little peculiar (but not necessarily surprising) that he fetishizes them, as we can see in the airport scene at the end of the novel when he insists upon being served only the bonus coffee from a completed loyalty card and not the nine others that he had paid for; as he says, 'It's only the remaining one I want. The extra one' (*R*, 279).

The narrator's paradoxical stance towards remainders is that he needs them, and yet he wants to control them. There is a neat, small moment of this when he first meets Naz: 'He looked just like I'd imagined him to look but slightly different, which I'd thought he would in any case' (R, 80). Naz exceeds the narrator's preconception of him, but this excess was apparently already part of that very preconception. Another interesting version of this problem of eliminating extraneous matter and influence comes when the woman playing the concierge in the apartment building re-enactment is instructed to wear a hockey mask. Because the narrator cannot remember the original woman's face, he insists that the re-enactor hide her own features so that they will not contaminate the recreated scene (R, 128). Likewise, much to the consternation of some of the prospective interior designers, the narrator insists that the portions of the building that he cannot remember be left blank so that the reality of the recreation does not impinge upon the memory:

> I'd left blank stretches in my diagrams [...] stretches of floor or corri-
> dor that hadn't crystallised inside my memory. [...] I'd decided that
> these parts should be blank in reality, with doorways papered and ce-
> mented over, strips of wall left bare and so on. Neutral space. (R, 113)

The recreation thus mimics the narrator's fallible memory and not the purported past: the previous reality. Indeed, at one point the narrator admits that perhaps the memory that he is trying to recreate is not of one single building which he had experienced in his past, but rather an amalgamation of different experiences, even films: 'Maybe it was various things all rolled together: memories, imaginings, films, I don't know. But that bit's not important. What's important is that I remembered it and it was crystal-clear' (R, 76). This is a key passage as it shows that the narrator is trying to create (or recreate) something from his own mind, not necessarily something from the archive of the world. The re-enactment creates something that had not previously existed in such a configuration. The 're' of 're-enactment' is actually superfluous, a remainder or reminder of a different concept. To take a line from Derrida's (1981: 206) reading of Mallarmé's *Mimique*, the re-enactments are 'mimicry imitating nothing [...] a double that doubles no simple'. The bank heist re-enactment, or more precisely enactment, is in effect a repetition of an event which has never previously occurred.

Another way of construing the act of re-enactment is as a very specific type of allegory. For the narrator, the re-enactments have meaning because they reference some 'event' within his memory, whether that event was an actual historical event or some trick of his own recall. They have no meaning in and of themselves, at least not for him. In this way they are signs; but they can only function as signs if they correspond perfectly to his imagination: any surplus or deviation has to be expunged. Likewise, the process of allegoresis only works if there is an approximate coincidence between the re-creation and the imagined original. Allegory depends upon a tension between the signifier and the signified: if they coincide too much then the scene is literal and not allegorical, but if they diverge too much (that is, if there is an excess at the level of the signifier), then the allegory breaks under the strain (see Whitman, 1987: 6–9). Allegory thus depends on excess, on a remainder (that is, a divergence between signifier and signified) that it necessarily tries to contain.[1] With the re-enactments, it is almost as if the act of re-creation turns into an allegory of itself; and, in fact, that is what the bank heist turns out to be:

> Occasionally I'd let my eyes run out to corners, looking, like the other re-enactors, for an edge, although I knew there was no edge, that the re-enactment zone was non-existent, or that it was infinite, which amounted in this case to the same thing. (R, 261)

The narrator even remarks that passers-by were 'all doing it just right', even though they did not know they were part of the re-enactment (R, 260). This involuntary and unselfconscious participation is analogous to what Jon Whitman (1987: 3–4 et passim) calls interpretive allegory, where an allegorical significance is divined from a text without any regard to it being deliberately 'programmed' into it by its author. With interpretive allegory, the allegorical initiative belongs to the reader. Likewise, the narrator begins to construe the whole world within the aura of re-enactability, without regard for the specific technological dispensation of Naz and Time Control. Indeed, the value of the bank heist is that it is a re-enactment, and not that it is an act of stealing money. The narrator thus transvalues the whole world into the sphere of the re-enactment. As he says of the bag of cash:

> Its money was like rubbish to me: rubbish, dead weight, matter – and
> for that reason it was valuable, invaluable, as precious as golden fleece
> or lost ark or Rosetta Stone. (*R*, 266)

The value of the robbery comes from the act of symbolic hypostasis which he is staging, and not the symbolic hypostasis in which the
Bank of England engages when it prints money, the one we tend to
believe in when we spend English pounds and pence.

The allegorical mode can also be seen in Naz's increasing enthusiasm for what the narrator is trying to do, although Naz is attracted to
a different aspect of the enterprise:

> Yes, Naz *was* a zealot – but his zealotry wasn't religious: it was bu-
> reaucratic. And he *was* drunk: infected, driven onwards, on towards
> a kind of ecstasy just by the possibilities of information management
> my projects were opening up for him, each one more complex, more
> extreme, my executor. (*R*, 218)

Naz's enthusiasm, initially, is directed towards the *process* of allegoriza-
tion and not the product. He remains servile to the materiality of the
signifier, that which he can continually manipulate and arrange, and
not to the mysterious epiphanic experience towards which the narrator is striving. However, while the narrator's drive seems teleological,
like Naz he is also captivated by the process of re-enactment. When
asked which re-enactment worked best, he cannot provide an answer
since he does not look at each re-enactment as a discrete quantifiable
event: 'The realness I was after wasn't something you could "do" just
once and then have got: it was a state, a mode – one that I needed to
return to again and again and again' (*R*, 223). He does not embark
on these re-enactments for a result, rather it is about the act of doing
it itself, repeatedly, like an addiction. Indeed, his immediate instinct
after the first run-through in the apartment building is to do it again.
Of course, recreating the original run-through brings its own logistical issues, and when the third run-through does not work out again he
decides to move on to something else. At one point, the narrator even
wants to re-enact the re-enactments, with new re-enactors playing the
parts of the previous re-enactors. Naz's enthusiasm for this idea is the

first manifestation of a mania for this mad project that exceeds the merely bureaucratic zeal he had first evinced.

The narrator is imposing his own sensibility on the world, moulding it to accommodate his mind. Thanks to his cash settlement, he has the resources to do this on a fairly large scale, even if the scale is not quite as vast as he desires. He forces his worldview, or *Weltanschauung*, one created through lack and absence, onto the world, thereby creating a world of lack and absence. He is, within a certain scale, godlike, and consequently harbours a few delusions of grandeur. He may have vanquished God, but he remains in thrall to the shadow, a shadow in which he has installed himself as God's supplement. When, during the first re-enactment he commands the motorcycle enthusiast to leave a patch of oil uncleaned so that he can 'capture' it later, the enthusiast asks what he means by the word 'capture': 'It meant whatever I wanted it to mean: I was paying him to do what I said. Prick' (*R*, 142). This is not unlike Humpty-Dumpty informing Alice that a word 'means just what I choose it to mean – neither more nor less' (Carroll, 1994: 100). This lexical authoritarianism is part of a larger pretence. The narrator has the power to create his individual hypostasis in material form: 'My pyramid was like a Pharaoh's pyramid. I was the Pharaoh' (*R*, 255). As he says elsewhere, 'I wasn't bound by the rules – everyone else was, but not me' (*R*, 209). The apartment building he has reconstructed is rather like a dollhouse, but one into which he can walk, or not, when he so chooses. He even has a model made of the apartment building – a simulation of the simulation – and plays with this miniature re-re-enactment while simultaneously manipulating the people in the full-scale re-enactment:

> I lifted the model up and rested it against the window sill so I could look down on the model's head poking out at the same time as I looked at the real one. The distance made them both look the same size. (*R*, 153)

The 'reality' of the so-called 'real' re-enacted is compromised by the fact that it can itself be re-enacted or simulated. Unsurprisingly, this double-order simulation sometimes supplements the first-order simulation:

> The next day I placed my model on my living room floor. I moved the figures around once more and issued instructions down the phone to Naz as I did this – only today I didn't go and look. Just knowing it was happening was enough. (R, 154)

The simulation supplements, takes the place of the thing it represents; and this chain of supplementarity has its own logic which goes on and on. If a re-enactment was already, following from Derrida, a double that doubles no simple, then, logically, this chain of supplementarity can be extended indefinitely. Thus we get the Kafkaesque detail of the supervisors who watch the re-enactors in shifts so that the re-enactments can continue without the narrator having to be present in person (R, 166). This desire is the logical conclusion of the narrator's project, a re-enactment that, once sparked by his initiative, can continue on without his involvement. It parallels Clairwil's desire for the ultimate crime, as expressed in the Marquis de Sade's *Juliette*:

> I would like [...] to find a crime which, even when I had left off doing it, would go on and have a perpetual effect, in such a way that so long as I lived, at every hour of the day and as I lay sleeping at night, I would constantly be the cause of a particular disorder, and that this disorder might broaden to the point where it brought about a corruption so universal or a disturbance so formal that even after my life was over I would survive in the everlasting continuation of my wickedness. (Sade, 1968: 525)

The true sign of godlike power is this act of indefinite creation. For the narrator, the motivation for all this supplementation is the feeling of inauthenticity he suffers after the accident (and, perhaps, the Sadean villain is victim to an analogous inauthenticity). The mysterious, ambiguous accident has *deconstructed* the narrator, to use the word in the trivial sense in which it has entered the vernacular. As the narrator recounts of his hospital stay at the beginning of the novel:

> Later still, during the weeks I sat in bed able to think and talk but not yet to remember anything about myself, the Settlement was held up to me as a future strong enough to counterbalance my no-past, a moment that would make me better, whole, complete. (R, 6)

The narrator is after a moment which would *restore* him, restore him to a state which he had perhaps never experienced in the first place. And, with his freshly-acquired resources, he keeps going after this restoration again and again. But these re-enactments, rather than reconstructing his fragmented self, testify to and exacerbate his fragmentation. As Paul de Man (1986: 84) writes of translations, themselves linguistic re-enactments, they 'disarticulate, they undo the original, they reveal that the original was always already disarticulated'. Indeed, during his physiotherapy the narrator remarks that he had always felt inauthentic:

> Even before the accident, if I'd been walking down the street just like De Niro, smoking a cigarette like him, and even if it had lit first try, I'd still be thinking: *Here I am, walking down the street, smoking a cigarette, like someone in a film.* See? Second-hand. (*R*, 24)

The point of the whole exercise of the re-enactments is to create moments where he might feel real. What he's after, at least at first, is not the events he remembers, but the event of recollection, that is, the fact that he had remembered various incidents. But, once the project is underway, it becomes more about the fact that certain scenes or events are memorable, that is, *capable* of being remembered or reproduced. More and more, as the project progresses, he keeps thinking of scenes *as he is experiencing them*, thinking that he would like to re-enact them. In a sense, his project is, following from (or re-enacting) Walter Benjamin, how to live in the age of techno-logistical reproduction.

This leads to the question of the tension between fetishizing the remainder while eliminating the surplus matter: the problem of the residual, as it were. All the effort and work that goes into the re-enactment – Naz's speciality: the surplus matter of the logistics of re-enactment – has to be hidden: the work of simulation must be dissimulated. And this is done in order to produce these moments of authenticity for the narrator, epitomized by the first of the men gunned down in gang warfare:

The truth is that, for me, this man had become a symbol of perfection. It may have been clumsy to fall from his bike, but in dying beside the bollards on the tarmac he'd done what I wanted to do: merged with the space around him, sunk and flowed into it until there was no distance between it and him – and merged too with his actions, merged to the extent of having no more consciousness of them. He'd stopped being separate, removed, imperfect. [...] And so I had to re-enact his death: for myself, certainly, but for the world in general as well. No one who understands this could accuse me of not being generous. (R, 184–5)

Here, he takes his personal perspective, 'The truth ... for me', and re-enacts it not just for his own benefit but for the world in general. Thus, contrary to a Nietzschean ethics, he imposes *his* truth as a universal. The narrator achieves this (fleeting) sense of not being inauthentic in a moment that was not coordinated by Naz. It was an involuntary accident, not unlike a Proustian madeleine or a misstep on an uneven cobblestone path. There are two other such moments for him: the temporarily disappearing blue goop from his car and the time when he needlessly plays the role of a beggar outside his stockbroker's office: 'Demanding money of which he most certainly had no need. [...] That's what made him feel the most real' (R, 224). In a sense, play-acting as a beggar is an improvised re-enactment, where everything feels just right, but without any pre-meditated plan.

Of course, what he realizes is that life is always susceptible to re-enactment, that all experiences are potentially repeatable. Any act can be re-enacted. This comes up in the narrator's discussion with Samuels, the robber, about how banks stage simulations, or as he calls them 'pre-enactments' of robberies (R, 241). The idea of the pre-enactment spurs the narrator to commit the bank robbery at the novel's end: a re-enactment where almost no-one knows what exactly what is going on. The re-enactors think it is a re-enactment, whereas the bank tellers and police think it is a real robbery, which would be for them a re-enactment of a different sort, the pre-enactment of moves they have already rehearsed in preparation for such an eventuality. In this sense, the scene recalls Borges's story 'Pierre Menard, Author of the *Quixote*', where it is claimed that a passage from Menard's fragmentary *Don Quixote* is thematically and stylistically superior to its counterpart in Cervantes's original even though the texts are absolutely identical. The words are the same, but the context is different. The 'repetition' – the fact that repetition is always possible and always available, even imperfectly – thus robs the original of *something*. As Baudrillard (1983: 146) writes, 'The very definition of the real has become: *that of which it is possible to give an equivalent reproduction.* [...] The real is not only what can be reproduced, but *that which is always already reproduced,* the hyperreal, which is entirely in simulation'. The simulation trumps the original thereby consigning the original to re-enactability.

With the bank heist, the narrator explains to Naz that, even though the bank staff do not know that they are participating in a re-enactment, they will still be aware of being in a re-enactment, albeit of a different kind: 'they've been trained to do exactly what the re-enactors have been trained to do. Both should re-enact the same movements identically' (*R*, 242). The plan is thus to confuse the event, to make enactment and re-enactment indistinguishable, without any difference or remainder between the two:

> Yes: lifting the re-enactment out of its demarcated zone and slotting it back into the world, into an actual bank whose staff didn't know it was a re-enactment: that would return my motions and my gestures to ground zero and hour zero, to the point at which the re-enactment merged with the event. It would let me penetrate and live inside the core, be seamless, perfect, real. (*R*, 244–5)

Eliminating the remainder between re-enactment and enactment is returning to a kind of 'event degree zero'. This plan doesn't work, but then again maybe it did, just in a different register; as the narrator says:

> I don't know. But I know one thing for sure: it was a fuck-up. It went wrong. Matter, for all my intricate preparations, all my bluffs and sleights of hand, played a blinder. Double-bluffed me. Tripped me up again. I know two things: one, it was a fuck-up; two, it was a very happy day. (*R*, 259–60)

The thing that gets in the way is a remainder: there is some surplus matter between all the intricate preparations for the event and the event itself. In this case, the excess is an absence of matter: a kink in the carpet in the warehouse where the robbery was rehearsed is absent the real bank, leading one of the re-enactors to trip, fire his gun, and kill himself. The re-enactment then becomes real, all too real:

> But it was a re-enactment. That's the beauty of it. It became real while it was going on. Thanks to the ghost kink, mainly – the kink the other kink left when we took it away. (*R*, 273)

This leads the narrator to commit an authentic act, one which unfortunately involves murder:

> I did it because I wanted to. Seeing him standing there in Four's position as I stood in his, replaying in first my mind and then my body his slow fall, I'd felt the same compulsion to shoot him as I'd felt outside Victoria Station that day to ask passers by for change. Essentially, it was the movements, the positions and the tingling that made me do it – nothing more. (*R*, 276)

Even then, it is not quite perfect as he says over the dead body that it should be on its side. There is always something left over:

> 'Isn't it beautiful?' I said to Naz. 'You could take everything away – vaporise, replicate, transubstantiate, whatever – and this would still be there. However many times.' (*R*, 277)

This passage has implications for McCarthy's claim that his novel can be read as an allegory for art. The problem of excess – of the remainder that cannot be accounted for – is exactly the problem raised by allegory since allegory involves an excess of signification. If *Remainder* is an allegory then, by definition, it is about something *more* than just a story of a man who suffers an unspecified accident which leads him to waste an excess of money. If this allegory is about art (or artistic activity) then it would posit art not as the paring away, but *as* the surplus matter – and surplus matter would be another name for irony, that which exceeds interpretive understanding. Art then both palliates and exacerbates ontological uncertainty in the precession of (its own) hyperreality.

Note

1 Because of this, Paul de Man (1983: 209) argues that allegory is related to irony in that with both 'the relation between sign and meaning is discontinuous'.

Works Cited

Baudrillard, Jean (1983) *Simulations*, trans. by Paul Foss, Paul Patton and Philip Beitchman. New York: Semiotext(e).

Beckett, Samuel (1957) *Proust*. New York: Grove.

Carroll, Lewis (1994) *Through the Looking Glass*. London: Penguin.

de Man, Paul (1983) 'The Rhetoric of Temporality', *Blindness and Insight*, 2nd edn. Minneapolis: University of Minnesota Press.

de Man, Paul (1986) 'Conclusions: Walter Benjamin's "The Task of the Translator"', *The Resistance to Theory*. Minneapolis: University of Minnesota Press.

Derrida, Jacques (1981) *Dissemination*, trans. by Barbara Johnson. Chicago, IL: University of Chicago Press.

McCarthy, Tom (2009) 'Interview with Radio Einz', 15 March, URL (consulted 8 January 2015): http://www.3ammagazine.com/3am/being-in-the-world-smoothly/

Nietzsche, Friedrich (1974) *The Gay Science*, trans. Walter Kaufmann. New York: Vintage.

Proust, Marcel (1992) *In Search of Lost Time*, trans. C. K. Scott Moncrieff and Terence Kilmartin, revised by D. J. Enright. London: Chatto and Windus.

Sade, Donatien Alphonse François (Marquis de) (1968) *Juliette*, trans. Austryn Wainhouse. New York: Grove.

Whitman, Jon (1987) *Allegory: The Dynamics of an Ancient and Medieval Technique*. Cambridge, MA: Harvard University Press.

7

'AN ETERNAL DETOUR'
REALITY HUNGER, POST-PROUSTIAN MEMORY AND THE
LATE MODERN SELF IN TOM MCCARTHY'S *REMAINDER*

Sebastian Groes

For in the brightness of art alone can be deciphered the baffled ec-
stacy that he had known before the inscrutable superficies of a cloud,
a triangle, a spire, a flower, a pebble, when the mystery, the essence,
Idea, imprisoned in matter, had solicited the bounty of a subject passing within the shell of his impurity, and tendered [...] at least an in-
corruptible beauty.

Samuel Beckett, Proust (1930)

In an essay on the power of cinema, George Orwell makes a bold
statement about the possibilities offered by film:

If one thinks of it, there is very little in the mind that could not *somehow* be represented by the strange distorting powers of film. A mil-
lionaire with a private cinematograph, all the necessary props and a
troupe of intelligent actors could, if he wished, make practically all of
his inner life known. He could explain the real reasons of his actions
instead of telling rationalised lies, point out the things that seemed to
him beautiful, pathetic, funny, etc. – things that an ordinary man has

to keep locked up because there are no words to express them. In general, he could make other people understand him. (Orwell, 1968: 9)

Besides being a perversely submissive celebration of a new artistic medium by an artist expressing himself in words, this is also a utopian, naive take on what film can achieve. Yet the urgency of the desire for communicating what it is to have – and *be* – consciousness locked inside a body, which makes the experience of being human just as elusive as it is miraculous, is telling. We detect a hunger for understanding consciousness, making genuine and meaningful communication with other people, understanding human behaviour, and for truth and knowledge.

Tom McCarthy's novel *Remainder* (2005) struggles with the same desire for understanding human consciousness. With a view to restoring a proper sense of selfhood and achieving meaningful communication with other people, the protagonist enacts Orwell's fantasy. The novel tells the story of a nameless, amnesiac narrator who, after being traumatized by an accident which involves 'something falling from the sky', receives eight million pounds (*R*, 5). He experiences an epiphany about his past in a bathroom and, rather than lying in bed pondering and probing his memory like Marcel Proust, proceeds to reconstitute his former self by attempting to recreate that childhood memory in reality through contextual association. He buys a building and uses 're-enactors', actors who have to play specific roles and generate phenomenological impressions, to evoke and metonymically expand the memory experienced in the bathroom. The attempted recovery of his former self fails, however, sparking an ever deepening quest for control over 'the real' by replicating increasingly violent real life events. The novel ends with the attempt to execute a carefully rehearsed bank robbery, a project which again fails, and we leave the protagonist when he escapes on a private plane doing endless loops, postponing his capture by the authorities, until the fuel runs out.

One way of interpreting McCarthy's enigmatic novel is by focusing on its intellectual and literary procedures in relationship to the protagonist–narrator's memory, which, has been erased due to his head trauma:

I don't even remember the event. It's a blank: a white slate, a black hole. I have vague images, half-impressions: of being, or having been – or, more precisely, being *about* to be – hit; blue light; railings; lights of other colours; being held above some kind of tray or bed. But who's to say that these are genuine memories? Who's to say my traumatised mind didn't just make them up, or pull them out from somewhere else, some other slot, and stick them there to plug the gap – the crater – that the accident had blown. Minds are versatile and wily things. Real chancers. (*R*, 5)

The proliferation of metaphors of memory – from 'slate' and the 'black hole' to the 'crater' and 'chancer' – yields a complexly stratified archaeology of conceptualization of memory, ranging from classical and Modernist conceptions to postmodernist and speculative realist thinking. The reference to the slate refers back to the Aristotelian conception of the self as a *tabula rasa* in *On the Soul* (Book III, chapter IV), which presupposes that man has no innate knowledge, but that knowledge is established only through experience and perception; there is no 'nature' but only 'nurture'. In the tension between the various references to light and the black hole we find an interest in the work of Plato, which thinks about memory as a form of remembering of things which already exist inside ourselves but that we have forgotten, an idea which is diametrically opposed to the Aristotelian conceptualization. The vague images and half-impressions refer to the late nineteenth and early twentieth century, with the Impressionist and Modernist interest in time, consciousness and memory, and the foregrounding of subjective perception as a way of understanding the world in painters from Claude Monet to Salvador Dalí and in writers from Conrad to Beckett. The allusion to confabulation injects a level of epistemological complexity and doubt, whilst the emphasis on randomness in the passage remind us of the distinctly postmodern challenge to conventional conceptions of 'the real', that is, the erasure of the boundary between fact and fiction and the idea that mediation of experience fundamentally challenges the narrator's authenticity. There is further speculation about the mind through some form of migratory memory ('pull them out from somewhere else'), a spatialization of the mind as a machine ('slot') and a return to a biological metaphor with the reference to 'crater'. The confused, panicky layering of metaphors itself expresses the narrator's struggle to make sense of his amnesia. This chapter bores its way through these layers of thinking about memory to suggest that *Remainder* forms an investigation of the state of the human experience at the start of a turbulent and troubled twenty-first century, renegotiating some of the underpinnings of postmodernist thinking in favour of an experimental, late Modernist conceptualisation of the mind and memory.

The Perpetual Present, Amnesiacs and 'the real': Beyond Postmodernism, or Before

Remainder is a reconsideration, and critical revaluation, of the cultural period that the text is trying to break free from: postmodernism. Although published in 2005, the novel was written in 2001, at the tail end of postmodernism.[1] In an interview with *The Believer* magazine, McCarthy says:

> I've read Baudrillard, but Plato said it all. The idea of the simulacra being a copy without an original, which is Baudrillard's big selling point – it's in the *Sophist* by Plato. Lots of people described *Remainder* as a very postmodern book, because there is this guy reenacting very stylized moments in a bid for authenticity, and in the postmodern era, they say, we don't have authenticity. But I was thinking as much of *Don Quixote*, the first novel, or one of the first novels, which is exactly the same. It is about a guy feeling inauthentic in 1605 and in a bid to acquire, to accede to authenticity, he reenacts moments from penny novels, the kind of TV of its day. So I think you have to be a bit careful about this cult of newness, the idea that somehow, post-about-1962, we're suddenly postmodern – It just ain't so. There's always a precedent. (Alizart, 2008)

McCarthy is defending himself against charges of postmodernism as his novel at first glance seems to resolutely embody various postmodernist tropes, from the figure of the amnesiac, the obsession with feeling inauthentic, epistemological and ontological uncertainty, hyper-mediatization and Spectacle, a criticism of late capitalist consumerism, the proliferation of simulacra, the breakdown of conventional signification, the deferral of a conclusion, the narrator's affectless voice – which chimes in with Fredric Jameson's (1992: 10) 'waning of affect' and J. G. Ballard's (1995: v) 'death of affect' – cultural and historical relativism and the modern subject's entrapment in a perpetual present. While *Remainder* may seem to demonstrate some of postmodernism's key tropes, I am arguing that it is actually a key intellectual 'hinge text' that struggles with, or moves away from, some of the postmodernism concepts just identified. As Zadie Smith (2008) notes, *Remainder* 'clears away a little of the deadwood, offering a glimpse of an alternative road down which the novel might travel, with difficulty, travel forward. We could call this constructive deconstruction'.

One focused way of thinking through McCarthy's tussle with postmodernism is via *Remainder*'s representation of memory. One defining characteristic of the postmodern period was its thinking about time, history and memory; according to some critics, the postmodernist experience was characterized by the loss of historical depth, of memory and by an experience dominated by a 'perpetual present'. Jameson (1992: ix) famously noted that it 'is safest to grasp the concept of the postmodern as an attempt to think the present historically in an age that has forgotten how to think historically in the first place'. Jameson also noted that 24-hour news broadcasting and the general acceleration of late capitalist existence was creating a 'perpetual present', because there was perpetually new news (see, for example, Jameson, 1985). Not only was the postmodern condition an ahistorical experience, but newness was itself impossible, trapping us into an endless recycling of past ideas and discourses. Metaphorically, this perpetual present resulted in, and from, social and cultural amnesia and a celebration of cultural superficiality: the internationalizing forces of globalization created an energetic, dynamic exchange of people, culture and ideas, but it also entailed a levelling out of cultural depth and richness.

A related line of thought conceptualising this assumed ahistorical, amnesiac condition runs via thinkers such the philosopher duo Gilles Deleuze and Felix Guattari, and the Marxist critics David Harvey and the aforementioned Jameson. They see the postmodern experience as a breakdown of traditional meaning-making processes. Because of the acceleration of the postmodern experience, and sheer scale of new connections associated with economic and cultural globalization, a breakdown in the conventionally stable relationship between signifier and signified manifested itself, leaving us with a swirling vortex of signifiers whose meaning is elusive and continually postponed. These thinkers argue that the postmodern experience creates a rupture in conventionally stable, linear signification, which is dependent on the ability of the mind to frame its experience in chronological, essentialist terms. In temporal terms, the experience of the self, events and the world is no longer unified: the organic structures that once provided us with deep structures allowing us to root ourselves in a deep history and traditional societal structures (such as the family and community) are lost and we become ahistorical and atemporal. In the light of this context, Deleuze and Guattari detect a shift in the dominance of two different types of memory:

> Neurologists and psychophysiologists distinguish between long-term and short-term memory. [...] The difference between them is not simply quantitative: short-term memory is of the rhizome type, and long-term memory is arborescent and centralised (imprint, engram, tracing, or photograph). Short-term memory is in no way subject to a law of contiguity or immediacy to its object; it can act at a distance, come or return a long time after, but always under conditions of discontinuity, rupture, and multiplicity. Furthermore, the difference between the two kinds of memory is not that of two temporal modes of apprehending the same thing; they do not grasp the same thing, memory, or idea. The splendour of the short-term Idea: one writes using short-term memory, and thus short term ideas, even if one reads or rereads using long-term memory of long-term concepts. Short-term includes forgetting as a process; it merges not with the instant but instead with the nervous, temporal, and collective rhizome. Long-term memory (family, race, society, or civilization) traces and translates, but what it translates continues to act in it, from a distance, off beat, in an 'untimely' way, not instantaneously. (Deleuze and Guattari, 2004: 15)

Postmodernity entails a shift towards rhizomic short-term memory, at the expense of long-term memory, which, as the word 'splendour' suggests is not necessarily a strictly negative experience because long-term memory entraps us in traditional, conservative meaning-making processes. Traditional, stale humanist structures such as the family and nation state may be rethought through the multiplicity of new, creative connections and meanings that may be forged through processes and thinking that involve short-term memory.

It is no surprise, then, that an army of amnesiacs populated post-modern culture, with protagonists suffering memory loss in, for instance, Martin Amis's *Other People* (1979) and *Yellow Dog* (2003), Michael Ondaatje's *The English Patient* (1992) and Steven Hall's *The Raw Shark Texts* (2007), to *Johnny Mnemonic* (William Gibson's story of 1981 and the film of 1995), *Total Recall* (1990), the *Bourne Identity* series (2002, 2004, 2007, 2012), and *Run, Lola Run* (1998). Amnesia, and the figure of the amnesiac, became metaphors for a condition in which we are no longer able to situate ourselves coherently and organically in a historical long view because conventional processes of identification have broken down. Christopher Nolan's film *Memento* (2000) encapsulated a postmodern condition in which, along the lines of Deleuze and Guattari's argument, a shift had taken place from long-term to short-term memory, with tragic consequences.

Remainder appears to be yet another amnesiac novel extending postmodern concerns into the twenty-first century. It is tempting therefore to situate McCarthy's novel among two specific 'postpostmodernist' artistic collectives. McCarthy could be said to belong to a group identified by Richard Bradford as the 'New Postmodernists'. Bradford includes Will Self, John Lanchester, Nicola Barker, Candida McWilliam, Ali Smith, Toby Litt and David Mitchell in this category as their work 'execute[s] a calculated and premeditated shift away from an implied mindset, outside the novel, that involves the plausible, the rational and the predictable; [...] the writers themselves are as astutely aware of the taxonomy of postmodernism as its theorists' (Bradford, 2007: 67).[2] These New Postmodernists thus work with the ideas offered by postmodernism, yet engage with and execute them in a less theoretical, more creative manner. McCarthy does not fit into this group because of his attraction to the high-theoretical, philo-sophical (especially Derridean) paradigms of postmodernism, and to Speculative Realism, which offers sets of rules of representation that dominate his fiction. Neither does McCarthy's poetics chime in with the aesthetics of the New Puritans, whose manifesto-anthology *All Hail the New Puritans* (2000) attempted to move decisively away from the baroque exuberance of writers such as Rushdie and Amis. This new generation of writers, including Alex Garland, Geoff Dyer, Rebecca Ray and Scarlett Thomas, shunned poetic license, meta-phor, rhetoric, rooting their prose narratives in real places and times. Indeed, in the spirit of Aristotle and Leavis's Great Tradition, the ninth point in their manifesto declared themselves moralists whose texts feature a recognizable ethical reality, which is a clear rejection of the amoral cultural and social relativism that the decadence of post-modern thinking in its more radical form had come to be associated with.[3] McCarthy does not fit into this group because he is aiming to salvage and redirect some of the radical and subversive thinking that postmodernism produced while the anti-intellectualism of the Puritans rubs up against his philosophical interests. And, as the arche-ology of metaphors I elucidated at the start of this chapter suggests, McCarthy is not aiming for purity, but for a messy complexity that imitates modern life.

McCarthy's representation of memory can help us clarify his nov-el's relationship to postmodernism: his protagonist takes us beyond the amnesiac as simply a figure of superficiality and dehistoricization, exposing this idea itself as a clichéd shorthand that misinterpreted some of postmodernism's underpinnings. McCarthy's novel chal-lenges, for instance, the simplicity of the perpetual present thesis, and it is therefore helpful to situate him among thinkers who chal-lenged the ahistorical and amnesiac associations of postmodernism. In *Tangled Memories* (1997), Marita Sturken notes:

> The postmodern condition has often been theorized as a context in which all sense of history is lost, amnesia reigns, and the past is van-dalized by the pastiche forms of the present. [...] I argue that post-modernism's relationship to the past is not ahistorical or amnesiac.

> Although memory's relationship to original experience is difficult if
> not impossible to verify, this does not make memory any less crucial.
> [...] Cultural memory is produced and resides in new forms. Indeed,
> it can often be disguised as forgetting. (Sturken, 1997: 16–17)

Just as Deleuze and Guattari argued for a shifting balance in the relationship between short- and long-term memory, Sturken identifies that our individual and collective memory has become increasingly complex, calling for a different, more subtle approach to our
understanding of memory. This memory-forgetting dynamic finds
its expression in the misrepresentation and/or repression of subversive events, ideas and discourses by more comfortable narratives, as
Raphael Samuel has pointed out about Thatcherite memorial and
historical procedures in *Theatres of Memory* (1994). In Mark Currie's
work we find, with the help of Derrida, another, even stronger rejection of the Jamesonian 'perpetual present' thesis:

> I'm not sure I agree with Jameson when he concludes [...] that the
> function of news media is 'to help us forget' or create a 'perpetual
> present'. The speed with which events are consigned to the past could
> more convincingly be analysed as a flight from the present, as an im-
> patience to narrate current events, to hurry everything into the past
> while it is still happening. This makes it a new way of remembering, of
> archiving, that actually displaces the experiential present tense with a
> historical self-consciousness. Historical self-consciousness does not
> then mean the same thing as historiographic self-consciousness: it is
> the sense that one is a narrative, or that one is part of a narrative of
> history, so that the present is experienced as if always already narrated
> in retrospect. (Currie, 1998: 97)

For Currie, the postmodern narrative consciousness is not determined by amnesia but by a perpetual archiving process, that is, the
perpetual creation of memory, in new forms. We could add to this
present-past dynamic a prospective, future element, as Derrida
(1996: 36) reminds us in *Archive Fever*: 'It is a question of the future,
the question of the future itself, the question of a response, of a promise and of a responsibility from tomorrow. The archive: if we want to
know what that will have meant, we will only know in times to come'.

Currie's reference to experiencing the present 'as if always already narrated in retrospect' comes close to the speculative realists' idea that the present has, from a future perspective, already played itself out, a mode of narration which McCarthy explores even more fully in C (2010).

Thus, instead of presenting us with another amnesiac who symbolically stands for a loss of cultural and historical depth, *Remainder* is actually a subtle move away from thinkers such as Jameson, but simultaneously also from Derrida for whom experience is largely a textual affair. As the emphasis on the physical head trauma suggests, McCarthy thinks of the mind and memory as, at least to a large degree, phenomena produced by the brain; McCarthy thus brings back an emphatically embodied experience. The bulk of the novel's second chapter is taken up by the description of the narrator's revalidation, which leaves no doubt that McCarthy is making a deliberate shift away from postmodernism's idealistic, utopian faith in textuality towards a revaluation of materiality: 'you'd find so much to analyse, so many layers, just so much *matter*' (R, 187) notes the narrator when observing a tarmac road. McCarthy also foregrounds the central role of the brain in the human experience: 'The part of my brain that controls the motor functions of the right side of my body had been damaged. It had been damaged pretty irreparably, so the physiotherapist had to do something called "rerouting"' (R, 19). McCarthy describes damage to the frontal and temporal lobes, the brain areas that are used for 'motoric memory skills', which pertains to procedural memory, but the novel foregrounds this physical trauma in relationship to declarative, autobiographical memory.

This description of this rerouting process in McCarthy's novel is striking for its resemblance with Robert Pepperell's reconceptualization of human consciousness and memory in *The Post-Human Condition* (1995). Pepperell calls the process by which memories are created and thoughts may be activated 'canalization':

> The principle of least resistance allows us to maintain comprehension because we are not having to set up new cases for each input, thus stability is maintained. If the scene is completely new or overwhelm-

ing (by analogy with rivers, a flood), then the energy input into the body will not be able to follow pre-established paths and new ones will have to be created. When an unfamiliar stimulus enters the body it will try to create a new path; he more powerful the stimulus the more significant the new path. [...] Each path may be discrete inasmuch as it relates to a particular memory, but not isolated insofar as it will be connected to many other paths through which it might be activated. The transformed potentiality represents the sum of all such paths that contribute to a thought even though they occur in widely differing areas of the mind at once. In this sense, we regard thought as being *distributed* rather than localised. (Pepperell, 1995: 81)

Remainder's narrator uses a similar metaphor for his recovery of motoric skills:

Rerouting is exactly what it sounds like: finding a new route through the brain for commands to run along. It's sort of like a government compulsorily purchasing land from farmers to run train tracks over after the terrain the old tracks ran through has been flooded or landslid away. The physiotherapist has to route the circuit that commands the limb and muscles through another patch of brain – an unused, fallow patch, the part that makes you be able to play tiddlywinks, listen to chart music, whatever. (*R*, 19)

As the 'crater' metaphor already indicated, land and geography are presented by McCarthy as analogous to the brain, an idea that resembles Pepperell's metaphor. McCarthy gives us an anti-classical image of memory not as something fixed (as in traditional metaphors from Plato's wax tablet to Freud's *Wunderblock*) but as a phenomenon that is decentralized and distributed, a process of constant reworking of memories. The model of memory that emerges then, is, in Margaret E. Gray's words,

the discovery that memory is not so much the retrieval of fixed facts as it is the ability to reorganise information. One important organizational category, for instance, is contextual association. We remember a loved one's face not in association, but in association with specific contexts or networks of activity: walking the dog, reading the newspaper. (Gray, 1992: 69)

The narrator is very much aware that he can only get his memory and selfhood back through 'contextual association'. Memory as continuous process is not necessarily a postmodern characteristic, though, but a metaphor for modernity in more general terms. The ability to reorganise and recategorise information reminds us of the late modernist image of continuous re-ordering and re-interpreting of autobiographical memory into a protean archive in Samuel Beckett's *Krapp's Last Tape* (1958). McCarthy's representation of amnesia is not associated with the schizophrenic metaphorically construed as a cultural crisis; rather, the trauma is literalised and embodied by the figure of the post-traumatic stress disorder (PTSD) sufferer as a real condition, signalling a shift away from postmodernism. Indeed, in the de-historicized landscape of *Remainder* – although the reference to the technology falling from the sky teases us into believing this is a post-9/11 novel – there are hardly any details that allow us to root the novel in a specific time. McCarthy's novel chimes in, temporally speaking, with the post-historical worlds created by Beckett.

'I – am – real': *Remainder* and the Possibility of the 'Real'

Another example of McCarthy's quarrel with postmodernist forms of representation happens not in the thinking about memory, but in the novel's thinking about the status of the real. A key example takes place during the episode involving the conversation with a homeless person (*R*, 52–6), whom the protagonist subsequently takes out for dinner. At the end of this passage the narrator reveals that this part of the story never actually happened: 'The truth is I've been making all this up – the stuff about the homeless person' (*R*, 58). Here we are potentially presented with a twist comparable that in Ian McEwan's *Atonement* (2001), where the perverse ending reveals that what we have read is a protracted, wilful act of fabulation. McEwan manipulates our readerly expectations and empathetic qualities to suggest the primacy and power of fiction over reality, which does not have the right 'to arrogate to itself the primary ontological position', as Alistair Cormack (2013: 76) has observed. The motive for McCarthy's protagonist pulling the rug from under the reader's feet is different, however. Whereas in McEwan subjectively invented narrative will win out over 'the real', in McCarthy the reversal dictates that the protagonist wants the real to triumph over fiction. This rehabilitation of the boundary between fact and fiction, and the hunger for at least the possibility of 'the real', becomes clear from the revalidation episode in Chapter 2, for instance:

> To cut and lay new circuits, what they do is make you visualise things. Simple things, like lifting a carrot to your mouth. For the first week or so they don't give you a carrot, or even try to move your hand at all: they just ask you to visualise taking a carrot in your right hand, wrapping your fingers around it and then levering your whole forearm upwards from the elbow until the carrot reaches your mouth. [...] Understanding this, and picturing yourself lifting the carrot to your mouth, again and again and again, cuts circuits through your brain that will eventually allow you to perform the act itself. That's the idea.
> But the act itself, when you actually come to try it, turns out to be more complicated than you thought. [...] you take a carrot – they bring you a fucking carrot, gnarled, dirty and irregular in ways your imaginary carrot never was, and they stick it in your hands – and you know, you just know as soon as you see the bastard thing that it's not going to work. (*R*, 19–20)

This passage forms one of many allegories through which we can read McCarthy's partial rejection of postmodernism. The passage is a correction of, for instance, Jean Baudrillard's idea of the simulacrum, whereby the laws, models and discourses shape the material world – 'the real' – around us: utopian idealism triumphs over realism. McCarthy's passage subverts this by suggesting that, however much you try to rehearse a scene in the imagination, reality will always be radically different, and arrogates to itself a primary ontological position. This is the narrator's *manqué* throughout the novel: no matter how much he rehearses an imagined reality or memory, the divide between the real and the imagined is irrecoverable. Whereas the postmodernists reveled in the feeling of inauthenticity, the tone of McCarthy's novel is one of suppressed despair. Therefore *Remainder* smacks of David Shields's *Reality Hunger: A Manifesto* (2010), in which the author sets out to 'write the *ars poetica* for a burgeoning group of interrelated (but unconnected) artists in a multitude of forms and media [...] who are breaking larger and larger chunks of "reality" into their work' (Shields, 2010: 3).[4] In McCarthy, 'the real' is back in a realistic naming strategy (Greg; Catherine; Marc Daubeney; Nazrul Ram Vyas; Matthew Younger), by setting the story in recognizable locales (Soho's Old Compton Street; Brixton's Coldharbour Lane and Ritzy Cinema), and in a reference to the Blueprint Café, which, contrary to a joke about simulacrum, refers to the actual café in London's Shad Thames (*R*, 80). But even though there is the sense that the divide between the real and the imagined is recovered, the problem remains that it is impossible to actually attain that reality; the challenges that postmodernism puts to our understanding of the real have left us with hunger for the real without any chance of achieving it.

Plato and Proust, Modernism and Memory: The Semiotics of Contextual Association

The depiction of PTSD and the resulting alienation and solipsism of the protagonist should alert us to the idea that we should not look for *Remainder*'s specific move beyond postmodernism, but to a return to Modernism. Or, rather, a move beyond postmodernism through a revaluation of Modernist obsessions such as memory, temporality, the subjectivity of an alienated and isolated experiential self, and Surrealism. Just as McCarthy prefers Plato's simulacrum over Baudrillard's version, it is instructive to investigate in more detail how beneath McCarthy's amnesiac there lies a deep engagement with, but also a correction of Proust – the Modernist master of memory – and his neo-Platonist conception of individual memory, as well as of the intellectual and cultural context that shaped Modernism's obsession with memory in more general terms.

The episode with the homeless man is instructive for McCarthy's thinking about memory. The episode ends with a key phrase: the narrator does not engage with the man because 'I didn't want to, didn't have a thing to learn from him' (*R*, 56). Indeed, during the re-enactment of the narrator's potential memories of himself, he notes: "'No,' I said. "We can't expect everything to work perfectly straightaway. It's a learning process'" (*R*, 146). This emphasis on learning-as-remembering points to the Platonic idea that memory is not the acquisition of new knowledge, but of re-remembered knowledge already present in us, proving that our souls are immortal. For Plato, learning-as-remembering is a reconstitution of the Ideal self, and the homeless man is unable to help the narrator remember who he is.

While there are overt references to Plato and his philosophy throughout *Remainder* – 'Plato Road' (*R*, 57), for example – McCarthy's Plato comes to us through Proust, whose conception of memory was neo-Platonist. As Robert Champigny (1962: 124) notes: '[Proust] does not write in order to invent; he writes in order to discover and recover: reflective possession, not constructive action, is the ultimate purpose'. In *Remainder*, this Platonic approach is also the dominant way of thinking about art. The protagonist remembers being taught making a sculpture in art class, and the teacher states: "'Your task isn't to create the sculpture," he said; "it's to strip all the other stuff away, to get rid of it. The surplus matter." (*R*, 87). Again, art is presented as discovery through taking away, taking out, by finding the Ideal beauty beneath the mess of quotidian concrete reality. In an early work, *Proust and Signs*, Deleuze (1972: 4) points out that Proust's conception of memory is Platonic and explores the idea that memory-as-learning turns the subject into an 'apprentice' who needs to acquire forgotten knowledge through the interpretation of signs: 'There is no apprentice who is not "the Egyptologist" of something'. This is the 'search' in the title of Proust's project:

> One might invoke Proust's Platonism: to learn is still to remember. But however important its role, memory intervenes only as the means of an apprenticeship which transcends recollection both by its goals and by its principles. The Search is oriented to the future, not to the past. (Deleuze, 1972: 4)

This future-orientedness of the decoding process is a condition that is at the heart of the behaviour of the nameless protagonist, albeit with a subtle difference: whereas Proust aims to make sense of the archived past with a future perspective in mind, in McCarthy there is no past archive to decode. The attempt to reconstitute the self through signifiers and sensory input – the Parisian flat on the fifth, sixth or seventh floor (R, 65); the floor with a repetitive pattern (R, 146); the concierge (R, 67); the motor bike enthusiast (R, 67); a nondescript middle-age couple (R, 67); the black cats on red roofs (R, 65); frying/cooked liver (R, 64, 65); piano music (R, 65), etc. – also fails because the hermeneutic process which McCarthy calls encryption (a semiotic tradition drawn from Bram Stoker, Joyce, Cocteau, Pynchon and Burroughs) experiences blockage.

In order to understand the reason behind, and implications of, the interpretative blockage in *Remainder*, it is useful to compare the key moment in McCarthy's novel – the bathroom episode – with Proust's famous madeleine episode. Both passages relate so-called involuntary memories, which Samuel Beckett conceptualizes eloquently:

> But if, *by accident* [...] the central impression of a past sensation recurs as an immediate stimulus which can be distinctively identified by the subject with the model of duplication (*whose integral purity has been retained because it has been forgotten*), then the total past sensation, nor its echo nor its copy, but the sensation itself, annihilating every spatial and temporal restriction, comes in a rush to engulf the subject in all its beauty of its infallible proportion. (Beckett, 1965: 72)

Involuntary memory chimes in with Platonic conceptions of memory, as it proposes we are remembering something that is already present in us, yet forgotten: our Ideal self, the deepest source and essence of our being. When Marcel dips a madeleine cake in a cup of tea in *À la recherche du temps perdu*, memories of his childhood in Combray come flooding back.[5] This moment is iconic, but the significance, meaning and truthfulness have been disputed since the novel was first published. The temporality of the passage is incredibly complex (the past and present tense are competing and mingling), the artificiality is foregrounded in the image of the theatre and the Japanese game with paper stresses that this episode is first and foremost a *written* exercise in memory retrieval. In Proust, we have two moments: the moment of actual rediscovery and the moment of revelation of the meaning. The madeleine episode is highly ambiguous because both the rediscovery of the memory itself as well as the elucidation of its meaning are difficult – a struggle taking two and a half pages. Deleuze (1972: 12) notes that 'Proust cites the madeleine episode as a case of failure [... yet] the madeleine looked like a real success from a certain viewpoint: the interpreter had found its meaning, not without difficulty, in the unconscious memory of Combray'. The failure of the madeleine episode forms a correction of the original Platonic conception of experience, which argues that abstract, Ideal concepts exist independently, separately from concrete human experience. This is why Proust and McCarthy are interested in semiology, and it brings to mind Roland Barthes's 'Myth Today', which argues that the abstract signified cannot exist without the concrete signified:

> For what we grasp is not at all one term after another but the correlation which unites them: there are, therefore, the signifier, the signified, and the sign, which is the associative total of the first two terms. Take a bunch of roses: I use it to signify my passion. Do we have here, then, only a signifier and a signified, the roses and my passion? Not even that: to put it accurately, there are only 'passionified' roses. (Barthes, 2000: 97–8)

Semiology thus allows for a correction of Plato's world view, arguing that the abstract and the concrete cannot exist independently from one another.

This is where the 'function' of art comes in, namely, to create an object or experience that unites the abstract Ideal with the concrete, everyday. Deleuze notes:

> At the end of the Search, the interpreter understands what had escaped him in the case of the madeleine: [...] that the material meaning is nothing without an ideal essence which it incarnates. The mistake is to suppose that the hieroglyphs represent 'only material objects'. [...] Now the world of art is the ultimate world of signs, and these signs, as though *dematerialized*, find their meaning in an ideal essence. Henceforth, the world revealed by art reacts on all others,

and notably on the sensuous signs; it integrates them, colors them with an esthetic meaning and imbues what was still opaque about them. Then we understand that the sensuous signs *already* referred to an ideal essence which was incarnated in their material meaning. But without art we should not have understood this, nor transcended the law of interpretation which corresponded to the analysis of the madeleine. This is why all the signs converge upon art; all apprenticeships, by the most diverse paths, are already unconscious apprenticeships to art itself. At the deepest level, the essential is in the signs of art. (Deleuze, 1972: 13)

In the acceptance of the world as composed of signs referring to an ideal essence, and through the translation and analysis of these signs into literature, the artist is able to fathom the depths of his or her being. It is, as Beckett also argues in the epigraph to this chapter, in the imaginary, written space of literature that the meaning of memory is discovered and elucidated, and connected to Ideal essence.

McCarthy's thinking about memory is related to Proust's neo-Platonism, yet strikingly different. In *Remainder*, the only memory event takes place when the narrator visits a bathroom at a party, and he experiences a sensory flashback that gives him – possibly – a glimpse of his childhood. This memory event is worth quoting at length:

It happened like this. I was standing in the bathroom with the door locked behind me. [...] I was standing by the sink looking at this crack in the plaster when I had a sudden sense of déjà vu.

The sense of déjà vu was very strong. I'd been in a space like this before, a place just like this, looking at the crack, a crack that had jutted and meandered in the same way as the one beside the mirror. There'd been that same crack, and a bathtub also, and a window directly above the taps like there was in this room – only the window had been slightly bigger and the taps older, different. Out of the window there was a roof with cats on them. Red roof, black cats. It had been high up, much higher than I was now. [...] There'd been liver cooking on the floor below – the smell, the spit and sizzle – and then two floors below that there'd been piano music. [...] I remembered it all, but I couldn't remember *where* I'd been in this place, this flat, this bathroom. Or when. [...] I couldn't place this memory at all.

> And yet it was growing, minute by minute as I stood there in the
> bathroom, this remembered building, spreading outwards from the
> crack. (*R*, 60–1)

After his jocular use of carrots as homage to the madeleine in Proust's
work, this passage presents us with an example of involuntary memory achieved through a visual trigger and subsequent metonymic expansion involving all senses. The episode is, in Bergsonian terms, a
mémoire pure, a 'pure memory' because it is involuntary rather than
what Bergson and Proust considered a second order of memory, the
mémoire-habitude, habitual memory, which the protagonist clings on
to during his repetitious re-enactments. Yet, what we are presented
with here is the opposite of a flashbulb memory, as in the case of
the madeleine, in which everything is perceived as crystal clear and
embodied, but this retrieval occurs through the reactivation of an
engrammatically inscribed memory. Susanna Nalbatian (2003: 60)
defines the engram as 'the physical change or neuronal change in the
brain both ingrained, originally, and later triggered by sensory signals
– visual, auditory, gustatory, olfactory and tactile'. *Remainder*'s memory event is not bounded, but associative, unclear and unfinished, and
its status and truthfulness are profoundly uncertain. This suggests
that the slow unfolding of the memory through the act of contemplation is not possible: the enactment of this fragment with the help of
money – the Orwellian fantasy we started with – fails not only due
to a lack of artistic and creative perspective, but because the episode
itself is a fiction – a phantom memory.

The qualification of this experience as 'déjà vu' is telling in this respect as another point to make is that the key to understanding the
memory lies in the verbal, not visual or other sensory stimulus, exploration of the memory, which the protagonist fails to achieve. Douwe
Draaisma writes about déjà vu, exploring its connection with two related phenomena, depersonalization (when everything and everyone
including ourselves are experienced as strange, machinic or dream-
like) and 'word alienation' (the experience of familiar words becoming alien). Draaisma writes:

the apparently so different phenomena of déjà vu, depersonalisation and word alienation are expressions of the same process. The starting point of the hypothesis is that the familiar feeling of a perception is due to associations between that perception and earlier experiences. These associations help date experiences in the past: the vaguer and weaker the associations, the greater the apparent time interval between the current and remembered experience. Because of a temporary decrease in psychic energy or reduced concentration, the associations that under normal circumstances feel familiar to us can be lacking or weakened. According to that hypothesis, word alienation is due to a lack of associative links between a word and semantic memory, as a result of which the word is experienced as no more than a sound. Depersonalisation is said to be the consequence of the complete absence of associations, so that not only the words but *all* aspects of the situation lose their familiarity. A déjà vu, finally, is said to arise when the associations are not completely absent, but are weak and small in number. The consciousness then has the illusion that the current experience is a memory of an event from a distant past. (Draaisma, 2004: 157–8)

These three phenomena exist on a sliding scale of disassociation, in which déjà vu sits in between depersonalisation, the strongest form, and word alienation, the weakest. The protagonist experiences all three of these phenomena, but the categorisation of the episode as déjà vu suggests that the memory is a very weak one. *Remainder* thus resonates with Nolan's *Memento* in which the wrong interpretation of scraps of information leads to the repetitious constructions of theories about a murder. McCarthy's novel does something different: although the memory traces are strong, they do not allow for a (former) reality to be reconstituted as this reverses of the Platonic process: the re-enactment is a constructive approach rather than a process of discovery, and can therefore never work; whereas Proust writes his way towards essence, the narrator's attempted literalisation of the scraps of memory by staging them in reality, in the hope of somehow merging them, aims to recreate the Ideal essence of the self in concrete reality.

When the attempt to reconstitute the essence of his self fails, the protagonist turns obsessively to establishing other events because the sensation it generates is pleasurable and addictive. Again we have to turn to Proust to understand McCarthy's procedure. Beckett notes:

> The identification of immediate with past experience, the recurrence of past action or reaction in the present, amounts to a participation between ideal and the real, imagination and direct apprehension, symbol and substance. Such participation frees the essential reality that is denied to the contemplative as to the active life. [...] Reality, whether approached imaginatively or empirically, remains a surface, hermetic. Imagination, applied – a priori – to what is absent, is exercised in vacuo and cannot tolerate the limits of the real. Nor is any direct and purely experimental contact possible between subject and object, because they are automatically separated by the subject's consciousness of perception, and the object loses its purity and becomes a mere intellectual pretext or motive. But, thanks to this reduplication, the experience is at once imaginative and empirical, at once an evocation and a direct perception, real without being merely actual, ideal without being merely abstract, the ideal real, the essential, the extratemporal. (Beckett, 1965: 74–5)

This process suggests the rationale behind the proliferation of re-enactments, which are reduplicating events to turn something factual into something actual, lived, and substantial, allowing the protagonist to get a glimpse of the essence of other events and objects. The problem is that the repetitious nature of the re-enactments, rather than allowing for a transfiguration of imagination into real experience (and vice versa), destroys the transformative process and collapses back into regressive habit. Proust distinguished between 'the profound self', triggered by first order memory, and 'the quotidian self', produced by habitual memory. This allows us to read *Remainder* as an indictment of a late Modern condition in which even the glimpse of the profound, non-habitual self reveals nothing but an empty shell, yet it is the thrill of the glimpse itself which has become our main drive. McCarthy's novel thus strips down postmodernism's celebratory powers, and returns us to an experimental, late Modernist critical mode which argues that knowledge about oneself and the world is increasingly hard to interpret.

Notes

1 Postmodernism's massive gravestone was provided by Martin Amis's final installment of his London triptych, *The Information* (1995), a formalistic rehearsal of postmodern tropes and ideas without much meaningful or new to say.

2 Bradford (2007: 67) continues: 'Their novels incorporate many of the mantras that their readers [...] would recognize as guarantees to intellectual hauteur but while the theorists write in a manner that variously bores and alienates the ordinary reader the novelists invite them in. It may or may not be the case that we are, as participants in the Postmodern Condition, experiencing an unprecedented intellectual and cultural apocalypse, an unbidden and all-pervasive state of nihilism, but what is evident is that fiction writers have seized upon this as a saleable commodity. Their style is alluring, by varying degrees elegant, friendly and transparent, and once the reader becomes attuned to this they are offered commodified thrills: multinarratives with no cohering pattern, horrible descents into the grotesque, arbitrary switches between the plausible and unimaginable. The New Postmodernists are in truth engaged in a programme that undermines the jargon-ridden pomposity of their academic counterparts'.

3 As Blincoe and Thorne (2000: xvi) put it: 'We are moralists, so all texts feature a recognisable ethical reality'.

4 This movement is characterized by a 'deliberate unartiness: "raw" material, seemingly unprocessed, unfiltered, uncensored, and unprofessional. [...] Randomness, openness to accident an serendipity, spontaneity; artistic risk, emotional urgency and intensity, reader/viewer participation; an overtly literal tone, as if a reported were viewing a strange culture; plasticity of form, pointillism; criticism as autobiography; self-reflexivity, self-ethnography, anthropological autobiography; a blurring (to the point of invisibility) of any distinction between fiction and nonfiction: the lure and blur of the real' (Shields, 2010: 5).

5 'And as soon as I had recognized the taste of the piece of madeleine dipped in lime-blossom tea that my aunt used to give me [...] immediately the old grey house on the street, where her bedroom was, came like a stage-set to attach itself to the little wing opening on to the garden [...] and with the house the town, from morning to night and in all weathers, the Square, where they sent me before lunch, the streets where I used to do errands, the paths we took if the weather was fine. And as in that game in which the Japanese amuse themselves by filling a porcelain bowl with

water and steeping in it little pieces of paper until then indistinct, which, the moment they are immersed in it, stretch and shape themselves, colour and differentiate, become flowers, houses, human figures, firm and recognizable, now all the flowers in our garden [...] and the good people of the village and their little dwellings, and the church and all of Combray and all its surroundings, all of this which is assuming form and substance, emerged, town and gardens alike, from my cup of tea' (Proust, 2003: 50).

Works Cited

Alizart, Mark (2008) 'Interview with Tom McCarthy', *The Believer*, URL (consulted 12 October 2012): http://www.believermag.com/issues/200806/?read=interview_mccarthy

Ballard, J. G. (1995), 'Introduction', in *Crash*. London: HarperPerennial.

Barthes, Roland (2000) 'Myth Today', in Susan Sontag (ed.) *A Roland Barthes Reader*, pp. 93–149. London: Vintage.

Beckett, Samuel (1965) *Proust*. London: John Calder.

Blincoe, Nicholas and Matt Thorne (2000) 'Introduction: The Pledge', in *All Hail the New Puritans*, ed. Nicholas Blincoe and Matt Thorne. London: Fourth Estate.

Bradford, Richard (2007) *The Novel Now: Contemporary British Fiction*. Oxford: Blackwell.

Champigny, Robert (1962) 'Proust, Bergson and Other Philosophers', in René Girard (ed.) *Proust: A Collection of Critical Essays*, pp. 122–31. Engelwood Cliffs, NJ: Prentice-Hall.

Cormack, Alistair (2013) 'Postmodernism and the Ethics of Fiction in *Atonement*', in Sebastian Groes (ed.) *Ian McEwan: Contemporary Critical Perspectives*, pp. 70–82. London: Bloomsbury Academic.

Currie, Mark (1998) *Postmodern Narrative Theory*. Basingstoke: Palgrave.

Deleuze, Gilles (1972) *Proust and Signs*, trans. Richard Howard. New York: George Braziller.

Deleuze, Gilles and Felix Guattari (2004) *A Thousand Plateaus: Capitalism and Schizophrenia*, trans. Brian Massumi. London: Continuum.

Derrida, Jacques (1996) *Archive Fever: A Freudian Impression*, trans. Eric Prenowitz. Chicago, IL: University of Chicago Press.

Draaisma, Douwe (2004) *Why Life Speeds Up as You get Older: How Memory Shapes Our Past*. Cambridge: Cambridge University Press.

Gray, Margaret E. (1992) *Postmodern Proust*. Philadelphia: University of Pennsylvania Press.

Jameson, Fredric (1985) 'Postmodernism and Consumer Society', in Hal Foster (ed.), *Postmodern Culture*, pp. 111–25. London: Pluto.

Jameson, Fredric (1992) *Postmodernism, or The Cultural Logic of Late Capitalism*. London: Verso.

Nalbatian, Suzanne (2003) *Memory in Literature: From Rousseau to Neuroscience*. Basingstoke: PalgraveMacmillan.

Orwell, George (1968) 'New Words', *The Collected Essays, Journalism and Letters of George Orwell*, ed. Ian Angus and Sonia Orwell, vol. 2 of 4, pp. 3–11. New York: Harcourt, Brace and World.

Pepperell, Robert (1995) *The Post-Human Condition*. Oxford: Intellect.

Proust, Marcel (2003) *The Way by Swann's*, trans. Lydia Davis. London: Penguin.

Shields, David (2010) *Reality Hunger: A Manifesto*. London: Hamish Hamilton.

Smith, Zadie (2008) 'Two Paths for the Novel', *New York Review of Books* 55(18): 89–95.

Sturken, Marita (1997) *Tangled Memories: The Vietnam War, the AIDS epidemic, and the Politics of Remembering*. Berkeley: University of California Press.

8

Post-Humanism and the Distributed Consciousness in Tom McCarthy's *Remainder*

Nick Lavery

Tom McCarthy has said that his work as a whole can be understood as 'a kind of grand anti-humanist manifesto' (Rourke, 2010). His novels, *Remainder* in particular, locate themselves at a point at which the ongoing breakdown of ideas and concepts inherited from the humanist tradition reaches what N. Katherine Hayles (1990: 282) calls its final stage, the 'denaturing of the human'. Reading Doris Lessing's *The Golden Notebook* (1962), which embodies this final stage through the psychological breakdown of its protagonist alongside a fragmentation of the text, Hayles summarizes what is at stake:

> The question that comes sharply into focus as breakdown approaches is whether individual consciousness, as it has been traditionally constituted in the Western tradition, can provide the unified context necessary to bring these splintering fragments together. Or more accurately, since what we are reading is a fictional representation of that consciousness, whether the conventions of realistic narratives can continue to constitute individual consciousness as a putative source for 'genuine art', or whether the disintegration of the subject will pre-

cipitate a crisis in representation which makes a traditional novel impossible to write. (Hayles, 1990: 255–6)

Writing on technology and the novel, McCarthy argues against the 'liberal-humanist' model of literary work as a 'form of self-expression, a meticulous sculpting of the thoughts and feelings of an isolated individual', claiming that the more novels he writes, the more convinced he becomes that 'what we encounter in a novel is not selves, but networks' (McCarthy, 2010). As I will argue in this chapter, the renegotiation of subjectivity in relation to contemporary advances in technology and neuroscience does not imply a crisis of representation for McCarthy, who defines the novel as a form inherently split between what it can and cannot articulate. Individual consciousness, as it has traditionally been constituted and embodied in the conventions of literary narrative, has always been a product of material and technological processes flowing beyond the boundaries of the individual. In this chapter, I argue that McCarthy's work embodies the post-human in its understanding of consciousness, and its representation in the novel, as determined by a complexity that it cannot express.

Remainder begins with an admission of inarticulacy by the narrator which hints, in its ambiguity, at several possible readings: 'About the accident itself I can say very little. Almost nothing. It involved something falling from the sky. Technology. Parts, bits. That's it really: all I can divulge. Not much, I know' (*R*, 5). Sebastian Groes (2016: 20) reads 'bits' as referring to both 'material parts of technology' *and* 'the basic units of information in computing'. The novel can be read in terms of both a Cartesian opposition between individual consciousness and matter *and* between a distinctly contemporary consciousness and the technological networks within which it is situated.

There is a similar ambiguity at work in the idea of post-humanism itself. For Suzanne Bow and Colin Wright (2001: 300), there is a distinction to be made between celebratory post-humanism, or 'extropianism' – the 'Promethean dream of a technologically assisted dematerialization of the human' – and critical post-humanism, which 'interrogates the imbrication of the embodied human with other entities – potentially animate, inanimate, informatics – and the extent to which this imbrication militates in favour of a perhaps more radical de-centering of the human' (Bow and Wright, 2001: 302). McCarthy takes 'post-humanism' to mean the former when he dismisses it as a 'dreadful fantasy': 'We are eminently human, and this is nothing to be proud of. To be human is to be that experience of repetition and non-self-coincidence that constitutes us. [...] Fantasies about the future – who cares?' (Critchley, 2010: 111). At the same time, he rejects any straightforward correspondence between the operation of the brain and consciousness, arguing against the idea that 'you can transfer neuroscience to the cultural arena': 'We don't think in our brains, we think in language and culture' (Critchley, 2010: 117). *Remainder*'s opening continues with the narrator justifying his inarticulacy in terms of brain damage and trauma. He claims to retain only 'vague images, half impressions' of the accident, explaining that minds 'are versatile and wily things. Real chancers' (*R*, 5). The next paragraph complicates this, by mentioning the 'terms of the Settlement' that legally prohibit him 'from discussing, in any public or recordable format (I know this bit by heart), the nature and/or details of the incident, on pain of forfeiting all financial reparations' (*R*, 13). The opening lines acquire a new layer of meaning, as does the reference to a mind whose interjections go against his contractual obligations to silence.

McCarthy has since repeated and developed this technique in *Satin Island*. The narrator, U, mentions that what he is writing is determined partly by confidentiality agreements relating to the Koob-Sassen project he has been working on, while also claiming that 'the Project', as is it subsequently referred to, is in some sense resistant to articulation, 'a project formed of many other projects, linked to many other projects' whose complexity renders it 'well-nigh impossible to say where it began and ended, to discern its "content", bulk or outline' (*SI*, 12–13). Describing his boss's brief on the project, he mentions that he is being vague 'in part because I'm obliged to be vague; but in part because he was quite vague as well' (*SI*, 48). Like the 'Project', the 'Settlement' stands in for a complexity that cannot be directly acknowledged:

> The Settlement. That word: *Settlement. Set-l-ment.* As I lay abject, su-
> pine, tractioned and trussed up, all sorts of tubes and wires pumping
> one thing into my body and sucking another out, electronic metro-
> nomes and bellows making this speed up and that slow down, their
> beeping and rasping playing me, running through my useless flesh
> and organs like sea water through a sponge – during the months I
> spent in hospital, this word planted itself in me and grew. *Settlement.*
> (R, 6)

Note the distinctive structure here, in which the ostensible point being made is delayed by description and digression, necessitating a
hyphen and reiteration. A similar image is also used in *Satin Island*:
U finds the dying Petr 'propped up in a bed with these tubes leading from his chest (one from each side) towards a translucent plastic
receptacle about the size and shape of a car battery' (*SI*, 121). Both
hint at what is omitted in the narrator's description of the accident,
a 'blank: a white slate, a black hole' involving 'Technology. Parts,
bits' (*R*, 5). The Settlement complements this blank. The narrator
describes it as 'held up to me as a future strong enough to counter-
balance my no-past, a moment that would make me better, whole,
complete' (*R*, 19). As Pieter Vermeulen (2015: 25) points out, the
narrator's trauma, 'far from registering as a psychologically significant
event, is merely mobilized as a device that triggers and structures the
plot': in 'indirectly funding the events that make up the novel's plot',
through the eight million pounds that make up the Settlement, it
'provides the novel with the narrative capital it needs to keep going
for some 280 pages'. The accident and the Settlement both contribute to the novel's narrative drive, and both determine the limitations
of what the narration can express. Both, moreover, are inadequate as
concepts through which to express the complex relation between the
body of the narrator and technology.

Remainder has been characterized, by Patricia Waugh and Jennifer
Hodgson (2012: 15), as making use of a literary mode embodying
'disconnection in its blank or hyper-reflexive, or comically disjunc-
tive form', a mode which Waugh (2011: 78) elsewhere describes as 'a
kind of thought-experiment, allowing the reader to enter a character's
consciousness conceived in entirely Cartesian terms, [...] an alter-

native, disturbed and purely introspective consciousness, one that moves through a dead, hypertrophied or glassy world'. This mode reflects both a 'hyper-reflexive world of "cool" where money is able to hire an army of networked agents, project managers and special-effects workers specialized in the materialisation of corporate "vision"' and 'the dangerous splitting of mind, body and world that lurks in the Platonic and the Cartesian' (Waugh and Hodgson, 2012: 16). The gap between articulation and experience, or between consciousness and the body, can be understood as fundamentally Cartesian. The way in which this gap is formulated in *Remainder*, however, emphasizes both the role of particular cultural processes in defining what can be articulated, as well as a contemporary interpenetration of the body and technology. For Kiene Brillenburg-Wurth (2011: 119), the post-human 'both fulfils scientific visions of the endless extensions of a liberal or autonomous humanist self subjecting the world to its free will *and,* as a critical concept, presents a means to dismantle that liberal self by expressing the very fluidity, multiplicity, and difference on which it is based'. *Remainder,* accordingly, both restates and questions Cartesian dualism.

This continues when the narrator begins to describe his feeling of inauthenticity, hinting at the impetus for his re-enactments as he does so. The first hint is in a reference to a 'photographically clear memory' (*R,* 17) at the end of the first chapter. The claim is inconspicuous for the moment, but sets up what follows. The next chapter begins by describing the narrator's recovery through the 'rerouting' of his brain. The narrator's claim that rerouting 'is exactly what it sounds like: finding a new route through the brain for commands to run along' (*R,* 19) echoes the ambiguity of the opening. He describes it as 'sort of like a government compulsorily purchasing land from farmers to run train tracks over after the terrain the old tracks ran through has been flooded or landslid away' (*R,* 19). Subsequent elaboration however reveals the model of the mind at work as distinctly contemporary. In order to 'cut and lay new circuits' in the brain, the protagonist is made to 'visualize' things. The example given is of lifting a carrot (*R,* 19). Actually lifting a carrot is taken to be a matter of visualizing doing so, and breaking down the action into a series of motions which must be understood and pictured (R, 19–20). As the narrator points out, the actual experience does not correspond to this model. The protagonist's training leads him to think of his hand, fingers and brain as 'active agents, and the carrot as a no-thing', but the physical carrot is 'more active' than him (R, 20). The feeling of the carrot as physical object is 'enough to start short-circuiting the operation' (R, 20), in an ironic reference to the technological aspects of the model.

The narrator's experience here has been read by Waugh (2013: 26) in terms of 'a disconnection of mind from body so Cartesian that every movement has to be relearned intentionally'. The narrator's chosen metaphor of new train tracks emphasizes this aspect. References to circuits, short-circuits, and visualization tie the sequence to the model of the mind Karen Barad summarizes as 'representationalism'. For Barad (2008: 125), 'the asymmetrical faith in our access to representations over things is a contingent fact of history and not a logical necessity; that is, it is simply a Cartesian habit of mind'. The influence of this habit on cognitive science's adoption of a computational model of the mind has been traced by Hayles. She introduces *How We Became Posthuman* (1999) with an account of how Alan Turing's 1950 paper 'Computing Machinery and Intelligence' – in which he set out the imitation game, or Turing test – defines intelligence in terms of 'the formal manipulation of symbols rather than enaction in the human life-world' (Hayles, 1999: xi) while also establishing a 'distributed cognitive system in which represented bodies are joined with enacted bodies through mutating and flexible machine interfaces' (Hayles, 1999: xiv). The sequence from *Remainder* hints at a form of representationalism grounded in technology. Soon after, the narrator comes to understand his situation in terms of a fundamental opposition between mind and matter, while latching on to a particular form of technology which will define his model of consciousness.

At first, the narrator acknowledges that the form of his treatment does not correspond to actual embodied experience: 'in the normal run of things you never *learn* to walk like you learn swimming, French or tennis. You just do it without thinking how you do it: you stumble into it, literally' (R, 21). He soon finds something which does function in this way, however: cinema. Robert De Niro's character in *Mean*

Streets has no such gap separating him from his actions: 'He doesn't have to think about them, or understand them first. He doesn't have to think about them because he and they are one' (*R*, 23). He and they are one because 'thinking', according to the model of the mind at work in the narrator's recovery, corresponds closely to film. Discussing this with a friend, the narrator is persuaded that the gap between his consciousness and his actions is universal, that he is 'just more usual than everyone else' (*R*, 24). The rest of the novel implies however that he is trying to establish a relation between himself and his environment modelled on film, beginning with his use of a filmic register to describe fantasies which he would 'play, refine, edit and play again' (*R*, 25) in his mind on the next page. The narrator comes up with the idea for his first re-enactment when experiencing a 'sudden sense of déjà vu' (*R*, 60), looking at a crack in plaster on the wall of a bathroom at a party. He sees the building he will recreate 'crystal-clear, as clear as in a vision', while conceding that he cannot place the memory (*R*, 61), later describing it as 'various things all rolled together: memories, imaginings, films. I don't know. But that bit's not important. What's important is that I remembered, and it was crystal-clear' (*R*, 76). His evasions and claims to uncertainty here echo the novel's opening description of his accident. By recreating this vision, he hopes to bridge the gap between his consciousness and experience by replicating a mental visualization in reality. Following on from the model of thought taught to him in therapy, he understands such visualizations to be a universal feature of consciousness, and his own inability to think in this way as a result of irreparable brain damage (*R*, 19). The novel questions the universality of this model by drawing out the technological aspects of representationalism through reference to cameras. Later on, the re-enactments' relation to cinema is indirectly signalled by the narrator's repeated insistence on having no cameras, or other forms of recording, used (*R*, 120, 147, 148, 182, 229), along with the suggestion that the narrator wants to take the place of the absent camera. As McCarthy puts it, he wants 'to "be" in some kind of movie *without there being a movie*' (Hart et al., 2013: 668). He 'scan[s]' the imagined building in his mind, 'moving from left to right and back again' (*R*, 66); hires a set designer on the principle that 'you only have to make the bit the camera sees look real' (R, 114); runs through scenarios in his imagination in which bad ones 'cut in' to good ones (R, 126); applies for a filming licence for one re-enactment (R, 182); runs through another at half speed 'like in an action replay on TV' (R, 197); imagines a brain editing visual impressions (R, 197); and has a re-enactment set up like a film but for him instead of an audience or cameras (R, 229). The narrator's relation to the outside world is not universal. Though he frames it in terms of a broad Cartesian distinction between mind and matter, it is determined by an explicitly representationalist model of the mind which finds its actual embodiment in the relationship between the camera and the film set.

Building on her reading of Turing, Hayles summarizes several defining features of post-humanism:

> The post human view privileges informational pattern over material instantiation, so that embodiment in a biological substrate is seen as an accident of history rather than an inevitability of life. Second, the post human view considers consciousness, regarded as the seat of human identity in the Western tradition long before Descartes thought he was a mind thinking, as an epiphenomenon, as an evolutionary upstart trying to claim that it is the whole show when in actuality it is only a minor sideshow. Third, the post human view thinks of the body as the original prosthesis we all learn to manipulate, so that extending or replacing the body with other prostheses becomes a continuation of a process that began before we were born. Fourth, and most important, by these and other means, the post human view configures human being so that it can be seamlessly articulated with intelligent machines. (Hayles, 1990: 3)

Remainder's implied model of thought can be understood in terms of these features. This model is articulated most clearly in the narrator's depiction of Naz, to whom he delegates the increasing volume of information accompanying his re-enactments.

The term 'whirring' is first used to compare Naz's mind to an actual computer, its repetition throughout the rest of the novel hinting at something withheld by the narration. The term is repeated twice in the paragraph in which it is first used: 'Naz's palmtop organizer [...]

was lying face up on the table, but Naz wasn't using it. Instead, he was logging his requirements in his mind, translating them into ma-noeuvres to be executed. I could tell: something was whirring behind his eyes. [...] The thing behind Naz's eyes whirred for a while.' (*R*, 82) Whirring, or variants 'whirred' and 'whir', are used in descrip-tions of Naz throughout (*R*, 84, 127, 149, 215, 217 (twice), 218, 236, 250, 274). The final reference describes the 'thing behind his eyes' as having stopped, placed within a broader metaphor of Naz's break-down as 'like a computer crashing – the way the screen, rather than explode or send its figures dancing higgledy piggledy around, sim-ply freezes' (*R*, 274). The narrator also describes this breakdown in terms of data or information: 'figures, hours, appointments, places, all abandoning their places, all abandoning their posts and scrambling for the exits, sweating their way out of him, rats scurrying from a sink-ing ship' (*R*, 281). As with the metaphor of the crashing computer, this forms a more developed instance of a recurring term used to de-scribe Naz. 'Processing' is first used as a synonym for 'whirring' in the same context: 'his eyes went vacant while the thing behind them whirred, processed' (*R*, 84). 'Processing' is repeated to a similar ex-tent as 'whirring', applied not only to Naz but to other characters and to the narrator himself (*R*, 84 (twice), 91, 92, 96 (twice), 188, 217). As with the references to a 'photographically clear memory', the use of the term 'processing' picks upon a seemingly innocuous way of de-scribing consciousness and subtly hints at the technological under-pinnings of the Cartesian dualism it is used to articulate. McCarthy emphasizes the different registers at work through a contrast between such computational terms and more human ones: 'it struck me as I waited that all great enterprises are about logistics. Not genius or in-spiration or flights of imagination, skill or cunning, but logistics' (*R*, 183). He also emphasizes ways in which these terms don't fit the pro-tagonist's thought processes. The narrator, planning the re-enactment of a bank robbery (later transferred to a real bank), 'calculate[es]' that if one of the participants 'slightly tripped on purpose, this would pre-vent him tripping by mistake' (*R*, 238), an assumption later proving to be a fatal error. While 'calculated' could be read as a synonym for 'thought' or 'conjectured' here, the error's repercussions later on reveal the arbitrary nature of the narrator's assumption, and its distinction from 'calculation' as strictly defined.

Looking at references to 'thinking' in itself, we find them occupying the same space as 'whirring' and 'processing': brief pauses during which one or another character receives and considers some kind of information. The term is first applied to the protagonist in a sentence placed between dialogue spoken by him and Mark Daubenay, his lawyer: 'I thought about this for a while, then said' (*R*, 40). Thinking produces a pause in dialogue, suggestive of the processing of information. The dynamic is then repeated, with the roles reversed: 'Daubenay thought about this for a moment' (*R*, 41). This continues when the narrator offers to buy a homeless teenager a meal: 'He looked up at me with his mouth still hanging open, thinking. I wasn't a Christian soul-hunter, and he could tell I wasn't police.' (*R*, 53) The moment is distinct within the novel in that the protagonist seems to be attempting to determine the thought processes of another person, perhaps in a hint at the empathy we might expect him to be in the course of developing here, if we follow Zadie Smith's (2009: 85) reading of the sequence. The logic of these assumed thought processes leads to the teenager assenting; we learn shortly afterwards that the entire episode has been made up by the narrator (*R*, 56). Subsequent references to thought follow on from and develop the dynamic used to describe Daubenay, and the use of 'whirring' and 'processing' to describe Naz; in other places, pauses or silences between dialogue occupy the same space (*R*, 65, 79, 84, 169 (twice), 181, 189, 211, 212 (twice), 232, 242).

Another description of Naz develops this pattern: 'Naz's whole body tensed. He was completely static for a while, his musculature suspended while the calculating part of him took all the system's energy. After a while the body part switched back on' (*R*, 250). Naz is split into two: a 'system' incorporating various apparently separate parts, and a machinic assemblage of those parts. This split refers back to the first description of Naz as a kind of prosthesis, a component of the narrator: 'He was like an extra set of limbs, tentacles spreading out in all directions, coordinating projects, issuing instruction, executing commands. My executor' (*R*, 73). The system of which he is a component is described in the neo-corporate terms picked up on by Waugh and Hodgson: Naz solves the narrator's problems with 'communicating' his 'vision' (*R*, 73). The brief description of Naz's 'ancestry' hints at the history of this idea and its relation to computing: Naz comes from a 'long line of scribes, recorders, clerks, logging transactions and events, passing on orders and instructions that made new transactions happen. Facilitators. That made sense: Naz facilitated everything for me' (*R*, 73). The passage hints at the idea of the narrator as not so much an individual as a system made up of transactions. The implicit model of thought as the processing of information established throughout the novel has important consequences, as laid out by Hayles (1999: 160), who writes that '[w]hen system boundaries are defined by information flows and feedback loops rather than epidermal surfaces, the subject becomes a system to be assembled and disassembled rather than an entity whose organic wholeness can be assumed'. Individual consciousness is linked to technology through the implicit definition of thinking in terms of whirring. While the narrator's use of this metaphor confirms his sense of control over his employees – 'thinking' is defined as information-processing, a brief pause before they carry out his wishes – its application to his own thought processes hints at a separate agency guiding his own actions.

Satin Island builds on this linking of thought with the operations of computers and the flow of information through U's reflections on buffering. The first reference to the idea comes near the start of the novel, when a Skype call freezes. The description, like that of Naz's breakdown, blurs the distinction between human and machine: 'I'm lacking, she began to tell me – but just then the audio dropped. Her face froze in mid-sentence too [...] a little circle span in front of her, to denote buffering' (*SI*, 9). The spinning circle is later described as whirring, in a possible reference to the earlier novel:

> I'd spend long hours staring at the little spinning circle on my screen, losing myself in it. Behind it, I pictured hordes of bits and bytes and megabytes, all beavering away to get the requisite data to me, [...] its pure, unfiltered content as it rushed into my system, which, in turn,

whirred into streamlined action as it started to reorganize it into legible form. The thought was almost sublimely reassuring. (*SI*, 68)

It is unclear whether U is referring to his computer or to himself when he mentions his 'system', an ambiguity recalling those at work in *Remainder*. U is more prone to reflection than the earlier novel's protagonist, and develops this thought into an analogy between consciousness and buffering:

> Staring at this bar, losing myself in it just as with the circle, I was granted a small revelation: it dawned on me that what I was *actually* watching was nothing less than the skeleton, laid bare, of time or memory itself. Not our computers' time and memory, but our own. This was its structure. We require experience to stay ahead, if only by a nose, of our *consciousness* of experience. (*SI*, 68–9)

U's faith in these comparisons stems from a lack of self-awareness. His interpretation misses out on the situated, contextualized nature of these revelations. His first experience of buffering is a direct encounter with it, in an airport, surrounded by screens; his elevation of it to a model for consciousness follows on from problems with the bandwidth in his office. The novel signals this from the start, by running through the history of the Turin Shroud. U mentions that the image 'isn't really visible on the bare linen', and only became so in the late nineteenth century on a photographic negative, before being disproven a few decades later by radiocarbon dating (*SI*, 3). There is an irony here in the U's hinting at an awareness of how technology determines meaning while remaining unaware of the contemporary form of this process at work in his use of metaphor in the same passage: 'We see things shroudedly, as through a veil, an over-pixelated screen' (*SI*, 3). U's own veil is the over-pixelated screen.

Reflecting on the prevalence of media technology in contemporary life, U is struck by the 'truly terrifying thought that the Great Report [a vaguely defined report on contemporary experience U works on throughout] had *already been written*. Not by a person, nor even by some nefarious cabal, but simply by a neutral and indifferent binary system that had given rise to itself, moved by itself and would perpetuate itself: some auto-alphaing and auto-omegaing script – that's what it *was*'. (*SI*, 123) The passage develops on McCarthy's reading of Michel de Certeau's *The Practice of Everyday Life* (1980), which 'presents all the various axes and apparatuses of society – its laws and institutions, trading systems and technology – as parts of a giant "scriptural system"' (McCarthy, 2015). Within this system, U intuits that people function as 'no more than actions and commands within its key-chains' (*SI*, 124). He further begins to understand the Koob-Sassen Project as 'evil', worming its way 'into each corner of the citizenry's lives, re-setting ("re-configuring") the systems lying behind and bearing on virtually their every action and experience, and doing this without their even knowing it', picturing 'its very letters (the *K* a body-outline, the *S*s folds of cloak, the hyphen a dagger hidden between these), slinking up staircases in the night while people slept, [...] its very vagueness render[ing] it inherently and unambiguously bad' (*SI*, 124). Consciousness – buffering – is defined in recognizably post-human terms, as an epiphenomenon deriving from the flow of information across human bodies and technology, its form determined by forces beyond the individual. At the same time, however, it is defined as separate from those forces in its inability to articulate them. *Satin Island*'s incongruous image of words creeping up staircases 'like a silent assassin' (*SI*, 124) – following on from *Remainder*'s description of the Settlement embedding itself into the narrator's body and growing – emphasizes a disjunction between articulation and material reality. Our awareness of this disjunction, a revised form of the dualist gap between consciousness and experience, can form the basis of a post-human reading.

Zadie Smith (2009: 83) terms *Remainder*'s narrator 'the Enactor', suggesting that 'protagonist' would be 'a word from another kind of novel'. Another example of this kind of novel, Steven Hall's *The Raw Shark Texts* (2007), is identified by Daniel Lea, who reads both as responding to a wider literary interest in authenticity through their toying with 'the mutual compatibility of biological and self-posited authenticity', and a shared view 'that the integrity of the individual as autonomous, self-determining agent is tied to a pathos of harmonious being-in-the-world' as well as 'the fear that the expression of that agency is problematized by discourses of social and cultural conditioning that shadow each action or ethical choice with the inauthenticity of the precursory echo' (Lea, 2012: 464). A moment early on in *Remainder* shows the narrator attempting this harmonious being-in-the-world through fictional narrative. Smith identifies inconsistencies during the sequence in which the narrator takes a homeless teenager to dinner. The waitress is described first as 'an old woman with big glasses', then as about 'eighteen, nineteen' (*R*, 54). The last description forces the Enactor to admit that he has been making this up: 'The waiter came back over. He was ... She was young, with large dark glasses, an Italian woman. Large breasts. Small.' (*R*, 56). Smith (2009: 84) describes this as a 'nervous breakdown' that signals a shift in the text away from the 'anti-literature hoax' or 'wind-up' of the first fifty pages. The aside that ends the chapter, when the narrator, explaining why he didn't in fact talk to the teenager, mentions that he hates dogs (*R*, 56) is significant in Joanna Gavins's (2013: 90) reading: 'the manner in which the narrator reveals his misreporting can be seen to shape the estranging nature of his unreliability. [...] the narrator suddenly increases the distance between himself and authorial audience through his casual and cold-hearted confession'. The narrator's conspicuous lack of empathy builds throughout the novel, culminating in a plan to kill all of his employees by loading them onto planes and blowing them up, and a moment at which he kills one of them for no apparent reason (*R*, 276). Of the latter, Gavins (2013: 93) notes that not only 'are the authorial audience at this moment made finally and disturbingly aware of the narrator's complete lack of empathy, but their estrangement from him is further fostered by ongoing suggestions within the narrative that his entire account may be a fabrication'. The opening of the chapter – 'The day came, finally. Then again, perhaps it didn't' (*R*, 259) – supports this, as does the close of the previous one, in which the narrator claims never to have been near cordite, belying his previous claims to have smelt it (*R*, 258).

The suggestion that the narrator's account of events may be a fabrication, alongside his pronounced lack of empathy, emphasizes the inadequacy of the way in which he understands the mind to work, and how this affects his perspective on his situation and actions.

The narrator's lack of empathy is signaled throughout by moments of what Vermeulen (2012: 550) calls 'dysphoric, subjectless affect', points at which the novel 'provides the reader with an ethically and affectively charged situation [...] only to leave a blank failure of response where the reader is led to expect an elaboration of this situation' (Vermeulen, 2012: 558). This failure of response is often tied to the way in which the narrator's consciousness, and those of others, are defined by technology. When Naz comes up with the plan to murder all of his employees, the narrator's relation to the plan is mediated by representations seen in his 'mind's eye' (R, 254), 'beautiful' images of dematerialization which run through his mind 'again and again and again' (R, 255). McCarthy describes Remainder as following 'very consciously' on from J. G. Ballard's Crash (1973), which he reads as depicting 'this alienated world where we've got all these screens in front of us', where 'events in the world just become narratives on TV' and the 'only real thing is lived violence' (Orwell, 2008: 3). Where Satin Island depicts a contemporary form of this alienation in U's constant engagement with screens, Remainder posits a correspondence between a particular psychological model of consciousness and visual technologies, showing the workings of that model through the narrator's alienation from the violence of his actions. A complementary understanding of thought in terms of information-processing is also used to depict his lack of empathy. While Naz does go along with the Enactor, there are hints of hesitation which the latter ignores. When the first re-enactment involves throwing multiple cats off roofs, Naz's question 'Doesn't it upset you?' is misinterpreted (R, 146). When the narrator first suggests the bank robbery, Naz's response is 'a long, long pause. When Naz eventually spoke, his voice was very deep and very slow' (R, 242). Descriptions of Naz during the conversation in which he suggests murdering all of the other employees emphasize a resistance that is neither recognized by the narrator as such, nor expressed in dialogue (R, 253–6). The narrator explains Naz's acquiescence to his decision to transfer the bank robbery re-enactment to a real bank by describing how the latter's 'talent for logistics had become inflamed, blown up into an obsession that was edging into a delirium. [...] He looked unhealthy, sick through lack of sleep. [...] Like me he'd become an addict' (*R*, 243). McCarthy in interview references this passage, linking it to the use of the computer metaphor to describe his breakdown, confirming that Naz's motivation in the novel is 'an obsession with information' (Gavan, 2013). McCarthy describes this aspect of the novel as an 'an allegory for Fascism or, to be more precise, Stalinism: [the narrator] needs to kill everyone he's worked with in order to take the process to its end. [...] The logical extension of information management is totalitarianism' (Gavan, 2013). The narrator ends this reflection on Naz by applying this metaphor to himself: 'I hadn't stopped to calculate the chances of his accepting or rejecting my order before I issued it; it hadn't even occurred to me – but if it had, if I'd been capable of stopping and calculating, I'd have thought it through and realized that there was no question but that he would go along with it' (*R*, 244). When he then asks the same question of himself, the answer implicitly relies on the same logic: 'Why had I decided to transfer the robbery to re-enactment to the bank itself? [...] to be real – to become fluent, natural, to cut out the detour that sweeps us around what's fundamental to events' (*R*, 244). This detour is consciousness, which the narrator understands as fundamentally separate from material reality. However, the way in which consciousness is defined in terms of technology – implicitly in *Remainder* and explicitly in *Satin Island*'s use of 'buffering' – positions it as emerging from the individual's interconnections with technology. The gap between consciousness and matter is used to hint at the conditions for the emergence of the former.

The violence of the later chapters leads to the question of motivation, which the narrator refuses to address. McCarthy describes a recurring dynamic, whereby the narrator has his employees look up words, as 'central to the whole way he kind of ends up conceptualizing and also performing the stages of his eventually psychotic and catastrophic trajectory', claiming that his protagonist is 'killing people because of definitions in the dictionary by the end!' (Orwell, 2008: 3–4) At one point, the narrator asks Naz to have the meaning of the word 'residual' looked up. The definitions returned by his employees define the term as an adjective tied to particular processes

'Of or pertaining to that which is left – e.g. in mathematics.' [...] 'In physics,' Naz continued, 'of what remains after a process of evaporation; in law, that which – again, remains of an estate after all charges, debts, etc. have been paid. [...] Residual analysis. [...] Residual heat. [...] Residual error.'(*R*, 248–9)

There is of course an implicit reference to the title of the novel here. The narrator has been prompted to look up the word by someone using it like a 'thing', which Naz corrects to a 'noun' (*R*, 249). The term 'thing' is used in *Satin Island*, to describe 'a piece of electronic hardware', the material embodiment of uncertain processes: 'Maybe a receiver, a detector, wavelength modulator, I don't know' (*SI*, 149). Barad (2008: 130) relates representionalism – which 'separates the world into the ontologically disjointed domains of words and things, leaving itself with the dilemma of their linkage such that knowledge is possible' – to '*Thingification*' – 'the turning of relations into "things," "entities," "relata"'. A similar idea is referenced indirectly when U gives an example of one his employer's aphorisms, drawn from critical theory: '*What are objects? Bundles of relations* ... ' (*SI*, 40). 'Relata', as an abstract noun implied by language, is similar to both 'remainder' and 'residual'. These terms, as nouns, or discrete things, cannot fully represent their referents. The attention paid to grammar here is significant, in showing how the very inadequacy of these terms reflects their emergence from processes and relations. In mistaking adjectives for nouns, the narrator identifies the gap between language and reality established at the start of the novel by 'the Settlement'.

The terms 'Residual' and 'Settlement' are a product not only of language and culture, but of the flow of information through intersubjective networks. The narrator has Naz text his employees by phone to ask the meanings of certain words. In positing a causal link between these definitions and the narrator's actions, we might equally posit a link between his actions and his place within these networks. Claiming that the narrator kills people because of words in a dictionary relies on a focus on, as Hayles puts it, information rather than material instantiation. An emphasis on information over the material accompanies advances in communications technology. In 2016, the narrator could look up the words instantly on a smartphone. This would both heighten the complexity of the networks surrounding him while also making it easier to read his actions in terms of information flow rather than intersubjectivity. Andy Clark (2003: 45) predicted, shortly before the publication of *Remainder*, that 'we will one day live in a world in which, thanks to some easy-to-access implant or wearable device' we will be able to look up words instantly. The implication, for Clark, is that 'our sense of self, of what we know of who we are, is surprisingly plastic and reflects not some rigid preset biological boundary so much as our ongoing experience of thinking, reasoning, and acting within whatever potent web of technology and cognitive scaffolding we happen currently to inhabit' (2003: 45). He develops here on extended mind theory (Menary, 2010), according to which objects such as phones or notebooks can form part of the self, based on the flow of information. Applying this model to the narrator allows us to understand his actions and understanding as determined by a self which stretches beyond the body, incorporating complex technological and intersubjective networks. In aligning consciousness with the flow of information, however, it may also mask the complexity of these networks. To move beyond a reading of *Remainder* in which the narrator murders because of words or, by his own account, because of 'the movements, the positions and the tingling, [...] nothing more' (*R*, 276), we need to address how this reductive narrative represents complexity.

Writing in 1999, Hayles notes the ambiguity at work in post-humanism, positioning critical post-humanism as defined by active engagement:

> I view the present moment as a critical juncture when interventions might be made to keep disembodiment from being rewritten, once again, into prevailing concepts of subjectivity. [...] If my nightmare is a culture inhabited by post humans who regard their bodies as fashion accessories rather than the grounds of being, my dream is a version of the post human that embraces the possibilities of information technologies without being seduced by fantasies of unlimited power and disembodied immortality, that recognizes and celebrates finitude as a condition of human being, and that understands human life is

embedded in a material world of great complexity, one on which we depend for our continued survival. (Hayles, 1999: 3)

In its implicit engagement with information and technology, *Remainder* depicts this process. The narrator frames his actions and understanding in terms of a fundamental Cartesian opposition between mind and matter, while overlooking the specific cultural and technological context of his situation. In framing this opposition in terms of articulation, however, he hints at the way in which his own consciousness is defined in terms of technology, and emerges from his body's position within networks which flow through him and beyond him. *Remainder* argues that the denaturing of the human can be written into the novel through an attention to what literary consciousness cannot express, and why.

Works Cited

Barad, Karen (2008) 'Posthumanist Performativity: Toward an Understanding of how Matter comes to Matter', in Stacy Alaimo and Susan Hekman(eds) *Material Feminism*, pp. 120–54. Bloomington: Indiana University Press.

Bow, Suzanne and Colin Wright (2001) 'Introduction: Towards a Psychoanalytic Reading of the Posthuman', *Paragraph* 33(3): 299–317.

Brillenburg-Wurth, Kiene (2011) 'Posthumanities and Post-textualities: reading *The Raw Shark Texts and Woman's World*', *Comparative Literature*, 63(2): 119–41.

Clark, Andy (2003) *Natural-Born Cyborgs: Mind, Technologies, and the Future of Human Intelligence*. Oxford: Oxford University Press.

Critchley, Simon (2010) *How to Stop Living and Start Worrying*. Cambridge: Polity.

Gavan, David (2013) 'Existential Ground Zero', *Gorse*, 25 September, URL (Consulted January 2016): http://gorse.ie/existential-ground-zero/

Gavins, Joanna (2013) *Reading the Absurd*. Edinburgh: Edinburgh University Press.

Groes, Sebastian (2016) 'Information Overload in Literature', *Textual Practice*, DOI: 10.1080/0950236X.2015.1126630.

Hart, Matthew, Aaron Jaffe, and Jonathan Eburne (2013) 'An Interview with Tom McCarthy', *Contemporary Literature* 54(4): 656–82.

Hayles, N. Katherine (1990) *Chaos Bound: Orderly Disorder in Contemporary Literature and Science*. Ithaca, NY: Cornell University Press.

Hayles, N. Katherine (1999) *How We Became Posthuman: Virtual Bodies in Cybernetics, Literature and Informatics*. Chicago: University of Chicago Press.

Lea, Daniel (2012) 'The Anxieties of Authenticity in Post-2000 British Fiction', *MFS Modern Fiction Studies*, 58(3): 459–76.

McCarthy, Tom (2010) 'Technology and the Novel, from Blake to Ballard', *Guardian*, 24 July, URL (consulted January 2016): http://www.guardian.co.uk/books/2010/jul/24/tom-mccarthy-futurists-novels-technology

McCarthy, Tom (2015) 'The Death of Writing', *Guardian*, 7 March 2015, URL (consulted January 2016): http://www.theguardian.com/books/2015/mar/07/tom-mccarthy-death-writing-james-joyce-working-google

Menary, Richard (2010) *The Extended Mind*. Cambridge, MA: MIT Press.

Orwell, Roger (2008) 'What's Left Behind: An Interview with Tom McCarthy', *Static* 7: 1–4.

Rourke, Lee (2010) 'In Conversation: Lee Rourke and Tom McCarthy', *Guardian*, 18 September, URL (consulted January 2016): http://www.guardian.co.uk/books/2010/sep/18/tom-mccarthy-lee-rourke-conversation

Smith, Zadie (2009) *Changing My Mind: Occasional Essays*. London: Hamish Hamilton.

Vermeulen, Pieter (2012) 'The Critique of Trauma and the Afterlife of the Novel in Tom McCarthy's *Remainder*', *MFS Modern Fiction Studies* 58(3): 550–68.

Vermeulen, Pieter (2015) *Contemporary Literature and the End of the Novel: Creature, Affect, Form*. Basingstoke: Palgrave Macmillan.

Waugh, Patricia (2011) 'Thinking in Literature: Modernism and Contemporary Neuroscience', in David James (ed.) *The Legacies of Modernism: Historicising Postwar and Contemporary Fiction*, pp. 75–96. Cambridge: Cambridge University Press.

Waugh, Patricia (2013) 'The Naturalistic Turn, the Syndrome, and the Rise of the Neo-Phenomenological Novel', in T. J. Lustig and James Peacock (eds) *Diseases and Disorders in Contemporary Fiction: the Syndrome Syndrome*, pp. 17–34. London: Routledge.

Waugh, Patricia and Jennifer Hodgson (2012) 'Introduction', *Review of Contemporary Fiction: The Future of British Fiction* 32(3): 9–29.

9

STRUCTURES, SIGNPOSTS AND PLAYS
MODERNIST ANXIETIES AND POSTMODERN
INFLUENCES IN TOM MCCARTHY'S C

Martin Paul Eve

Mid-way through Thomas Pynchon's influential first novel, *V.* (1963), the reader is introduced to Kurt Mondaugen, a wireless radio operator stationed in the colonial German Südwest in 1922. Mondaugen is there to investigate a set of atmospheric disturbances ('sferics') that have been detected and that are resulting in a group of strange messages on his radio receiving device. The most notable of these messages, as decoded by the sinister Lieutenant Weissman, reads 'DIGEWOELDTIMSTEALALENSWTASNDEURFUALRLIKST'. As Weissmann interprets these characters: 'I remove every third letter and obtain: GODMEANTNURRK. This rearranged spells Kurt Mondaugen. [...] The remainder of the message [...] now reads: DIEWELTISTALLESWASDERFALLIST'. With some added spaces this message reads 'die welt ist alles, was der fall ist', widely known as the phrase that opens Wittgenstein's famous work of logical positivist philosophy, the *Tractatus Logico-Philosophicus* (1921): 'The world is all that is the case'. Mondaugen replies to Weissman, in a fashion that sounds as 'curt' as his name, that he has 'heard that somewhere before' (Pynchon, 1995b: 278).

When it comes to having 'heard that somewhere before', much the same could be said when reading the works of Tom McCarthy after Pynchon. For these themes of cryptanalysis, anagrammatic play, modernist (or at least Wittgensteinian) philosophy and radio waves – so prominent across Pynchon's oeuvre – also find a locus in Tom McCarthy's 2010 novel, *C*. *C* tells the life story of Serge Carrefax, a figure born at the turn of the technological revolution. A character blessed with analytical rather than emotional intelligence, Carrefax represents the blossoming and abrupt death of technological utopianism. After all, as the text notes with supreme irony, there is a belief in Serge's lifetime regarding war that 'the more we can chatter with one another, the less likely that sort of thing becomes' (*C*, 48). The twentieth century, of course, tells a very different story. McCarthy's text is also saturated with Pynchonian references that can be seen even by a comparison to the small portion of *V.* that I have quoted above. Indeed, the publisher even notes on the jacket of the first UK edition that *C* is 'reminiscent of Bolaño, Beckett and Pynchon'. Although the lineage of influence between the writers is never explicit, given McCarthy's and Pynchon's shared fascination with literary irony, metafictive reflexivity, single-letter acronymic titles (their ironic hallmarks of technological rationality and the language of applied science), an interest in wireless telegraphy, cryptography and technology, and a model of characterization that is more functional-pragmatic than emotional-empathetic (Eve, 2014: 28–9), it is far from surprising that many reviewers draw comparisons between the writers (see, for just two examples, Burn, 2012; Tayler, 2010).

This affinity between Pynchon and McCarthy stands for more than this specific relation, however. As almost the archetypical postmodernist, it is difficult but to read a writer's relationship to Pynchon as a metonym for a relationship to postmodernism, in its many guises. While McCarthy has already been diagnosed by Justus Nieland (2012: 570) as a 'forensic scientist of modernism', in this chapter I instead situate McCarthy within a broader intertextual scope that stretches into the postmodern frame. Indeed, from this starting point of a resonance between McCarthy and Pynchon, I suggest that it would make sense to treat seriously the situation of McCarthy within postmodernism, or at least to investigate how his novels interact with this classification.

Such an analysis of McCarthy's postmodernism, I contend, is overdue and can be thought through a threefold series of 'structures', 'signposts' and 'plays' for more reasons than to create my Derridean pun of a title. In the first section, 'Structures', I will examine how the formal elements of McCarthy's writing – at the paragraph, sentence, and novel level – imitate many of the postmodernist experimental and ludic features of temporal disorientation while beginning to explore some of the contradictions in thinking about McCarthy's work as a return to any preceding generic style. In 'Signposts' I will unearth some of the ways in which McCarthy's text points to itself in the metafictional tradition, signalling its historical placement but also thereby warning the reader of the techniques that must be deployed to understand its ludic form. This primarily draws upon the historical ungroundedness of McCarthy's quasi-historical novel. Finally, in 'Plays', I will look at some of the explicit textual resonances with and re-enactments of the postmodern canon, including the works of Don DeLillo and J. G. Ballard.

Through such a progression it is my intention to show that *C* can be read profitably within the generic histories of postmodernism and not just through a modernist filter. Indeed, with its echoes of Pynchon, DeLillo and Ballard I want to argue that, like *Remainder*, *C* is a novel about the classificatory history of twentieth-century literature; that most metafictional of fictions, a text about genre, a literary-historical fiction, concerned with the history of literature.

As a final note before proceeding: I choose not to define the terms 'modernism' or 'postmodernism' *in toto* outright. This is not only because it is tedious to encounter every essay that undertakes this task, but more importantly because it is impossible and always selective. I instead opt here to make clear the aspect of (post)modernism to which I am referring at a given moment, be it epistemology vs. ontology, ludic play, temporal distortion or any of the other characteristics frequently assigned under these taxonomies. That said, it is important to acknowledge Lyotard's (1984: 79) well-known proposition about cultural postmodernity (even if not specific to postmodern literature) that 'the postmodern is undoubtedly part of the modern'. The boundaries between modernism and postmodernism are neither strictly temporal nor thematic or stylistic. It can seem, when dealing with postmodernism, as though the contemporary reader is caught within the same bind faced by Justice Potter Stewart in defining pornography: 'I shall not today attempt further to define the kinds of material I understand to be embraced within that shorthand description, and perhaps I could never succeed in intelligibly doing so. But I know it when I see it' (Supreme Court of the United States of America, 1964). Furthermore, it is important to note that there is a large degree of critical effort at present that is devoted to charting the resurgence of modernist-like literary practices in contemporary writing (perhaps most prominently, James, 2012). What I will begin to suggest here, however, is that although C knowingly toys with modernist structures, it can equally be said to deploy postmodernist tropes, through its formalist elements (its structures), through the ontological destabilisation of its histories (its signposts to nowhere), and through its re-enactments of its intertextual affiliations (its plays).

1. Structures: McCarthy's Formal Postmodernism

To begin with some remarks on the postmodern form and structure of McCarthy's novel: C is, undoubtedly, a disorientating read. Indeed, as the text itself puts it, in one of its metatextual moments, 'the next few scenes are confusing' (C, 58). Although not obfuscating in its narrative to the same extent as the modernist Ulysses (1922) or the postmodern Gravity's Rainbow (1973), the reader can feel constantly wrong-footed, several steps behind his or her authorial guide. Evidently, this places the novel in the tradition of experimental work favoured by the high modernists and postmodernists in which difficulty plays a core role. As I will demonstrate in the next section this is partly a result of the text's 'clever clever' game-playing and its relationship to history. However, it is also evident that the novel is extremely rich in terms of its linguistic and structural signification and it is to the playful elements of the novel's language that I first turn here.

To begin to see evidence of how McCarthy encodes a ludic mode through moments of metafictional reflexivity, usually centred around linguistic games – a trope found in much postmodernist writing – consider, as an example, how the reader is told, early in the text, that:

> Serge gets stuck on words like 'antipodean' and 'fortuitous', and even ones like 'tables'. He keeps switching letters around. It's not deliberate, just something that he does. (C, 38)

This instance is just the first of many in which McCarthy distils the novel's totality into a microcosmic metonym at the levels of language, of theme, and of authorship. Firstly, in terms of language, when Serge confuses the letters in 'tables', McCarthy asks us to consider whether the character might be the 'ablest' (the most competent to deal with the trials of modernity?), in a 'stable' condition (with his stagnation and focus on blockage, to which I will return), whether he might 'be last' to survive, or whether he is simply playing with a 'lab set', an apparatus that proves so fatal for his sister. Secondly, and as just one example, at the thematic level, this passage connects with the 'tilting' table of the séance later in the novel where Serge rigs a device to interfere with a medium's trickery (C, 230). In this sense, Serge's early 'switching letters around' in the word 'tables' parallels the rearrangement of letters that he later conducts on the medium's table. Finally, in terms of authorship, all moments of metafiction suggest an easy (or perhaps lazy) reading in which we might consider whether there is a parallel between McCarthy and Serge; is Serge, in some way, the 'author' of C? McCarthy's novel, I would argue, tends to stop just short of such metatextual gimmickry. After all, the linguistic playfulness does not occur consistently throughout the novel. It seems, rather, that the flattening of diegetic levels that is suggested by McCarthy's metatextual play even demonstrates self-awareness of the metafictional tradition and works to signal this.

When this metafictional linguistic playfulness does surface again in C, it does so in a way that is derived from much modernist but also postmodern fiction. As an example from a work of high modernism, this can be seen in the wrecked anagrammatical play of *Ulysses*'s 'annos ludendo hausi' for 'Iohannes Doulandus' pointed out by Don Gifford (1988: 560–1). This ludic mode is continued, however, in Pynchon's *V.* with Kurt Mondaugen's aforementioned message but also in *Gravity's Rainbow* where the phrase 'medoshnicka bleelar medoometnozz in bergamot' appears to contain many of the book's most pertinent phrases, including: Enzian, Blicero, zero, kabbala and doomed (Pynchon, 1995a: 746; Weisenburger, 2006: 373). Anagrammatic play features consistently through *C*: the puns on *insect*/*incest* run throughout the novel and connect to the text's thematic preoccupations. In this case, the family connotations of *incest* followed shortly by *insect* (a trope connected to death at the end of the novel) seem to relate to Serge's sister, thereby binding the narrative of *C* to Freud's Wolf Man case. Indeed, Freud's patient, Sergei Pankejeff (the 'Wolf Man'), suffered from a variety of nervous conditions in the wake of his sister's suicide, including depression and severe constipation, all of which happen to McCarthy's similarly-named character Serge. Again, the effect of McCarthy's playfulness in the novel is to structurally bind chronologically disparate elements together (family/incest → death/insect) in a way that is linguistically ostentatious, thereby metafictionally highlighting the readerly act of interpretation: a most postmodern trait.

At the microcosmic level, however, the disorientation and aesthetic swirling in the novel is also a result of the text's micro-prolepsis (its brief jumps forwards in time and/or knowledge). By this, I mean the fact that the text makes no concession to the reader's lack of foreknowledge of events only later revealed, in spite of its otherwise overwhelmingly linear, chronological character (on which I will say more shortly). Take, as an example, the instance at the beginning of the novel where Carrefax senior is sending for a doctor to tend to his pregnant wife and the 'F's and 'Q's in his telegraphy system are substituted ('F' [..-.] and 'Q' [--.-] being inverse codes in the Morse system) (*C*, 6). The reader is, though, aware at this stage neither that early telegraphy will form a central thematic tenet of the novel nor that such a prototypical system has been developed by the character. Only a few pages later, this is explained in more detail to the reader

(*C*, 12). The length of stretch between mystery and resolution here is not substantial enough to make the work as taxing as many of the high postmodernist fictions, but it does immediately call to mind their 'difficulty' and plays on temporal distortion (say, for example, the mediations on time in Kurt Vonnegut's *Slaughterhouse-Five* [1969]).

That said, while epistemic play is a frequent feature of all fiction and may even be intrinsic to its form, particularly within modern and postmodern varieties, *C* is curious in its presentation because it chooses to conceal information from the reader only for brief periods before revealing its hand. It is also an outlier in this respect because the chronological macro-structure of the novel is entirely linear; a mode that does not always lend itself to abrupt retrospective enlightenment (for a counter example, one could compare the temporal leaps of Graham Swift's *Waterland* [1983] and the moment of grim revelation in that text that is facilitated by its final analeptic shock). Although there are portions of Serge's life that are not narrated (i.e. the text's chapters are non-adjacent in chronological terms), *C*'s quadripartite structure of 'Caul', 'Chute', 'Crash', 'Call' moves definitively forward in time through the life of Serge Carrefax. Although this may, at first, sound more like a realist mode than a postmodern styling, this structure actually shows, in terms of literary history, why *C* appears to do something different from the forms of modernist epistemic play to which it pays homage. Indeed, while the dark tone of McCarthy's war-saturated novel might induce a temptation to think that this text is a dystopian historical novel in which the critical force of history is bought to bear on the present – a didactic text that might warn us of the dangers of the past repeating (which depends upon cycles and historical analogy) – *C* does not seem to be wholly convinced by the logic of cycles and repetition. Instead, its structure is aptly C-shaped. The homophonic titles of the first and last sections of the text ('Caul'/'Call') imply the loop, the cycle, but eventually shy away from it in a differentiated repetition. Likewise, the cleansing instructions of Serge's doctor at the clinic are to think in terms of change, not cycles: 'things mutate', he notes, 'that is the way of nature – of good nature. [...] You though, [...] have got blockage, [...] instead of transformation, only repetition' (*C*, 105).

To reiterate: through the fact that its first and last section titles sound identical, in conjunction with the above in-text diagnoses of 'repetition', *C* hints that the reader should expect to see parallels and cycles. This then extends to the interpretation of the generic structures within which *C* might be read; echoes of and affinities with modernism and postmodernism. However, Serge seems incapable of closing the loop (and such repetition is presented, as above, as a pathology) and so, while his death bears the hallmarks of his childhood, the repetition is imperfect. This changes the focus in the novel's historiography from an epistemology of similitude (in which we would *know* and recognize elements of the past by their resemblance to the present) to one of a fresh ontology (in which the present is a newly transformed world and way of *being*, evolved out of the past but distinct from it). Such a focus is the classic shift in dominant – from epistemology to ontology – charted by Brian McHale and that he claims defines the postmodern novel, situated at the heart of *C*'s historiography (McHale, 1986).

To demonstrate further this ontological mutation, which is reflected in McCarthy's language, consider also the textual collocation of *incest* with the name of Serge's sister, Sophie (imperfectly repeated as Sophia), at the end of the novel that harks back to the familial near-voyeurism at the village fair scene and his sister's use of his penis as a telegraph key in the life of young Serge (*C*, 22, 60–1, 253). Yet, at the moment of Serge's death it is not the term *incest* that appears, which characterizes his childhood and where it 'all began' (*C*, 252), but rather it is an *insect* bite (*C*, 304–10). Through such moves and linguistic play, McCarthy's text invites 'pattern-making and pattern-interpreting behavior' from its readers (by implying an affinity between chronologically distant moments in the text) only to frustrate such text-processing (by showing and stating that such affinity is always imperfect in its analogy), a trope of interpretative refusal that, again, McHale famously ascribes as a core feature of the postmodern novel (McHale, 1979: 88).

This attitude towards time and cyclicality – enacted at the micro and macro levels in the text – also brings implications for *C*'s placement as a postmodern historical novel, to which I will now turn. Such complicated dynamics, where each structural description of text and history seems only partially to fit, or is complicated, resists wholeness and only gives *almost*s. Within such a framework, these, then, are at least some of the structures of C: almost-repetitious, almost-analogous and, as I will now show, almost-historiographic.

2. Signposts to Nowhere: McCarthy's Postmodern Historiography

If C is almost many things, there is at least some certainty in the fact that parts of the text are *definitely* metatextual. There are, however, several more direct instances where a metatextual function can be ascribed to this work, but that also contribute to an understanding of the novel's generic placement, primarily in its role as a work of historical fiction. One of the foremost of these aspects is the text's cryptic references to the plane of Lieutenant Paul Friedrich 'Fritz' Kempf, against whom Serge fights in an aerial battle in the later part of the novel and upon which I will now undertake some historical unpicking before returning to its postmodern implications. Kempf, a recipient of the iron cross, famously had the words 'kennscht mi noch' painted on the wings of his plane, a fact that C accurately re-conveys, and which, roughly translated, means 'do you still remember me?' (C, 173). Kempf was a member of squadron Jasta B (which was originally called Jasta 2 [VanWyngarden, 2007: 6]) and, later, Jastaschule I, and was credited with four victories over the course of the First World War, thereby narrowing the potential date for Serge's encounter with him to four specific moments (VanWyngarden, 2007: 90). Two of Kempf's takedowns were of Sopwith Camel aeroplanes (on 20 October 1917 and 8 May 1918 respectively) and one a Sopwith Pup (5 June 1917), both types of single-seater biplane, but a victory is also logged to him on either 29 or 30 April 1917 against a two-seater plane (a BE2e) (Franks et al., 1996: 179; VanWyngarden, 2007: 39). At no point in the war that I have managed to find did Kempf down an RE 8 aircraft (of the type in which Serge flies).

As with all historical fiction, however, it is unwise to mistake the aesthetic use of historical detail for a correlation with reality. At some point in all historical fiction the connection with reality is severed. Indeed, C's dogfight is not based upon any one specific account and there was no figure called 'Serge Carrefax' who was shot down, although the allusion to Kempf rather than the more renowned 'Red Baron' (von Richthofen) could be said to narrow McCarthy's potential sourcings. Pinpointing such data is not, though, the purpose of this historical digression. It is rather to show, by example, that C's aesthetics and content presuppose, or at least insinuate, an archive, regardless of whether one exists. The level of specific historical detail here – that the reader is given the markings of one precise plane as Serge's foe – invites a type of paranoid reading that the text must ultimately frustrate. This is not a difference of type or kind to other historical fiction, which always relies on such a withdrawal from fact, but rather a difference of degree as to where a reading becomes 'paranoid', a difference of placing for where the suspension of disbelief is triggered. This trope resurges in much postmodern writing that intermingles fact and fiction within a metafictional context that explicitly seeks to situate history as merely another form of narrative.

To understand why C's form as a historical novel is postmodern rather than realist, though, it is first necessary to define the classical historical novel. After all, *all* historical fiction mixes fact and fiction. Commonly traced in origin to Walter Scott's *Waverley* (1814), the subtitle of which is *'Tis Sixty Years Since*, the first and most basic requirement of conventional historical fiction is that it be set at a historical time that is distant enough to exclude the author's direct experience, as a mature adult, of the period in question (see, for example, Lee, 2014). Certainly, this applies to McCarthy and C's chapters on the First World War. Where C begins to become more complex as 'historical fiction', however, is when the other criteria of the genre are brought into play. For Sarah Johnson, the aesthetics of writing and parameters of reading in historical fiction are strongly generically codified. As she puts it:

The genre also has unofficial rules that authors are expected to follow. To persuade readers that the story could really have happened (and perhaps some of it did), authors should portray the time period as accurately as possible and avoid obvious anachronisms. The fiction and the history should be well balanced, with neither one overwhelming the other. (Johnson, 2006)

Likewise, while noting that historical fiction is frequently more of a meditation on the present than on the past, Jerome de Groot adds that:

Historical fiction works by presenting something familiar but simultaneously distant from our lives. Its world must have heft and authenticity – it must feel right – but at the same time, the reader knows that the novel is a representation of something that is lost, that cannot be reconstructed but only guessed at. This dissonance, it seems to me, lies at the heart of historical fiction. (de Groot, 2010)

Against these criteria, C fares somewhat variably. For one, because the novel is set within four different periods, each characteristically differentiated from the previous, the background history is not so 'well balanced' against the fiction. Indeed, even the portions of the text that are most seemingly specific in their historical detail are actually fictional. Perhaps the most specific that we can be about most of the 'Chute' section of C is to say that it is set during the First World War and ends at its close, which lacks the traditional specificity of verifiable historical events and people that one would expect in realist historical novels such as Hilary Mantel's *Wolf Hall* (2009), even where such realist texts also use authorial license to 'warp' such details. Again, this is a difference of degree, not of type.

Secondly, we might query whether C is a historical novel that 'feels right' in terms of its periodization. Does it have the 'heft and authenticity' that de Groot requires? I would contend, in actuality, that the text does not and that very little in C 'feels right' at all. This comes about, at least in part, because the historical circumstances in the novel are mediated through a sociopathic character whose 'perceptual apparatuses refuse point-blank to be twisted into the requisite configuration' for the dissonance of which de Groot writes. Specifically, Serge is unable to grasp *perspective*: 'he sees things flat; he paints things flat' (*C*, 39). Yet, the type of doubled knowing gesture that is expected from a work of conventional historical fiction can only be achieved through a kind of parallactic performance of perspective, one in which the depth and richness of the period is painted from a known and perceived distance. The central character in *C* lacks these prerequisites, even as McCarthy possesses them. Indeed, *C* is a novel that seeks to give a double perspective precisely because of the disjunct between Serge and McCarthy. Serge's perspective, as related to him by his father, would render historical circumstances as non-discrete, as *flat*, positing that we might imagine that 'every exciting or painful event in history has discharged waves of similar detectability into the ether – why we could pick up the Battle of Hastings, or observe the distress of the assassinated Caesar. [...] These things could still be *happening*, right now, around us' (*C*, 198–9). In Serge's world, '"me" is every name in history; all times have fused into a *now*', negating the particularity of any re-performed, specific historical period (*C*, 189). On the other hand, McCarthy's novel is one that encourages the hunt for specificity and uniqueness through the sowing of historical detail and insinuated but obscure facticity into the work. Even when such eventual archival tracing is frustrated and Serge's worldview seems to win out, this results in a situation in which Serge's flattened perspective on history contrasts with some of *C*'s remarks on historiography.

Indeed, I argue that *C* should be considered a work of postmodern historiographic metafiction – a term coined by Linda Hutcheon to denote fiction that highlights its own fictionality while dealing with the *nature of history* (Hutcheon, 1988) – rather than as a more conventional historical novel, because of the many meta-narratorial statements within the work that conflate history with narrative. Building on the work of Hayden White, texts such as *C* perform the claim that the predominant difference between history and fiction is the former's claim to truth (White, 1975: 93–7). Firstly, to make this case, consider that *C*'s historiography is constructivist. In McCarthy's novel, history in its formal sense is written by the victors and usually consists of privileging 'great figures' and wars. This is perhaps most clear when Serge is flipping through the brochure for the Klodĕbrady

Baths. We are told, at this point, that 'the accompanying text gives the town's history, which seems to consist of a series of invasions, wars and squabbles over succession' (C, 85). Elements of personal narrative and 'secrets of the heart', however, are elsewhere revealed to be omitted from the official historical record in C and are referred to as 'clandestine history', a gesture that immediately pluralizes the truth of a singular historical record and summons a paradigm of 'history from below' (C, 290). At the same time, however, institutional history as recounted by Laura, a character who 'studied history at St. Hilda's College, Oxford', is shown by McCarthy to be entirely concerned with mythological narratives. Laura's 'history' dissertation was on Osiris and consists of recounting the 'well-known myth' and 'cosmology' of Ancient Egypt from an intra-diegetic perspective that speaks of the ancient gods as though they were factual occurrences: 'The sun itself entered the body of Osiris' (C, 280–1). For Laura, who comes from the heart of formal and institutional academic history at Oxford, myth-making and history-making are similar, if not the same.

As Serge's recording officer demands, then, asking for the history of their recent flight in the First World War section of the novel: 'Narrative, Carrefax'. Serge's reply demonstrates how history, in the formal senses that the novel critiques, elides specificity and is based on subjective reconstruction: 'we went up; we saw stuff; it was good' (C, 143). The result of this disjuncture between levels in C – in which we are shown the initial events but then given a reductive 'history' – is 'to both inscribe and undermine the authority and objectivity of historical sources and explanations', as Hutcheon (1988: 123) puts it. In this way, C critiques the historiographic underpinnings of realist historical fiction through a postmodernist approach.

Yet the stylistics of postmodern historiography incorporated by C are hardly a new phenomenon and I do not claim that they lead to coherent or useful ends. As Shawn Smith (2005: 2) noted, ten years ago, it is 'no longer new or revolutionary' to point out that 'history is a field of competing rhetorical or narrative strategies'. What makes this interesting, though, is that it is certainly the case that C re-performs not only modernist texts and tropes, but also, particularly with respect to its history, postmodernist techniques that came to prominence in the

1970s and 1980s. For comparison, take, for instance, the historico-paranoid phase of DeLillo's oeuvre, exemplified in *Libra*, where the character Ferrie encourages the reader to 'think of two parallel lines', one the life of Lee Harvey Oswald, the other the conspiracy to kill the President; bridging this gap is 'a line that cuts across causality, cuts across time. It has no history that we can recognise or understand. But it forces a connection' (DeLillo, 1989: 339). As well as speaking to the nature of conspiracy, destiny and agency, this is also, clearly, a metatextual meditation on the weaving of narrative through history of the kind shared by *C*. After all, writes DeLillo, this third line, like fiction 'comes out of dreams, visions, intuitions, prayers, out of the deepest levels of the self'. Such hints of historical specificity encourage the hunt – which is certainly the norm among those who study Pynchon and Borges, but also Joyce – and thereby cast the reader him- or her-self in the role of the postmodern detective; never certain that such efforts will result in epistemological surety and always aware that they are more likely to result in a destabilization of a previous worldview: ontological collapse, regardless of how helpful such a view may be. Through its micro-prolepsis and insinuated facticity, *C* contains the afterlife of this aspect of postmodern fiction. Like many postmodern historical novels, the archival signposts are often devoid of referents; signposts to nowhere.

3. Plays: McCarthy's Postmodern Re-Enactments

Finally, then, although one of the key reference points for *C* is Woolf's *Between the Acts* – a work featuring a nested play-within-a-play at its core bound to suggestions of war – I would like to end this piece with two comparisons to the postmodern authors whom McCarthy's novel most clearly invokes, these being J. G. Ballard and Don DeLillo. While I have, already, throughout this piece noted some affinities with Pynchon, it is worth just reiterating that these features include a shared fascination with single-letter, recurring titles, encrypted messages, overlapping points of reference, metafictional tropes, and plays on history.

This is not all, though, for echoes of postmodernity. For we might also consider whether C is a text that is riffing on the postmodern fiction of Ballard, a text situated in the 'angle between the walls', to borrow a Ballardian phrase. Consider, for instance, the resonance with the geometric perversions of Ballard's *The Atrocity Exhibition* (1970) that are echoed in several of C's passages such as this one:

> More than anything, it's what he hears in Petrou's voice, its exiled, hovering cadences – and what he sees in Petrou's face and body, his perpetual slightly sideways stance: a longing for some kind of world, one either disappeared or yet to come, or perhaps even one that's always been there, although only in some other place, in a dimension Euclid never plotted, which is nonetheless reflecting off him at an asymptotic angle. (C, 251)

It would be possible to select almost any passage from Ballard's experimental novel and to find much of McCarthy's work as a replication, or, if feeling uncharitable, a parody, of its style. Consider, for instance, Ballard's statement that 'these embraces of Travers's were gestures of displaced affections, a marriage of Freud and Euclid' (Ballard, 1990: 76), the last clause of which not only perfectly embodies the topological and geometric slants to C's curious sexual encounters (along with the previously discussed Wolf Man references that include Serge's sexual preference for rear entry) but also echoes exactly the above passage's mention of 'a dimension Euclid never plotted'.

More specifically, however, C's reference to Ballardian geometric tropes is ensconced within notions of subjunctivity; of a world hiding behind this world – 'a longing for some kind of world, one either disappeared or yet to come' – disallowed from coming into possibility but forever remaining on the cusp of realisation. In Ballard's text, such subjunctivity and ontological instability is engendered through a pluralisation of worlds, as it is in C. For *The Atrocity Exhibition* this is framed through notions of inner and outer worlds, with the inner being primarily concerned with the psyche. Indeed, at the core of *The Atrocity Exhibition* Dr. Nathan says that:

> Planes intersect: on one level, the tragedies of Cape Kennedy and Vietnam serialized on billboards, random deaths mimetized in the experimental auto disasters of Nader and his co-workers. Their precise role in the unconscious merits closer scrutiny; by the way, they may in fact play very different parts from the ones we assign them. On another level, the immediate personal environment, the volumes of space enclosed by your opposed hands, the geometry of your postures, the time-values contained in this office, the angles between these walls. On a third level, the inner world of the psyche. Where these planes intersect, images are born, some kind of valid reality begins to clarify itself. (Ballard, 1990: 47)

In other words, there is a mediated public sphere; a world of interpersonal relationships; and an inner landscape of the mind. In *C* this plays out slightly differently with a dysfunctionally narrated broad public and historical plane ('I liked the war' [*C*, 214]), mediated through a character who is incapable of forming meaningful interpersonal relationships in his localized world ("Turn around," he says. "I want to see your back" [*C*, 114]) and whose interior mental landscape is contoured and rocky (a space 'that seems to have become all noise and signal' [*C*, 178]). *The Atrocity Exhibition* and, to an extent, *C*, attempt to map the intersection of these spaces in new ways that avoid the sensationalized mediation of the first sphere, the usually sentimentalised depiction of the second, and the conventional Cartesian separation of the inner world from the outer.

Ballard, however, is the not the only other point of postmodern anchorage for *C*. Rather, on top of the Pynchonian allusions, one particular moment in the novel feels particularly motivated by a recreation of the themes of Baudrillardian simulation embedded in Don DeLillo's wonderful *White Noise* (1985). Indeed, towards the end of McCarthy's novel, Abigail relates to Serge her experience of watching tourists at the pyramids in Cairo, tourists who

> got their cameras out and started photographing them, although I don't know why because their photos won't turn out as nice as the ones in the book and brochures either. And they didn't even photograph the things for very long, because there was a buffet laid out on the deck, [...] but then of course they realised that they had to show

a certain reverence towards the Pyramids, while still not missing out on lunch, so they revered and ate and photographed all at once. (C, 262)

This relates to, but is not directly the same as, one of the most celebrated passages of DeLillo's novel, namely the incident with the 'most photographed barn in America':

> Several days later Murray asked me about a tourist attraction known as the most photographed barn in America. We drove 22 miles into the country around Farmington. There were meadows and apple orchards. White fences trailed through the rolling fields. Soon the sign started appearing. THE MOST PHOTOGRAPHED BARN IN AMERICA. We counted five signs before we reached the site. There were 40 cars and a tour bus in the makeshift lot. We walked along a cowpath to the slightly elevated spot set aside for viewing and photographing. All the people had cameras; some had tripods, telephoto lenses, filter kits. A man in a booth sold postcards and slides – pictures of the barn taken from the elevated spot. We stood near a grove of trees and watched the photographers. Murray maintained a prolonged silence, occasionally scrawling some notes in a little book.
> 'No one sees the barn,' he said finally. (DeLillo, 2011: 11–13)

These two passages, while overlapping, are ever so slightly different in their outcomes. DeLillo's text is concerned with the displacement of reality and the endless proliferation of simulacra engendered by mechanical reproduction in the era of late capital: 'We're not here to capture an image, we're here to maintain one. Every photograph reinforces the aura', he writes (DeLillo, 2011: 14). McCarthy's passage, on the other hand, effects the more pedestrian critique that is surely familiar to anybody who has acted as a flâneur among tourists: that the act of photographing, a form of mimesis, supersedes experiencing.

When McCarthy's statements are coupled with the large number of other postmodern allusions in the work, however, this passage changes in scope and becomes, instead, a re-play of exactly the taxonomic battle that I have been charting throughout this chapter. Indeed, McCarthy's tourists photographing the pyramids represent a three-way pull between the knowledge that their photography is an act that perpetuates the simulacra (the postmodern); the feeling of duty to return to a more conservative, reality-rooted approach to culture (a modernist epistemological quest where there really is a solid referent to find); and an overwhelming sense of tedium with the whole debate (eating and photographing all at once).

So, what does this all mean for McCarthy's novel? As I have argued in this chapter, despite the 'modernist' feel to and reference points within *C*, there are also a significant number of allusions to postmodern texts throughout McCarthy's work that have to date been overlooked. Elements of metafictional play in the text's structure, a form of historiographic metafiction that insinuates an archive, and a set of direct correlations to postmodern authors all contribute towards such a reading. To conclude, though, with an opening up: it is difficult to set *C* within one single paradigm and what I have sought to do here is to provide evidence against the singular dominance of a modernist reference point for the novel. The text's overarching structure implies that McCarthy does not simply endorse generic repetition, be this modernist or postmodernist. The closed cycle of the *O* is not given; it is, instead, a *C* – a near-miss for analogy and repetition, a quasi-cycle that implies plurality. This latent claim for generic novelty, or at least, for genre-fusion and mutation, can easily lead to claims of pastiche or lesser imitation. However, in its historical structure, *C* is a novel about the future and its differentiated repetition. It is also, in such a way and despite its harkings back to modern and postmodern forebears, a text commenting on the future of experimental literary genre. It is in this way, I contend, that *C* plays out its modernist anxieties and its postmodern influences.

Works Cited

Ballard, J. G. (1990) *The Atrocity Exhibition.* revised edn. San Francisco, CA: RE/Search.

Burn, Stephen (2012) "Men in Space,' Tom McCarthy's Complex Novel', *The New York Times*, February 24, URL (accessed January 2016): http://www.nytimes.com/2012/02/26/books/review/men-in-space-tom-mc-carthys-complex-novel.html de Groot, Jerome (2010) 'Walter Scott Prize for Historical Fiction: The New Time-Travellers', *Scotsman*, June 19, URL (accessed January 2016): http://www.scotsman.com/lifestyle/books/walter-scott-prize-for-historical-fiction-the-new-time-travellers-1-813580

DeLillo, Don (1989) *Libra*. New York: Penguin.

DeLillo, Don (2011) *White Noise*. London: Picador.

Eve, Martin Paul (2014) *Pynchon and Philosophy: Wittgenstein, Foucault and Adorno*. London: Palgrave Macmillan.

Franks, Norman L. R., Frank W. Bailey and Rick Duiven (1996) *The Jasta Pilots*. London: Grub Street.

Gifford, Don (1988) *Ulysses Annotated: Notes for James Joyce's Ulysses*. Berkeley: University of California Press.

Hutcheon, Linda (1988) *A Poetics of Postmodernism: History, Theory, Fiction*. New York: Routledge.

James, David (2012) *Modernist Futures: Innovation and Inheritance in the Contemporary Novel*. New York: Cambridge University Press.

Johnson, Sarah L. (2006) 'Historical Fiction – Masters of the Past', *Bookmarks Magazine*, January 20, URL (accessed January 2016): http://www.bookmarksmagazine.com/historical-fiction-masters-past/sarah-l-johnson

Lee, Richard (2014) 'Defining the Genre', *Historical Novel Society*. URL (accessed January 2016): http://historicalnovelsociety.org/guides/defining-the-genre/

Lyotard, Jean-François (1984) *The Postmodern Condition: A Report on Knowledge*, trans. Geoff Bennington and Brian Massumi. Minneapolis: University of Minnesota Press.

McHale, Brian (1979) 'Modernist Reading, Post-Modern Text: The Case of Gravity's Rainbow', in *Poetics Today* 1(1–2): 85–110.

McHale, Brian (1986) 'Change of Dominant from Modernist to Postmodernist Writing', in Douwe W. Fokkema and Hans Bertens (eds) *Approaching Postmodernism*, pp. 53–79. Utrecht: John Benjamins.

Nieland, Justus (2012) 'Dirty Media: Tom McCarthy and the Afterlife of Modernism', in *Modern Fiction Studies* 58(3): 569–99.

Pynchon, Thomas (1995a) *Gravity's Rainbow*. London: Vintage.

Pynchon, Thomas (1995b) *V.* London: Vintage.

Riffaterre, Michael (1978) *Semiotics of Poetry*. Bloomington: Indiana University Press.

Smith, Shawn (2005) *Pynchon and History: Metahistorical Rhetoric and Postmodern Narrative Form in the Novels of Thomas Pynchon*. London: Routledge.

Supreme Court of the United States of America. 1964. 'Jacobellis v. Ohio 378 U.S. 184'. URL (accessed January 2016): https://supreme.justia.com/cases/federal/us/378/184/

Tayler, Christopher (2010) '*C* by Tom McCarthy', *Guardian*, July 31, URL (accessed January 2016): http://www.theguardian.com/books/2010/jul/31/c-tom-mccarthy-novel-review

VanWyngarden, Greg (2007) *Jagdstaffel 2 Boelcke: Von Richthofen's Mentor*. Oxford: Osprey.

Weisenburger, Steven (2006) *A Gravity's Rainbow Companion*, 2nd edn. Athens: University of Georgia Press.

White, Hayden (1975) *Metahistory: Historical Imagination in Nineteenth Century Europe*. Baltimore, MD: Johns Hopkins University Press.

10

Tom McCarthy's *Remainder* and 'the Great Outdoors'

Arne De Boever

Welcome to the Great Outdoors

The following discussion of Tom McCarthy's novel *Remainder* is driven by a fascination with what the French philosopher Quentin Meillassoux early on in his book *After Finitude: An Essay on the Necessity of Contingency* calls 'the great outdoors', and specifically by the relation of that 'great outdoors' to fiction. In Meillassoux's words, the great outdoors is

> the *absolute* outside of pre-critical thinkers: that outside which was not relative to us, and which was given as indifferent to its own given-ness to be what it is, existing in itself regardless of whether we are thinking of it or not; that outside which thought could explore with the legitimate feeling of being on foreign territory – of being entirely elsewhere. (Meillassoux, 2008: 7)

As such, it poses a challenge to what Meillassoux calls correlationism, or thought that is caught up in the relation between reality and its human perceiver. If this is indeed the case, then this great outdoors also poses a formidable challenge to literature and specifically realist fiction as it is traditionally practiced.

Others have picked up on this. In his book *Alien Phenomenology, Or What It's Like to Be a Thing*, in which Meillassoux's great outdoors is a recurring concern, Ian Bogost (2012: 40–1) notes that literature's 'preference for traditional narrative acts as a correlationist amplifier'. 'Whether empathy or defamiliarization is its goal', he adds, 'literature aspires for identification, to create resonance between readers and the human characters in a work'. The 'whether' clause is important: for it indicates that *even* literature that would *mess* with traditional narrative – literature that would *defamiliarize* – would *still* be caught up in the correlationist bind, *as long as* it aims to create resonance between readers and characters. It may be, then, that it is nearly impossible for literature to break out of this bind – unless the literature in question is something like Ben Marcus's *The Age of Wire and String*, discussed later on in Bogost's book, and characterized by Bogost (2012: 82) as 'incomprehensible'. It is 'within that incomprehensibility', he argues, that something like a literature of the great outdoors becomes possible.

Interestingly, some of the work associated with Meillassoux's philosophy has been literary: *Cyclonopedia*, Reza Negarestani's cult 'novel' (if we can still call it that), has already had an important symposium dedicated to it (Keller et al., 2012), and the event brought together some of the most important voices in contemporary speculative realism. Indeed, Meillassoux himself has taken on the question of literature in his work on the great outdoors. His second book to be translated into English, *The Number and the Siren* (2012), is a study of Mallarmé's extraordinary poem *Un Coup de Dés* – and it is an impressive demonstration of how his philosophical thought can be developed through a meticulous, obsessive reading of a work of literature. However, *Un Coup de Dés* is of course a poem, and one that lends itself particularly well to Meillassoux's thought. What about the great outdoors and the rest of literature?

Graham Harman has pointed to the weird fiction of H. P. Lovecraft as a key resource for his object-oriented thought (not the same as Meillassoux's philosophy, but related to it) (Harman, 2012). Indeed, it is worth noting that Meillassoux himself has written about fiction in an essay titled 'Metaphysics and Extro-Science Fiction' (2010), a text I will return to in the final section of this article since its argument will prove to be of central importance to the reading of Tom McCarthy's *Remainder* that I develop. Clearly, fiction does have a place within these debates – even if this place is only beginning to be sketched out. In what follows, I contribute to this project.

My argument in this article will be, put simply, that *Remainder* opens up the realist novel onto what Meillassoux calls the great out-doors. Pushing the argument about realism that Zadie Smith has made about McCarthy's novel further, I argue that the book practices a *speculative* realism – and, more precisely, a speculative *materialism* – that seeks to write, even though this becomes nearly impossible to pull off, 'stories of uncertain reality, those in which the real crumbles gradually, from one day to the next ceasing to be familiar to us' (Meillassoux, 2010: 60) – *the material debris of the real.*

Meillassoux (2010: 60), whose words I have just quoted, associates this kind of story with 'extro-science fiction' (or XSF) and fore-grounds 'the dread uncertainty' that this 'genre' (for that is how he theorizes XSF) reveals. I read *Remainder*, which at first sight has noth-ing to do with XSF, as an XSF novel, opening up the kind of 'world' that Meillassoux associates with XSF. By doing so, however, I also re-think XSF outside of generic constraints, as a *modality* in which any novel in any genre can be written – whether it is a science fiction nov-el or a realist one. Indeed, it may even be, and here I am taking some distance from Harman's preference for Lovecraft, that it is in realist fictions that the weirdness of the XSF modality can truly be appreci-ated. For it might ultimately be in those places where one expects it least that the weird can ultimately come into the 'strange strangeness' (Morton, 2010: 38) of its own.

Very Little, Almost Nothing[1]

In the opening pages of *Remainder*, we are informed that the narrator has suffered an accident about which he is not allowed to speak – and which he does not appear to remember. 'It involved something falling from the sky', the novel's first paragraph states. 'Technology. Parts, bits. That's it, really: all I can divulge. Not much, I know' (R, 5). He is not allowed to speak about it because of an £8.5m settlement he has received as compensation. The settlement came through on the condition that 'you can't discuss the accident in any public arena or in any recordable format' (R, 8). Since he does not remember anything about the accident, this does not really pose a problem. It is worth noting that the novel thus, from the get-go, raises the problem of representation, easily associated in this context with trauma – i.e. easily assessable, critically, in the context of 1990s ethical criticism. However, I intend to show that the problem of representation as it is evoked here is actually different, related to the great outdoors rather than to trauma. But first, the novel.

Although the settlement that the narrator has received is large by any standard, it appears to be warranted. The novel's second chapter recounts how after the accident, the narrator had to relearn how to move again. This involves a cognitive, neuro-plastic process that is referred to in the novel as the 'rerouting' of the brain: 'finding a new route through the brain for commands to run along' (R, 19). For example, if you need to relearn how to pick up a pen, your physiotherapist will ask you to *imagine* picking up the pen first: to think, several times over, each and every movement that you would need to make to pick up the pen – as if the entire movement would be broken down into an Eadweard Muybridge series of photographs. In this way, circuits are cut through the brain 'that will eventually allow you to perform the act itself. That's the idea' (R, 20). In order to learn how to move again, the narrator thus needs to remake his brain. McCarthy's narrator learns this lesson first-hand.

Although the therapy is successful – the narrator does learn to move again – the particular procedure, which relies heavily on understanding in order to achieve doing, prevents him from feeling natural. Since every single one of his actions is shot through with consciousness, he feels he has lost touch with the real, and cannot 'just be'. Instead, all of his actions feel unnatural, 'second-hand' (R, 23). Consciousness overwrites his authentic contact with the real. In order to get rid of this feeling, the narrator embarks on a mad series of 're-enactments' that lead from the relatively innocent reconstruction of a building that he thinks he remembers to the re-enactment of a fake bank heist that ends in death and destruction. These projects are funded by the settlement he has received, and in particular by his sky-rocketing stocks. Going against his financial advisor, the narrator puts all his money in technology and telecommunications without diversifying or top-slicing. This speculation makes for huge gains but also risks tremendous losses. In fact, the re-enactment projects propel the narrator into such a high degree of exposure – linked in the book to his financial exposure, which puts him on the verge of collapse – that they will enable him to experience what he considers to be some tingling sense of the real. But this experience also arrives at the cost of other people's lives and indeed, given the novel's ending, possibly at the cost of his own life.

The narrator's authenticity problem is drawn out most explicitly when, shortly after getting out of the hospital, he goes to see Martin Scorsese's film *Mean Streets* at the Ritzy theatre in Brixton, London. What strikes him, as he is watching the film, is

> how perfect De Niro was. Every move he made, each gesture was perfect, seamless. Whether it was lighting up a cigarette or opening a fridge door or just walking down the street: he seemed to execute the action perfectly, to live it, to merge with it until he was it and it was him and there was nothing in between. (*R*, 23)

'He's natural when he does this', the narrator concludes. 'Not artificial, like me. He's flaccid. I'm plastic'. The narrator thus paradoxically associates De Niro, an actor in a film, with being natural. De Niro becomes the narrator's authenticity or reality fetish, the figure that represents everything that he is not.

When his friend Greg points out that he just means De Niro is 'cool' – 'All film stars are cool' – the narrator replies that this is not what it is about. 'It's about just being', he continues, 'De Niro was just being; I can never do that now' (*R*, 23). Reflecting later on this conversation, it suddenly hits the narrator that '[e]ven before the accident' he had 'always been inauthentic': 'if I'd been walking down the street just like De Niro, smoking a cigarette like him, and even if it had lit first try, I'd still be thinking: *Here I am, walking down the street, smoking a cigarette, like someone in a film*' (*R*, 24). The problem of the novel, then, is that the narrator's accident and specifically the care he received in its aftermath, intensified this feeling of inauthenticity to the point where it has become unbearable. It is through his accident and the therapy that follows it that the narrator learns something about his life that was already true before the accident.

Shortly after he has received the money of the settlement, the narrator embarks on another therapeutic project through which he intends to recover this real that he thinks he has lost or never had. It is a mad project that attempts to reconstruct, starting from a crack in the bathroom wall at the house of one of his friends, the entire world that is born from it. The project's foundational scene takes place at a party on Plato Road – the reference to Plato, whose theory of ideas is crucial to McCarthy's own philosophy, is not accidental (I will return to this later). 'I was standing by the sink looking at this crack in the plaster when I had a sudden sense of déjà vu':

> I'd been in a space like this before, a place just like this, looking at the crack, a crack that had jutted and meandered in the same way as the one beside the mirror. There'd been that same crack, and a bathtub also, and a window directly above the taps just like there was in this room – only the window had been slightly bigger and the taps older, different. (*R*, 60)

The déjà vu is described as a memory: 'I remembered it all', the narrator says, 'but I couldn't remember *where* I'd been in this place, this flat, this bathroom' (*R*, 61). What he does realize as his memory of this crack is expanding – he remembers the building in addition to the bathroom and the flat, the people in the building, and even the buildings surrounding that building – is that everything he remembers had been 'real'. 'I'd been real – been without first understanding how to try to be: cut out the detour. I remembered this with all the force of an epiphany, a revelation. Right then, I knew exactly what I wanted to do with my money. I wanted to reconstruct that space and enter into it so that I could feel real again' (*R*, 62).

Whether it is an actual building that is being remembered here, or whether the crack in the bathroom wall merely triggers a desire to return to the womb – 'You been giving birth in there?' someone asks when the narrator finally gets out of the bathroom (R, 63); when the crack is reconstructed later in the novel, we find out that it needs to have the colour of flesh (R, 121) – remains unresolved in the novel. Instead, the rest of the novel revolves around the narrator's obsessive reconstruction of this space as well as of other spaces catching his interest: a tyre shop, a murder scene, a bank.

To facilitate the reconstruction, the narrator engages Nazrul Ram Vyas, a man who is working for a company called Time Control. Here is how the narrator explains his project to Naz:

> I want to buy a building, a particular type of building, and decorate and furnish it in a particular way. I have precise requirements, right down to the smallest detail. I want to hire people to live in it, and perform tasks that I will designate. They need to perform these exactly as I say, and when I ask them to. I shall most probably require the building opposite as well, and most probably need it to be modified. Certain actions must take place at that location too, exactly as and when I shall require them to take place. I need the project to be set up, staffed and coordinated, and I'd like to start as soon as possible. (R, 78–9)

Ultimately, this is exactly what Naz will help the narrator to set up. But the 'politics' of the project, if that is a word that can be used in this context, appear problematic. From 'I want to' to 'I shall' to 'exactly as and when I shall', one senses the intensification of control in the narrator's description. Indeed, now that he has received a large amount of money through the settlement, it appears that he intends to exercise a fantasy of total control that will involve not simply buildings, but also people, and even the sun (R, 211).

Whereas some might ultimately not care about the buildings and the animals involved in the project (he has cats walk across the roof of the building opposite to his, and he cares very little about the fact that several of them crash to their deaths), it is ultimately around the involvement of people that some ethical and political questions are raised. Clearly, the narrator's project will have a tremendous influence on his employees' lives. Referring to them first as performers, he will later insist that they are not: 'All the ... performers', he goes – 'no, not performers: that's not the right word ... the participants ... staff ... ' (*R*, 83). Ultimately, he calls them 're-enactors' (*R*, 85). The important thing, however, is that they 'must be ... I mean, we'll need complete ... jurisdiction over all the space' (*R*, 83). His use of the term jurisdiction is telling: within the building, it is the narrator's *word* that is *law*. He will rule his building as a sovereign and micro-manage the lives of the re-enactors he engages. Meanwhile, 'I shall move throughout the space as I see fit' – the tone of grandeur is unmistakable (*R*, 84). Naz executes his boss's totalitarian fantasy without skipping a beat.

Re-enactors can live in the building, the narrator explains, but '[t]hey'll have to get used to being in two modes, though: *on* and *off* (*R*, 82). Like robots, he imagines them to operate according to a switch over which he has full control. Given these statements, it seems that what Naz is facilitating is not so much time control but life control: total control over the lives of those who are hired as re-enactors. This becomes perhaps most clear in the novel when the narrator orders a model of the building: 'a scale model' that has 'little figures in it' representing the different characters in the building:

> the motorbike enthusiast next to his bike, the pianist with his bald pate, the liver lady [a woman who is cooking liver all day] with her headscarf and her snake strands of hair, the concierge with her stubby arms and white mask [she wears a mask because the narrator cannot remember her face]. (*R*, 152)

Executing his fantasy of total control, the narrator will move around these figures in the model of his building like pawns on a chessboard. Of course, the people will be expected to follow his movements, as if he were moving the actual people around. If things were not already explicit enough, McCarthy also has his narrator marking the model with blood later on in the novel (*R*, 186). Importantly, it is his own blood and not that of the re-enactors. So the suggestion seems to be that he is not simply controlling the re-enactors from the outside, but that his own biological life is very much involved in this project as well. If this is indeed a project of life-control, as I have suggested, it is worth asking whose life is being controlled: the lives of the characters? Or the narrator's life? Perhaps both? By whom? Who is writing whom in this meta-fictional allegory of biopolitical realism?

To a certain extent, the question of the narrator's control over the re-enactors' lives is relevant for those who are involved in fixing up the building as well. Because of certain oversights within the reconstruction planning – oversights that may or may not have been made deliberately (*R*, 106) – workers are sometimes made to undo jobs they had already completed. Motivation, however, was not lacking: 'the people we'd hired were being paid vast amounts of money' (*R*, 107). The cynical assumption appears to be that as long as you pay people enough money, you can make them do anything. 'What was lacking, if anything was comprehension: making them understand exactly what it was that was required of them' (*R*, 107). The directive is very specific:

> And making them understand at the same time how little they needed to understand. I didn't need to make them share my vision, and I didn't want them to. Why should they? It was my vision, and I was the one with the money. They just had to know what to do. (*R*, 107)

Ask no critical questions. An order is an order.

The narrator notes that 'this wasn't easy' (*R*, 107). One major crisis is caused by the pianist, one of the characters that were part of the narrator's original vision of the building. A doctoral student in music, this man is required to run through Rachmaninov all day while making mistakes, retaking passages, and so on and so forth. It needs to sound as if he were *practising* Rachmaninov. Lying on the floor of the staircase one day, 'studying the way the light fell from the large windows onto the patterned floor [...] while the piano music looped and repeated in the background' (*R*, 146), the narrator suddenly sees the pianist walk up the stairs. 'This, of course, was physically impossible: I was listening to him practicing his Rachmaninov two floors above' (*R*, 147). The explanation is simple: what the narrator is hearing is a recording, the mechanical reproduction of the pianist practicing Rachmaninov. Although the pianist argues that 'it's the same thing, more or less', the narrator shouts that 'it is not! It is just absolutely not the same thing!' (*R*, 147). What makes his project successful, clearly, is that *real* people are involved in it. He is exercising his control not over characters, but over *real* people. It is as if the novel's biopolitical fantasy has become real. Indeed, McCarthy's own novel – and the tradition of realism in which it participates – is arguably complicit with the narrator's project. Its logic of conception arguably resembles that of the narrator's reconstructions.

For now, I want to focus on the fact that the reconstructions function as a kind of therapy for the narrator. He engages in them as a practice of care, in the hope that they will restore to him a sense of being real, first-hand, natural, authentic. As such, they appear to be successful. Checking out a building – the one that will eventually become his building – early on in the novel, the narrator 'felt a tingling start up in my right side' (*R*, 100). Thinking about how the entire scene of his déjà vu would fit in the building, '[t]he tingling became very intense' (*R*, 102). Experiences like this return again and again throughout the book and appear to be related to his project of experiencing the real. Perhaps because of this reason, the experiences are addictive. If he has them once during a particular re-enactment, he wants to do that re-enactment again, so as to have them again. He also tries to change the re-enactment – to slow it down, for example – so as to try to extend the feeling (one can think, for example, of a slowed-down scene in *Mean Streets* in which De Niro cruises through a bar in Little Italy, New York, with one girl on each arm and wearing no trousers). It is as if the narrator wants to disappear into these moments entirely and thus finally achieve the authenticity and reality he desires.

That is what happens later in the novel when, looking at the diagrams of a murder scene that he will want to re-enact, he goes into a trance.

> The longer I stared at these pictures, the more intense the tingling in my upper body grew. It had moved into my brain, like when you eat too much monosodium glutamate in a Chinese restaurant. My whole head was tingling. The diagrams seemed to take on more and more significance. (*R*, 179–80)

And so he 'drifted off' into the world that he was seeing. One and a half hours later, he wakes up looking into the concerned faces of Naz and a doctor. The doctor suggests that these trances, which will recur and intensify in the book, are linked to trauma. As such, they are pharmacological, both curative and poisonous:

> He's manifesting [...] the autonomic symptoms of trauma, [...] Response to trauma is often mediated by endogenous opioids. That is to say, the body administers its own painkillers – hefty ones. The problem is, these can be rather pleasant – so pleasant, in fact, that the system goes looking for more of them. The stronger the trauma, the stronger the dose, and hence the stronger the compulsion to trigger new releases. Reasonably intelligent laboratory animals will return again and again to the source of their trauma, the electrified button or whatever it is, although they know they'll get the shock again. They do it just for that fix: the buzzing, the serenity ... (R, 204)

The suggestion appears to be, as Naz notes, that the narrator is doing the same thing.

This reveals something rather disturbing about the narrator's therapy. Whereas he thought it was therapeutic, it might actually have been poisonous, no more than an elaborate way to return to the trauma from which he suffered (but which he does not remember and cannot talk about publicly) and to the opioids that his body released at that time. It is through this experience – through the tingling he appears to experience in this condition – that he thinks he is approaching the real. It might very well be that his trauma – the event that reconfigured his existence – operates for him as the real to which he does not have access. Not remembering it, and not being allowed to talk about it publicly, our narrator's existence is ultimately scripted by a foundational event that is inaccessible to him. It was a moment of near-dying that functioned as a kind of re-birth – but one that exposed to him the inauthenticity of his life. In response, the narrator is trying to get back to that originary moment (remember, in this context, how the crack in the bathroom wall is associated with birth) in order to access the real. But the process, although it takes place under the guise of therapy, is clearly pharmacological. Like a laboratory rat, the narrator is running against the inaccessible source of his trauma over and over again, only to experience that tingling feeling that he associates with the real.

But can trauma really settle the question of the real as it is raised in the novel?

The Question of Realism

Clearly, *Remainder* is a novel that is obsessed with the real, and as such the particular 'realism' it practices deserves some further consideration to see how it might fit in contemporary debates about realism. Let us consider a particularly pertinent one, in which McCarthy's novel eventually became involved.

On 24 July, 2000 *The New Republic* published literary critic James Wood's now famous review 'Human, All Too Inhuman'. In the review, Wood takes on what he calls 'the big, ambitious novel':

> The big contemporary novel is a perpetual-motion machine that appears to have been embarrassed into velocity. It seems to want to abolish stillness, as if ashamed of silence. [...] Stories and substories sprout on every page. [...] Inseparable from this culture of permanent storytelling is the pursuit of vitality at all costs. (Wood, 2000: 41)

Thomas Pynchon, Don DeLillo, Salman Rushdie, David Foster Wallace, and Zadie Smith are some of those mentioned as practitioners of the genre, a brand of realism that Wood labels 'hysterical'.

> Storytelling has become a kind of grammar in these novels; it is how they structure and drive themselves on. The conventions of realism are not being abolished but, on the contrary, exhausted, and overworked. Appropriately, then, objections are not made at the level of verisimilitude, but at the level of morality: this style of writing is not to be faulted because it lacks reality – the usual charge against botched realism – but because it seems evasive of reality while borrowing from realism itself. It is not a cock-up but a cover-up. (Wood, 2000: 41)

It is not because they offer the 'existence of vitality' that we should mistake this for 'the drama of reality' (Wood, 2000: 42).

'What are these stories evading?' Wood asks (2000: 42). One answer to this question is 'the possibility of novelistic storytelling'. With that comes 'an awkwardness about character and the representation of character' (Wood, 2000: 42). Whereas stories are usually generated by human beings, 'these recent novels are full of *in*human stories' – a phrase that Wood (2000: 42) considers to be oxymoronic, 'an impossibility, a wanting in both ways'. Ultimately, the stories that these big, ambitious novels offer 'defy the laws of persuasion' (Wood, 2000: 42). Their readers simply do not buy these tales, however alive, human, or connected their characters are presented to be. What these stories lack, in Wood's (2000: 42) view, 'is the human': they suffer from 'the crisis of character, and how to represent it in fiction'. He clinches the argument with a close-reading of Smith's *White Teeth*, deeming it 'all shiny externality, all caricature' (Wood, 2000: 42). This is opposed later in the review to a passage from Charles Dickens's *David Copperfield*, which does not fall into this trap – even though Dickens is also presented in the review as 'the parent' of hysterical realism. Wood's review ends with a clear question: 'Which way will the ambitious contemporary novel go? Will it dare a picture of life,' as Dickens offers us, 'or just shout a spectacle,' as the big, ambitious novel in Wood's view does (Wood, 2000: 45)?

I am not rehearsing this by now old debate because Smith needs saving – Wood also praises her in the review, and in any case she doesn't need saving and has responded to Wood's criticisms herself. In October 2001, and now in the aftermath of the September 11 terror attacks, Smith's 'This is How it Feels to Me' was published in the *Guardian*. Recalling James Wood's 'hefty, well-timed kick at what he called "hysterical realism"' – a term that she labels 'painfully accurate for the sort of overblown, manic prose to be found in novels like my own *White Teeth* and a few others he was sweet enough to mention' – she reveals that she in fact agrees with him, even though she also thinks the 'collective term' he proposes is 'too large a net, catching significant dolphins among so much cannable tuna' (Smith, 2001). Wood's review is not going to keep her from writing. She does suggest, however, that 'September 11 has made [the problem that Wood raises] more urgent and intractable'. Many others – most infamously, perhaps, Martin Amis in a series of pieces on the terror attacks now collected in his book *The Second Plane: September 11: Terror and Boredom* – had begun to reconsider the project of novel-writing in this light, or rather in this shadow – 'in the shadow of no towers', as the title of Art Spiegelman's book about the event put it (Amis, 2009; Spiegelman, 2004). As always, the novel pulled through, and I am now inclined to think that Smith's real answer to Wood's challenge only arrived many years later, in November 2008, when *The New York Review of Books* published her essay 'Two Paths for the Novel'.

Let us recall Wood's question, in his review of Smith: 'Which way will the ambitious contemporary novel go?' He offered two options: offer a picture of life, or shout a spectacle. Smith's title seems to reference Wood's question directly, and she too is laying out two paths, both involving the aesthetic of realism. On the one hand, she discusses Joseph O'Neill's novel *Netherland*, representative of a 'breed of lyrical Realism' that she considers to be 'perfectly done' (Smith, 2008). The problem is that *Netherland* is conscious of this, and furthermore 'has some consciousness' of the arguments that have attacked the 'credos upon which Realism is built: the transcendent importance of form, the incantatory power of language to reveal truth, the essential fullness and continuity of the self'. With some awareness of these arguments, *Netherland* turns out to be, in Smith's perceptive reading, an 'anxious novel': a post-catastrophe (i.e. post-9/11) novel in which the catastrophe isn't terror but realism itself. She goes on to lay bare some of the clichés that structure this book which 'places before us what it fears might be a tired effect'. In other words, *Netherland* 'recognizes that effect's inauthenticity, its lack of novelty, even its possible dullness – and it employs the effect anyway'. There are sites of authenticity in the novel but all of these are ultimately dismantled as a fake. And as it continues in its search for the 'real', *Netherland* can only do so anxiously, in the knowledge that this 'anxiety trace' – its marking and remarking, its tracing and retracing – may be the best there is for realist fiction today.

On the other hand, and still – though somewhat awkwardly – in the shadow of no towers, she turns to McCarthy's *Remainder* as indicating another possible path for twenty-first century fiction. Unlike *Netherland*, *Remainder* is 'fully conscious' of the theory that informs it, and according to Smith the novel's great challenge is 'how to write about it'. As she sees it, *Remainder* takes the path of the 'anti-literature hoax', a 'wind-up' that 'works through the things we expect from a novel, gleefully taking them apart, bit by bit'. This destructive project culminates in the narrative suffering what Smith calls, continuing the psychoanalytic language from her discussion of *Netherland*, a 'nervous breakdown': the novel explicitly reveals that the true reality it is supposed to give us access to 'was never there in the first place', and it's only after this has been exposed that the narrative rebuilding is allowed to begin. Let us have a closer look at the scene in question, and how it comes about.

When the narrator is drinking a cappuccino one day in 'one of those Seattle-theme coffee shops' (R, 49) where he has a loyalty card – because he is obsessed with the loyalty card filling up, he will be having more than one cup – he notices the people outside of the coffee place, specifically how they are looking 'just like me: completely second-hand' (R, 50): they 'acted out the roles' of characters in advertising. After his sixth cappuccino, however, he 'noticed a group of homeless people' and in this case his experience is entirely different: 'After a while I started thinking that these people, finally, were genuine' (R, 52). Like De Niro, the homeless are thus turned into an authenticity or reality fetish. And so the narrator 'decided that I would make contact with them'. Asking one of them to join him for dinner, they end up at a Greek restaurant – possibly another reference (after Plato Road) to Greek philosophy and the tension between form and matter that it contributed to the history of Western philosophy in which the narrator is caught up – where they are met by a waitress, 'an old woman with big glasses' (R, 54). The narrator 'ordered a bottle of white wine' and when the waitress comes back with the wine,

> My homeless person [note the possessive pronoun] watched her breasts as she leant over the table to pour it. I watched them too. Her

shirt was unbuttoned at the top and she had nice, round breasts. She must have been about his age, eighteen, nineteen. (*R*, 54)

At this point, one might still gather that they have changed waitresses. But when, a little further along, the narrator spills red wine over the white tablecloth and 'the waiter' comes back over (*R*, 56), the novel appears to be just as confused as the reader: 'He was ... She was young, with large dark glasses, an Italian woman. Large breasts. Small'. Clearly, the narrative is collapsing. And indeed, almost immediately, the narrator informs the reader that '[t]here wasn't any table. The truth is, I've been making all this up – the stuff about the homeless person. He existed all right, sitting camouflaged against the shop fronts and the dustbins – but I didn't go across him' (*R*, 56).

In other words: everything we have just been reading was invented. What we witnessed, in the chapter, was a moment of novelistic invention, during which several characters were called into being – the homeless person (who really existed, but did not participate in the events that were described), the waitress. Significantly, the descriptions of the waitress are infused with sexual desire, thus playing into the scene's ultimate conclusion that all of this is the narrator's fantasy. Indeed, the tingling that the descriptions of the waitress might produce in some readers might be related to the power-trip that the narrator is also having: *do you want a sexy waitress, the narrator seems to be asking? I'll give you a sexy waitress: I'll transform the old woman into a young one, enlarge her breasts, unbutton her shirt, and if you want her to go down on you while you are sipping your wine, I can arrange that as well.* It is an experience of the narrator's power, of the power over life that the narrator appears to have. And yet, after this demonstration, the narrator takes it all back again. None of this was real, it was all invented. But that doesn't mean the narrative can't go on: indeed, this is only the end of the third chapter. There is a lot more to come.

As I have already said, Smith reads this moment as a 'nervous breakdown', a moment where the narrative collapses. But there is more. Smith ties the scene – and I think she is correct to do so – to the genre of the novel's long-standing relation to realism and the 'credos upon which [it] is built: the transcendent importance of form, the incantatory power of language to reveal truth, the essential fullness and continuity of the self' (Smith, 2008).

The contrast that Smith develops between *Remainder* and O'Neill's novel *Netherland* is illuminating. As Urszula Terentowicz-Fotyga has noted in her article 'Unreal City to City of Referents', Smith argues that whereas *Netherland* is perfectly written and executes the credos of realism impeccably, the novel is nevertheless highly anxious about this perfection. Constantly referring to the clichés that characterize its language, it reveals itself to be a master of realism, but one troubled by anxiety. As Smith sees it, *Remainder* takes an entirely different track. The novel's 'minimalist narrative and withdrawal from linguistic bravado remind her [Smith] of Beckett, Joyce, and Kafka, writers who transgress the neat categorizations of realism and anti-narrative, modernism and postmodernism' (Terentowicz-Fotyga, 2009: 312). Samuel Beckett is mentioned early on in McCarthy's novel, during a scene in which the narrator is looking for re-enactors. One of the actors who has come to audition has 'prepared a passage to perform for us: some piece of modern theatre by Samuel Beckett' (*R*, 110). 'We don't want to hear that', the narrator says. He is explicitly not interested in acting, but in re-enacting. The irony is, of course, that what the re-enactors get involved in is ultimately very close to a Beckett play.

To situate McCarthy's particular realism, Smith turns to Alain Robbe-Grillet and his experiments with fiction-writing. Given that McCarthy has written the introduction for Robbe-Grillet's *Jealousy*, one assumes that this is no coincidence. In this introduction, which was also published in *Artforum*, McCarthy starts with the issue of realism. Critics have noted, he writes, that Robbe-Grillet's work, 'forswore any attempt to be "believable" or to engage with the world in a "realistic" way' (McCarthy, 2008: 392). McCarthy argues, however, that in this assessment

> [these critics] displayed an intellectual shortcoming typical of Anglo-American empiricism, and displayed it on two fronts: first, in their failure to understand that literary 'realism' is itself a construct as laden with artifice as any other; and second, in missing the glaring fact that Robbe-Grillet's novels are actually ultrarealist, shot through at every

level with the sheer quiddity of environments to which they attend so faithfully. What we see happening in them, again and again, is space and matter inscribing themselves on consciousness, whose task, reciprocally, is to accommodate space and matter. As Robbe-Grillet was himself fond of declaring: 'No art without world'. (McCarthy, 2008: 392)

It is, indeed, the unbearable weight of the realization that realism is a construct that triggers the anxiety of O'Neill's novel and the nervous breakdown in *Remainder*. What McCarthy adds to this, however, is that a narrative practice that responds to this can be read as 'ultrarealist'. In other words, as a practice that does not break with realism, but continues it in the ulterior regions where that first insight – realism is a construct – forces it to go.

It is a 'novel theory' of a kind, one that links up remarkably well with the theory of literature that McCarthy has developed in his book *Tintin and the Secret of Literature*. In this book, McCarthy asks whether the Belgian artist and writer Hergé's comic book series *Tintin* can be considered literature. The book operates from the assumption that it can, and lays bare – through creative close-readings of Hergé's life and work – the ways in which the comic books can be shown to operate 'like' literature. Indeed, McCarthy goes so far as to develop a theory of literature on the basis of his discussion of Tintin.

As the title of his book reveals, that theory revolves around the notion of the secret.[2] Literature presents us with a world, McCarthy notes, but a world that must ultimately remain secret. We cannot take a DNA test of a character, McCarthy notes. Ultimately, the life of a character is not known to us: not to the reader and not to the writer either. Thus, McCarthy quotes Derrida's statement that character-life ultimately remains 'eternally unreadable, absolutely indecipherable, even refusing itself to any promise of deciphering or hermeneutic', adding himself that 'the text creates the secret [...] making it readable through its own unreadability' (*T*, 146).

With reference to the French philosopher François Laruelle, whose work is sometimes associated with speculative realism, one could speak here of a textual 'hermetics' rather than a textual hermeneutics

– with readers being figured as 'hermeneuts' or 'hermetologists', followers of what he in a text on the secret calls 'another Hermes':

> He defines the essence of truth as a secret, but as a secret that in order to exist and to be made known needs none of the light of logos, none of the tricks of meaning, the strategies of interpretation, the horizon of the World, or the transcendent forms of appearance. Truth as secret exists autonomously prior to the horizontality of appearance. The secret enjoys an absolute precedence over interpretation; it is itself the Uninterpretable from which an interpretation emerges. It is the invisible that has never been visible because it is know from the outset to be invisible. (Laruelle, 2010: 20)

However, before things get too metaphysical we must point out that if the novel-theory McCarthy develops in the Tintin book and in *Remainder* can be read together, the secret (the authentic, the real) would be material – it would be *the secret of matter*.

For further proof, consider how Smith ties these concerns to a reading she witnessed in New York in which McCarthy was involved. The reading was organized by the International Necronautical Society and involved McCarthy as well as philosopher Simon Critchley, whose book *Very Little ... Almost Nothing* is alluded to in *Remainder*'s opening sentences. Being read was the society's manifesto. I quote here again from Smith's review. 'We begin', the manifesto goes, 'with the experience of failed transcendence. [...] Being is not full transcendence [...] but an ellipsis, an absence, an incomprehensibly vast lack scattered with [...] debris and detritus' (Smith, 2008). In this history of philosophy, this debris and detritus – this matter – is generally considered to be a corruption of perfect form (think, for example, of Plato, who is closely related to the birth of the narrator's re-enactment project, on Plato Road). But necronauts, as Smith points out – and we could add hermeneuts to the group – 'feel differently':

> They are 'modern lovers of debris' and what is most real for them is not form or God but the brute materiality of the external world. [...] In short, against idealism in philosophy and idealist or transcendent conceptions of art, of art as pure and perfect form, we set a doctrine of [...] materialism. (Smith, 2008)

There is another re-enactment that is described in the book that
captures the philosophical tension between form and matter that is
central to the novel. Smith also discusses it in her article. When the
narrator is getting a punctured car tyre replaced one day, he asks for
the windscreen washer reservoir to be refilled. After the boy working at the shop has poured a litre of the washer liquid into the reservoir, the narrator pushes 'the spurter button to make sure it worked'
(R, 159). But nothing comes out. 'It's all gone!' he concludes – and
he feels wonderful about it. '"Two litres!" I said, "Where has it all
gone?" They'd vaporized, evaporated'. As far as he can tell, the liquid
has 'transubstantiated', and he considers it to be a 'miracle' (R, 160).
When the narrator turns on his car to drive off, the liquid of course
comes gushing out of the dashboard, and he is covered by it. It turns
out there that there has not been a miracle after all. He will try to
enact one when he starts re-enacting this scene in a twenty-four hour
loop. He asks his collaborators to design a system that would have the
blue liquid evaporated. However, since one can never get the upper
hand on matter, this is not the fiction with which *Remainder* will conclude. Matter wins out over form: it is in matter that form collapses,
releasing an experience of the real.

What I would like to ask at this point is: how do both the examples
that Smith mentions in 'Two Paths for the Novel' relate to Wood's
plea back in 2001 for 'human stories' that would 'dare a picture of
life'? Neither one of them strikes me as particularly human. While
Netherland offers a perfectly executed lyrical realism, Smith's review
suggests that the 'real' story that is being told here is a profoundly inhuman one, on at least two levels: first, because it's the story of realist
fiction's struggle with realism itself, the credos upon which it is built;
second, because the attack on these credos – on the relation between
language and the world that it reveals – ultimately does reflect back on
the correlationism, the relation between the world and its human perceiver, in which realist fiction is caught up. Reading the novel's anxiety
trace means pushing the novel towards the limits of the human – but
importantly without necessarily migrating into the terrain of the hysterical realism that Wood attacked (and in Smith's view, rightfully so).

In *Remainder*, we are ultimately reading (as opposed to reading *about*) the narrative's 'nervous breakdown'. We are not reading here *about* the nervous breakdown of the narrator, or one of the novel's characters; it is the narrative's nervous breakdown *itself* that we read, and as such this novel tells an inhuman story that any story about a human being – however nameless or weird he or she appears – can only approach. What is being laid out here, in other words – even though Smith does not explicitly say so and may not want to push things quite this far – appears to be something like a third option in addition to 'picturing life' and 'shouting a spectacle': it's a plea for an inhuman, speculative realism that would move realist fiction from the correlationist logic of representation into the logic of the real itself. Isn't this what Smith is ultimately after in her reading of 'anxiety' in *Netherland* and of the 'nervous breakdown' in *Remainder*? These are not novels that use language to offer us, in a signification-theory-kind-of-way, direct access to the real; they do not follow the logic of representation. Instead, they are an integral part of the real, and the challenge before us appears to be to read them – and ultimately to write them – in this way. *Weirdly.*

Remainder as XSF

I want to argue now, in closing, that *Remainder*'s particular weirdness, and the intervention it makes in the history of realism, is illuminated when the novel is placed next to Meillassoux's great outdoors, and specifically his thoughts on literature and this great outdoors. For this, we need to turn to Meillassoux's essay 'Metaphysics and Extro-Science Fiction'.

In the essay, Meillassoux distinguishes between two regimes of fiction, one that he labels science fiction (SF) and one that he labels extro-science fiction (XSF). He points out that as far as its relation to science goes, SF preserves the existence of science. In SF, science 'may be profoundly transformed', he writes, 'but there will always *be* science' (Meillassoux, 2010: 27). In XSF, this is not the case: XSF thinks 'worlds outside science', '*where experimental science is im-*

possible in principle, rather than unknown in fact'. It's the latter that Meillassoux will be interested in – not because he is particularly interested in fiction, but because the distinction between SF and XSF will enable him to lay out a conceptual distinction that he deems to be of philosophical interest.

Meillassoux's discussion revolves around 'Hume's problem', familiar to readers of *After Finitude*. The problem involves a billiards match, 'during the course of which the laws of dynamics cease to apply' (Meillassoux, 2010: 30). How can we know, Hume asks, 'what truly guarantees – but also, what persuades us – that physical laws will continue to hold in a moment's time, given that neither experience nor logic can assure us of this?' (Meillassoux, 2010: 31). Meillassoux goes on to discuss Karl Popper's answer to this question: Popper argues that 'nothing could guarantee it, but moreover that this was a good thing, since there is nothing fantastic about these possibilities – they must be taken entirely seriously'. This is, Meillassoux (2010: 35) points out, the SF answer: 'Popper tells us that new experiences could refute our theories; but he never doubts that the existing, canonic experiments will always produce the same results in the future'. He thus confuses Hume's problem, which is ontological, with an epistemological problem. Meillassoux (2010: 36) argues, however, that Hume was interested in something else: 'Hume's problem mobilizes another imaginary, the imaginary of extro-science fiction, a fiction of a world become too chaotic to permit any scientific theory whatsoever to be applied to reality anymore'.

To illustrate, but also to further his thought on the problem, Meillassoux turns to an Asimov story that does both: it captures the XSF imaginary, since 'a totally unforeseen event [...] comes to pass' in it, but it is ultimately an SF story since this totally unforeseen event appears to *still* be explainable by the laws of science. That is why, Meillassoux argues, the story functions: narrative needs this SF resolution, and a world of 'pure chaos, a pure diversity ordered by nothing' risks rendering fiction impossible. In other words: with the XSF imaginary, fiction is able to go where science cannot – and evidently some kind of thought still happens there.

I will skip now, in the interest of time, the crystal-clear pages on Kant that follow in the essay, where the possibility of this 'some kind of thought' – consciousness – is discussed. I want to list, instead, the possibilities of extro-science fiction worlds with which Meillassoux's (2010: 50) essay concludes: type one worlds would be 'irregular, but not enough to affect science or consciousness' – as he notes, these worlds are not extro-science 'in the strict sense since they still allow the exercise of science'; the irregularity of type two worlds 'is sufficient to abolish science but not consciousness' – these worlds, he notes, 'are the real extro-science worlds' (Meillassoux, 2010: 52); finally, type three worlds: 'they represent lawless universes in which disordered modifications are so frequent, that [...] the conditions of science and those of consciousness alike, are abolished' (Meillassoux, 2010: 56–7).

Which brings him to his final question: how to write XSF? He lists three solutions, and it is worth asking how they match the three worlds described above: first, '[introduce] just one rupture without cause or reason' (he summarizes this as 'catastrophe'); two, 'nonsense' (this recalls Bogost's discussion of the Ben Marcus novel, to which I alluded in the opening pages of this article); or, three, write 'stories of uncertain reality, those in which the real crumbles gradually, from one day to the next ceasing to be familiar to us' (Meillassoux, 2010: 60). It is this third solution that he considers to '[express] most faithfully the XSF genre'. Meillassoux summarizes this as 'the dread uncertainty of the atmospheric novel', and notes that there probably aren't enough of these around 'to constitute a genre'. Indeed, at the beginning of his essay, too, there are some genre-related worries: some might argue that the SF genre already includes the XSF genre and that it thus makes no sense to separate between the two, in fact that the SF genre contradicts the very distinction he is trying to make. Like Meillassoux, I think this is not a worthwhile argument, in part because in my view, XSF is not a genre – I in fact think we do it harm to locate it under SF. One could ask here in what kind of contexts this experience of dread uncertainty is most profound: in recognizably weird contexts, where the literature we are reading is explicitly, openly trying to break with traditional narrative (as Harman seems to think when he proposes

Lovecraft's weird fiction as the key resource for object-oriented on-tology); or in familiar contexts, where the literature we are reading is realist, but is infected nevertheless by an incomprehensibility that begins to corrode fiction at large.

My own position is the latter, and as a consequence I do not think of XSF as a genre but as a modality of writing, which can be practiced in *any* genre.[3] It may of course be that certain genres lend themselves better to it than others, and it certainly may be that SF is one of those genres. Given Meillassoux's description of what he calls 'the atmospheric novel', however, and the ways in which in such novels 'the real crumbles gradually, from one day to the next ceasing to be familiar to us', I think a case could be made for the realist novel – of course, written in a certain modality – as a good genre for the practice of XSF. As the title of Harman's book already reveals, this very distinction between 'weird' fiction and 'realist' fiction may be precisely what is under discussion here, since the point of the XSF modality would arguably be to reveal the weird as real, and the real as weird.

So where does *Remainder* stand in relation to the three worlds that Meillassoux lists, and the three solutions for writing XSF that he proposes? Since the novel includes only one 'nervous breakdown' (to recall Smith's discussion of the book), I would argue that it fits best the first type of world that Meillassoux describes: 'irregular, but not enough to affect science or consciousness'. As such, the novel might not be extro-science 'in the strict sense' since it sticks to the rules of the game for the entire rest of the time. However, as far as Meillassoux's solutions go, *Remainder* is closest, in my view, to the third solution, which he deems to be closest to XSF: neither catastrophe nor non-sense, the novel offers a story 'of uncertain reality […] in which the real crumbles gradually, from one day to the next ceasing to be familiar to us'. As such, it qualifies, I have argued, as what Meillassoux refers to as an 'atmospheric' novel: ending high up in the sky, in a plane that is flying in circles until its fuel will run out, it evokes that 'dread uncertainty' that Meillassoux mentions, indefinitely speculating about the material debris of the real.

Notes

1 Some of the material in sections 2 and 3 of this article are part of the chapter on *Remainder* that is included in my book *Narrative Care: Biopolitics and the Novel* (Boever, 2013). The material appears here, however, in an entirely new theoretical framework and as such it has been thoroughly reorganized (in particular in section 2).

2 I have addressed this problematic in chapter 3 of my *States of Exception in the Contemporary Novel: Martel, Eugnides, Coetzee, Sebald* (Boever, 2012).

3 XSF is to genre what I've argued storytelling is to the novel in Walter Benjamin's essay 'The Storyteller' (Boever, 2008).

Works Cited

Amis, Martin (2009) *The Second Plane: September 11: Terror and Boredom.* New York: Vintage.

Boever, Arne De (2008) 'Politics and Poetics of Divine Violence: On a Figure in Giorgio Agamben and Walter Benjamin', in Justin Clemens, Nicholas Heron and Alex Murray (eds) *The Work of Giorgio Agamben: Law, Literature, Life,* pp. 82–96. Edinburgh: Edinburgh University Press.

Boever, Arne De (2012) *States of Exception in the Contemporary Novel: Martel, Eugnides, Coetzee, Sebald.* New York: Continuum.

Boever, Arne De (2013) *Narrative Care: Biopolitics and the Novel.* New York: Bloomsbury.

Bogost, Ian (2012) *Alien Phenomenology; Or, What It's Like to Be a Thing?* Minneapolis: University of Minnesota Press.

Harman, Graham (2012) *Weird Realism: Lovecraft and Philosophy.* Winchester: Zero.

Keller, Ed, Nicola Masciandaro and Eugene Thacker (eds) (2012) *Leper Creativity: Cyclonopedia Symposium.* New York: Punctum.

Laruelle, François (2010) 'The Truth According to Hermes', trans. by Alexander Gallloway. *Parrhesia* 9: 18–22.

McCarthy, Tom (2008) 'The of the Pressant' *Artforum* 46(10): 392–5.

Meillassoux, Quentin (2008) *After Finitude: An Essay on the Necessity of Contingency,* trans. Ray Brassier. New York: Continuum.

Meillassoux, Quentin (2010) 'Metaphysics and Extro-Science Fiction', in Florian Hecker and Robin Mackay (eds) *Speculative Solution,* pp. 25–60. Falmouth: Urbanomic.

Meillassoux, Quentin (2012) *The Number and the Siren: A Decipherment of Mallarmé's Coup de Dés,* trans. by Robin Mackay. Falmouth: Urbanomic.

Morton, Timothy (2010) *The Ecological Thought*. Cambridge, MA: Harvard University Press.

Smith, Zadie (2001) 'This is How it Feels to Me', *Guardian*, 13 October, URL (consulted 8 January 2015): http://www.guardian.co.uk/books/2001/oct/13/fiction.afghanistan

Smith, Zadie (2008) 'Two Paths for the Novel', *New York Review of Books* 55(18), 20 November: 89–95.

Spiegelman, Art (2004) *In the Shadow of No Towers*. New York: Pantheon.

Terentowicz-Fotyga, Urszula (2009) 'Unreal City to City of Referents: Urban Space in Contemporary London Novels,' in *Journal of Narrative Theory* 39(3): 305–29.

Wood, James (2000) 'Human, All Too Inhuman', *New Republic* 223(3): 41–5.

11

NEW INHUMANISMS
TOM McCARTHY AND SPECULATIVE REALISM

Andrew Gibson

One of the young McCarthy's lodestars, Maurice Blanchot, famously wrote of the importance of sustaining a passion for the outside.[1]
One way of presenting the intellectual history of the past four decades would be to suggest that they have witnessed an accelerating
shift from the passion for an outside conspicuous however minimally
or liminally in various of its major eminences – Derrida, Foucault,
Lacan, Lyotard – to an adjustment, reconciliation or capitulation to
an inside.[2] The patron saint if not prime mover of this turn – and probably its most notable representative – was Richard Rorty.[3] It is evident above all, perhaps, in contemporary presentism. Presentism is a
culture's more or less voluntary and conscious self-enclosure within
itself, within the horizons of its epoch and its forms of discourse and
knowledge, the conviction that no other culture has mattered or can
matter as it does, or rather, perhaps more pressingly, that no other
culture can matter to *it* more than it does, that it alone really speaks to
itself, tells itself about itself. A presentist culture has no outside and
no concept of one (save perhaps one that is peremptorily reducible
to its terms, which means that it is not really an outside at all). Thus,

on the one hand, a presentist culture is incapable of thinking the possibility of its own radical insufficiency, can no longer re-imagine itself. On the other hand, it can no longer hear the exteriority that is history, even as a distant alterity, intuition or trace; or, believing that it can no longer hear history, it turns history into a simulacrum to which (in what it takes to be its own worldly realism) it then resigns itself as all the history there is to know. By the same token, it has shut off any sense of the exteriority of the future, as that which may set our present terms at naught, or mean that we do not have to bear with them. Another way of saying this would be that a presentist culture risks being devoured by its own *hubris*. What interests me above all in this essay, however, is a specific conjuncture at which the hegemony of presentism has apparently come under threat, or begun to seem open to question, at least to some, and a new experiment with anti-anthropomorphic materialisms – with new inhumanisms – becomes possible and even necessary. The essay addresses the importance of that experiment, and the importance of the McCarthy experiment within it.

No doubt most cultures have been concerned to foster, preserve, promote and enhance the vividness of their claim to immediate historical attention and indeed superiority. How else do cultures survive? What cultures have ever sincerely entertained a persuasion of their own frivolity or irrelevance? Nonetheless, presentism, or what Quentin Meillassoux (2006a: 70) nicely calls 'communal solipsism', seems perhaps uniquely the hallmark of our culture, of its will to acquiesce in confinement to its own interiority. One might speculate on the reasons for this. One, very clearly, is the literal loss of alternative worlds. The most obvious disappearance of an exteriority has been the demise of Communism. But the postwar years have equally witnessed the progressive obliteration of the last faint residues of cultures that could offer Mauss, Bataille and even Lévi-Strauss at least a hypothetical position of exteriority from which to continue to think. Baudrillard's great example, the indigenous Philippine tribe, the Tasadays, discovered by anthropologists and disintegrating on contact with the outside world, remains luminous here; and if Baudrillard's major point is that the Tasadays are subsequently re-

turned to the jungle and 'preserved' (see Baudrillard, 1998), their reduction to a token of themselves is also a measure of the bankruptcy
of our much-vaunted ethics of respect for alterity.

For if presentist culture is indifferent to anything it is alterity. This
needs saying very starkly. The ethics of alterity was the specious mask
adopted by a process of relentless homogenization; alterity, yes, so
long as it has the measure of our norms, and they have the measure of
it. One world now prevails. To say that global capitalism has become
the only game in town is too glib, too partial, too ready-made an explanation, too easy a mystification of the vast contemporary drive to
seal the present into itself, the sources of which are no doubt complex
and various. We gave up some time ago on such classic distinctions
between a base and a superstructure. It nonetheless remains the case
that there is no longer an exteriority to capital, that outside its limits,
there is only death (a principal theme of this essay); or, to put the point
differently, as does Badiou, in a hegemonically presentist culture, the
only thing that can happen to us appears to be death (Badiou, 2001:
35; in our culture, mere death in itself becomes 'tragedy'). The defeat
of alterity is a defeat of the historical sense. It is also, more largely,
a failure of the kind of imagination of otherness *tout court* that was
part of what enabled the survival of the utopianisms. No doubt this
has partly to do with technology. Contemporary technology provides
ever more formidable resources not only for shoring up the present's
involvement with itself, but for the simulation of (historical) alterity
as presentness. It is perhaps the most formidable instrument for closure invented thus far. The media become global cage and specular
image, the mirror in which we ceaselessly look to confirm our present
identity, and to confirm it as the only one available and the only one
that matters. Given this, it is perhaps hardly surprising that intellectu-
als have increasingly accommodated to the historical shift, that the
spirit of critique seems endangered if not defunct, that deconstruction mutates into a presentist alibi, that erstwhile voices of fierce pro-
test, now increasingly steeped in a Kantian faith in 'the ontological
dignity of the positive' – one scarcely hears anything else; Artaud
redivivus would be fobbed off with CT – begin to announce the im-
minence of 'the good society'.[4]

These are some of the roots of contemporary presentism. Presentism, or rather, presentisms, for they proliferate with the bewildering rapidity of McCarthyist systems and, like McCarthy's systems, in myriad fields, as pragmatisms, soft ethicisms, social-democratic progressivisms, postmodern liberalisms and so on. Could the great early proponents of the radical movements of the sixties and after – feminism, postcolonialism, the queer revolution – have conceivably foreseen how their projects would serve at length as guarantees of present virtue? The notion that one might somehow date the onset of presentism is probably idle, but one can think of it, at least, as identifiable with the moment when postmodernism mutated into a kind of asymptotic Leibnizianism (all is, well, gradually becoming for the best in what is, well, gradually becoming the best of all possible worlds… vaguely, somehow).[5] That moment marked the major collapse of a theoretical project, and left lone if distinguished figures, prophetic voices like Badiou, Agamben, Rancière and Žižek – the recognition of their distinction being a marker of an encouraging reluctance, still discernible in the culture, quite to give up on what they express and represent – to play the role of cultural Voltaires.

But one might almost think that there were something to be said for the dialectical *Umschlag*,[6] after all, that there has been a reversal of the reversal.[7] For there have been signs in the past few years that the presentist turn is now being contested. To think beyond the anthropocentric or humanistic horizon, if only to think the absent trace of what it does not enclose, is a major manifestation of a passion for the outside. Grand theory was partly animated by a powerful anti-anthropocentric and anti-humanistic drive, of which the paradigm was perhaps Foucault's *Les mots et les choses* (1966). The past few years have witnessed the fitful emergence of a phenomenon, the appearance of new 'inhumanisms', that might seem like a radical extension of that drive, its assumption of stark new forms, its transmutation within new parameters. The 'inhumanisms' are various; neither philosophy nor aesthetics has any particular privilege relative to them; and no particular politics is immediately attached to them, save perhaps a politics of the objectionability of presentism.[8] This essay will put two of them together, both among the most encouraging productions of a generation twenty years younger than my own. My intention is partly to place them and root them in place, to provide supports for them, and to encourage them in explicating them, chiefly as sites of resistance to the prison-house of presentism. At the same time, however, I shall finally put myself at a certain distance from them, which may be partly generational, but is not just that.

The first is the philosophical movement known as speculative realism. There are signs enough by now that this movement scarcely existed at all and is already coming apart (see Bryant et al., 2011: 1–19). There was hardly likely to be a shared agenda that united a post-Badiouian speculative philosopher in the French tradition, Quentin Meillassoux, a radical and rigorous post-Nietszchean nihilist, Ray Brassier, a Deleuzean 'cyber-vitalist' (Bryant et al., 2011: 8) – if that is what he is; it is certainly not what is most important about his work – Iain Hamilton Grant, and a punk Heideggerian, Graham Harman, for more than a short length of time. But to dwell on this, or on the critiques of speculative realism – which have so far largely come from positions more conventional and familiar than the philosophers' own (see note 14) is to miss their exact significance. The significance of speculative realism, or of the philosophers who briefly grouped themselves under the speculative realist umbrella, is their passion for an outside, their recognition of the imperative need to think beyond the present in the present, to think what is exterior to it.[9]

If there is a single disposition that unites the major speculative realists, it is a decisive repudiation of the anthropocentric premise and of the presentist one which turned out to be its ineluctable *terminus ad quem*; for one might claim that presentism is always in fact a scaled-down anthropocentrism, a kind of kindergarten humanism (man may not be any longer exactly at the centre, but contemporary man certainly is – minus the patriarchal and heterosexual bias, of course). This spells the death of what the speculative realists call correlationism. Speculative realism seeks to have done with the correlationist parenthesis which it claims has dominated philosophy from Kant to postmodernism. Within the correlationist frame of reference, thought must revolve around the knowing subject, cannot 'step outside itself' to gauge the distance between what is 'in-itself' and what is 'for-us'. Exteriority thus becomes co-extensive with the human frame of reference, whether this last be perceptual, linguistic, discursive, ideological, communal or historical. By the same token, the thinker always exists in conjunction with his/her 'correlate' (as subject-object, noesis-noema, language-reference, discourse-theme, etc., etc.).

By contrast, the speculative realists dramatically foreground the radical other of correlationism itself. Here they move decisively beyond the structuralist and post-structuralist generation. The editors of *The Speculative Turn* perspicaciously note, specifically with reference to Derrida and exteriority, that what vitiates or at least limits the anti-humanism of the structuralist and post-structuralist generations is their very obsession with the linguistic mark. This inevitably means that they cannot finally countenance 'any possibility of a world independent of the human world [...] (as is neatly symbolized by Heidegger's famous crossing-out of the word "Being")' (Bryant and Harman, 2011: 4). Structuralists and post-structuralists even reverse back in the direction of humanism, leaving humans as ever 'in absolute [if more troubled] command at the center of philosophy', and surrendering the object-world to the physicists (Harman, 2009: 94). By contrast, the speculative realists refuse to take the linguistic turn. They abandon it and leave it behind them. For they take their bearings from an objectality – the word objectivity has misleading connotations – quite beyond the human-world or subject-object relation.

This is not a matter of any 'dull commonsense realism of genuine trees and billiard balls existing outside the mind' (Harman, 2009: 2). Speculative realism is a speculative and even a 'weird realism' (ibid.). Take for example the concept of the object at stake in Harman's eccentric Heideggerianism, the privilege he affords to *Zuhandenheit*, readiness to hand, as contrasted with *Vorhandenheit*, presence at hand. The object has no presence. It is rather what exists, obscurely and inexhaustibly, beyond all possible views of it and uses that may be made of it, as an invisible totality, as irreducible to representation or the *eidos* as *Dasein* itself. The *Zuhandenheit* of an object is primary, always and definitively inaccessible, its *Vorhandenheit*, its availability to employment or perception (to the correlation), secondary. Its objectal depths are precisely what free it from, hold it beyond any and all subjects and their views; in this respect, 'the real is whatever *resists* all trials of strength' (Harman, 2009: 91). However, objectal depths can never be grasped other than theoretically; the real in speculative realism is always a theoretical construction, though that does not make it the less refractory to correlationist treatment.

Harman's objectality is not Brassier's, Meillassoux's or Hamilton Grant's. Brassier's and Meillassoux's is rooted in scientific knowledge as Harman's is not, and is determined by the recognition of the 'arche-fossil', a material that bears the traces, not of prehistoric life, but of 'phenomena anterior even to the emergence of life [...] such as the radioactive isotope whose rate of decay provides an index of the decay of rock samples, or the starlight whose luminescence provides an index of the age of distant stars' (Brassier, 2010: 49). Here we glimpse an objectality 'anterior to the possibility of [human] experience' and to human representation, articulation (Brassier, 2010: 52). Indeed, it is not known to experience at all, exists only as trace, and therefore radically separates off the modes of existence of the human thing as the most minuscule of incidental parentheses. So, too, Hamilton Grant's account of Schellingian *Naturphilosophie* is concerned with 'becomings prior to mind, or nature', with nature as 'unconditioned' or 'unthinged', a nexus of forces for which 'finite human experience can provide no standard' (Hamilton Grant, 2008: 107, 109, 121) as is evident in the objectality of the 'the oldest formations of the earth' according to Schelling's geologism.[10]

The arguments for speculative realism are various. Firstly, there is the argument from the history of thought. Correlationism has run its course and its possibilities are by now exhausted. It is moribund, 'stale and fruitless', and has stripped the history of philosophy 'of its challenge' (Harman, 2009: 108), as we can see in its final winding-down from deconstruction, which had elegance and an extraordinary intellectual penetration and subtlety, to Rortean pragmatism, which had elegance and penetration, to the contemporary presentisms, which have none of them. Secondly, there is the argument from science. Kant's great Copernican revolution in philosophy is founded on and inseparable from a peremptory and curiously unmodern exclusion of scientific knowledge from the centre of thought. But this must not be allowed to continue, not least, because scientific knowledge presses on us ever more hardly. Then there are two arguments that are particularly Brassier's. Thirdly, the moral argument: correlationism cannot escape the suspicion of partiality and indeed the withering touch of a psychoanalytic anthropology, in that it flatters our persuasion of our own position and importance, for which there is no philosophical foundation. The proper business of philosophy has never been to tell us what we would like to hear. Fourthly, the philosophical argument: correlationism privileges epistemology over ontology. But the question of what, how and how adequately we know the world is not the end of all philosophical inquiry. *That* an object is is not 'a function of what it is' and cannot be reduced to it (Brassier, 2011: 62). So, too, Harman's distinction between the object and views of it refuses all conflation of the ontological with the epistemological question and reasserts the independence of the being of the object outside what is known or not known about it. Fifthly and finally, as Harman states with reference to the linguistic turn, '[i]t is not true that I have any more intimate access to language or consciousness or the conditions of speech-acts than I do to a pile of rocks. In both cases there is much that withdraws beyond my understanding' (Harman, 2009: 86). Indeed, to turn the linguistic turn otherwise is to begin to think human being as a special instance of *Zuhandenheit*.

It may be that the chief importance of the speculative realist moment will turn out to be above all the line a new generation of thinkers draws under correlationism: some of the paths they follow out of their critique – Harman's Heideggerianism, Hamilton Grant's Deleuzeanism and, if Adrian Johnston is right, Meillassoux's quasi-theological turn – bring worryingly familiar and even obvious problems along with them (Johnston, 2011). Brassier's determination to think the implications of modern science right down to the philosophical ground is likely to be a much more fertile alternative, but so far as I know he has yet to graft on to it what it surely requires, a politics and an aesthetics.[11] However, the materials for a post-correlationist aesthetics are emerging around us, the fiction of Tom McCarthy being I think a particularly notable example, above all C. But if the materialisms of the speculative realists do not coincide, nor does McCarthy coincide with them, nor am I going to try and show that.

C is inhabited by two principal forms of imaginative thought: one deals in what I shall call *formalisms*, the other in *singularities*. I use these two terms because I have not so far come up with better ones; they are to be understood as stripped of much of their previous baggage; a 'singularity' here is emphatically not Deleuzean, for example, and a formalism has nothing to do with Russian formalism. The terms come out of reading C, and have a sense that quite particularly refers to it. A formalism – the word McCarthy actually uses is 'formation', as in 'an intricate formation that suggests an irrigation system or the mechanism of a crane' (C, 14) – is a collection of units, elements or entities and their relations to which there are limits as precisely fixed as a frame, and as evidently defined as a line. There are formalisms that obviously obsess McCarthy: repetitions, of course (here the novel is faithful to the young McCarthy's ardent Derrideanism), but also mechanisms, systems, arrangements, networks, codes, processes, grids, layouts, matrices, wirings, webs, structures, geometries, patterns, diagrams, logics, mazes, zones, switchboards, nodes and relays, plans and orders, exchanges and connectivities, overlapping sequences, linking vectors and control lines, sets of principles, rules and instructions, intersections, formulae, mandalas... This points to what is effectively a formalism of the nth degree that McCarthy everywhere proposes.

The appearance of the formalism is a McCarthyist law: only in McCarthy can queues form spontaneously without there being anything to queue for (the relevant passage [C, 181] reads like a satire on the example of the queue in Sartre's *Critique of Dialectical Reason*).[12] Formalisms communicate, proliferate, cross one another, produce a palimpsest. Formalisms are not necessarily literal: a body, for example can have a 'motor' with 'engine-parts', or 'cogs and sprockets' (C, 16, 46). Nature and mechanism swap roles, their terms become interchangeable. A firefly 'puls[es] photically, in dots and dashes' (C, 254). The mobility of fleshliness can appear as a formalism: a mouth 'forms positions, holding each in place for several seconds before morphing to strike up the next one' (C, 22). Formalisms can appear in any sphere; sexual preferences, for example. They abound in the organic world, from the moth-system in the Hatching Room (C, 29) to the 'markings on a butterfly's wings' (C, 156). What matters, then, is not a literalism but a mode of thought. Formalisms are rigorously determined, but any given formalism may be susceptible to *décalage*. '[A]dditions creep into the rules, modifications' (C, 41). The young McCarthy was a great reader of the *nouveau roman*; if there is a particular *nouveau roman* to which C seems particularly close, it is Michel Butor's *La modification* (1957), a great literary practice of *décalage*. Modifications, modulations, yes – 'The shapes modulate as they repeat, their curves narrowing or widening, their lines arcing and flexing as they process across the glass' (C, 21) – but not transformations. Like that of Brassier, Harman or Sam Gillespie – not a speculative realist, but worth thinking about in connection with the speculative realists – McCarthy's atheist materialism is not Epicurean.[13] There is no version of the *clinamen* here.[14]

Formalism infects description. More strikingly, no novelist since Henry Green has been so committed to the generalized description, the pluralisation of detail: 'rowers are lowering their not-yet-charcoaled canoes from a jetty, while swimmers in trunks and bathing caps splash friends in paddle boats' (C, 60), etc. Really? Rather, if anything, surreally. There is even a kind of description as phenomenological *epoché* in C, description framed in itself and for its own sake, as in the description of the garden with which the first chapter ends (C, 4–5), familiar from Robbe-Grillet, as in the famous account of the tomato-slice in *Les Gommes*, but of which the paradigm in the *nouveau roman* would perhaps be the pages-long description of the movement of the leaves on the tree at the beginning of Claude Simon's *Histoire*. This practice may at times reach a certain level of abstraction: compare some of the passages about shapes and movements in C with the voiceover recital from Jacques Élie Faure on Velazquez in the beautiful opening sequence of Godard's *Pierrot le fou*, Godard being another love of the young McCarthy's.[15] Since McCarthy is a novelist, his formalisms also include those of language and literature, the systems of language and literature. The system of language is at issue in C from the reference to 'the F and Q firk-quirk' (C, 12) onwards.

The system of literature appears throughout C in the extent to which the literary tradition itself becomes a formalism and a storehouse of formalisms, as represented in the fact that C can batten indifferently but consciously on materials from classic novels – the pageant from Woolf's *Between the Acts* (C, 108), the Castorp/Behrens discussions in Thomas Mann's *Der Zauberberg* (C, 104–5), the upriver journey of Conrad's *Heart of Darkness* (C, 275–86). That C should make something of Spenser's 'Shepheardes Calender' (C, 19), a classically formulaic text, is indicative.

Alongside the formalisms, however, C presents a world of singularities. Of course, formalisms have their glitches. McCarthy in his cunning is aware that any given formalism may be subject to a glitch, like the uncorrected spelling errors that appear in the book itself. But a glitch is not categorically distinct from a formalism. Glitches are functions of formalism, incorporated within it, its necessary corollary. A singularity, by contrast, is a presentation of that which appears once and once only, here and now and only here and now. Singularities have traditionally been the very stuff of the novel; novels have almost always told us that they were concerned with singular worlds composed of singularities. The example *par excellence* would be Tolstoy's *War and Peace*. Tolstoy is the very antithesis of McCarthy: he is everywhere gripped by the singular, random occurrence, that which merely happened to happen. Compare his accounts of the war scenario with those in C, which heretically buck the classic accounts of the First World War battlefield (from Sassoon to Bion to Fussell) of war as chaos, disorder, mad chance as much as they do Tolstoy. In C, war is an ineluctable formalism, multiply and variously diagrammatic. Singularity in C is represented by the companionable howitzer shell that abruptly appears and travels alongside Serge's plane (C, 142), or the poor little louse that finally crawls out of the bogus spiritualist 'contraption' (C, 234). Singularity becomes derisory, comical. But singularities are also the remnants of a classic novelistic furniture, as with the cancer that 'upset[s] the delicate architecture of an ear' (C, 44), or Sophie's abrupt 'I've got a lover' (C, 73).

On the one hand, McCarthy has no interest in the staples of narrative representation: plot, characters, subjective perception, thematics, psychology, the drama of incident. The word 'narrative' appears in *C* only ironically (*C*, 250). On the other hand, the staples need to exist, if only in traces; but they need to be there so that the principle of formalism can incessantly repeat its grip. Networks are dense, people spectral. The 'whole of Egypt' may be 'one big, endlessly repeating pornographic film, like *Love's Madness* on a loop' (*C*, 271). Any notion of 'isolation' from the 'sea of transmission' – from the axiomatic priority of the formalism – is a 'fantasy' (*C*, 64). Any 'inconvenience caused to the overall machinery of empire by the interruption of the chain of orders [...] is negligible' (*C*, 250). So, too, you might think that buying an exquisite classic will mark you out in all your singularity, when in fact it just returns you to the principle of the formalism again:

> The Cook's tour [guidebook] told us we should read Herodotus, so as to come here not as tourists but as 'travellers,' 'individual explorers.' So we got that too. But now it turns out everybody else on our tour is carting round a copy of Herodotus. (*C*, 261)

The same disposition recurs at a variety of different levels of the text. 'One night', Serge 'sees a figure gliding' (*C*, 67) – a scrap of classic novelese, briefly, almost classically flung out, as in early Beckett;[16] but of course the instance is repeated, enters very shortly into a formalism again. It is not surprising – indeed, it is crucial – that, in *C*, a birth should be, not a difference within repetition, but subject to the principle of the formalism, rendered in formalist terms (*C*, 9–10). Whatever the degree of McCarthy's Derrideanism, the distinction, here, is important. Formalisms overtake anything at all: the *quodlibet* is a formalism, or subsumed within one.

The McCarthy of *C* has absolutely no interest in the correlationist problematic as it has dominated the novel, perhaps especially the English novel from Austen to McEwan. He has no interest in the concern, designated by the key quotation from Cowper in *Emma* at more or less the inaugurating 'correlationist moment', with the subject as 'Myself creating what I saw' (Austen, 1882: 295). The world exists anyway, prior to such a concern, in the anteriority of the formalism. The web is always already 'around the world' (*C*, 13). The novel is a different thing for McCarthy, as it is for his tradition, a recent European, intellectual tradition perhaps not best defined as strictly a tradition of the novel at all. McCarthy's work might be summed up as a post-correlationist, 'objectal' fiction. In the beginning was the formalism, the empty truth of the formalism. The formalism was always already there. There is no innocence before the formalism. What matters is not the content of any formalism but the formalism *as* formalism. That is why it is possible to speak of the formalism as an outside, to identify McCarthy's concern with formalisms with the inhumanism of the speculative realists, and to draw on both in the struggle with presentism. It might seem as though the eternal absorption of the singularity in McCarthy bespeaks the absolute absence of an outside. But something like the reverse is actually the case: what is at stake is rather the availability, everywhere, of the outside within the inside. This turns out to involve a thought of historicity, too; more importantly, a repudiation of presentism more or less as flat as those discoverable in speculative realism:

> The mistake most of my contemporaries make is to assume that they're the first – or, even when it's clear they're not, that *their* moment of looking is somehow definitive, standing outside of the long history of which it merely forms another chapter. (*C*, 278)

Yet, at the same time, historicity remains for McCarthy a generalized principle. Time just goes 'round and round' (*C*, 279); round and round, that is, as the eternal recurrence of the formalism.

Unlike the individual mechanism, the machine will repeat indefinitely, 'without a reason for doing so' (*C*, 285); which equally means that the outside is everywhere available within the inside; which means in turn that 'everyone's dead; the evidence alone is to be salvaged' (*C*, 278); or, as McCarthy (1999) puts it differently, in the *First Manifesto* of the Necronautical Society, 'death is a type of space, which we intend to map, enter, colonise and, eventually, inhabit'. In neither McCarthy nor the speculative realists is there any question of a return to the space of critique, nor (with the possible exception of Hamilton Grant) of any vitalism: there is no concept of Deleuzean becoming, the élan vital or the will to power or life in McCarthy, Meillassoux,

Brassier or Harman. In C, the gentle satire on the concept of 'a whole light and vibrant field of radiant transformations' in the spiritualism sequence is evidence enough of that in McCarthy's case (C, 235). Particular formalisms have only a transient and finite existence, they too die. The machine repeats indefinitely, but the individual mechanism is as mortal as the operator:

> An array of instruments greets them, strewn across shelves and benches, monometric flame and typesetting machines, phonautographs, rheotomes, old hotel annunciators and telegraph station switches – most of them opened, disgorged, their inner wiring spilling tangled, trailing from one level to another. (C, 35)

McCarthy is not a writer much given to sadness. In a novel where people also die, this is as sad as it gets. But then, in themselves, formalisms are inseparable from the work of death. McCarthy's thought is not a vitalism but a mortalism. According to Brassier, the speculative realist to whom McCarthy's work is closest, the Lyotard of *The Inhuman* asserts that the certain occurrence in the future of the death of the sun vitiates the 'ontological temporality' according to which philosophy has always constituted itself relative to a future, understanding that solar death is something that has *'already happened'*, is even 'the aboriginal trauma driving the history of human life'; which means that '[e]*verything is dead already*' (Brassier, 2010: 223). McCarthy shares Brassier's conviction of 'an anterior posteriority proper to physical death which seizes organic temporality but cannot be seized by it'. 'We are all necronauts, always, already', says the Necronaut Manifesto (McCarthy, 1999). Everything is dead already in C, in that formalism always precedes singularity, as, according to that great founding text for any mortalism, important for Brassier, too, Freud's *Beyond the Pleasure Principle*, through its growing intimacy with the truth of the formalisms, animate human singularity incessantly returns to the inanimate domain which had always already captured it from the start. The corresponding element in the domain of affect in C is Nabokovian anaesthesia (Nabokov being another enthusiasm of the young McCarthy's).

The mortalisms however are not (or not quite) the whole tale. Most of the most prominent criticisms of speculative realism so far have been unconvincing and provide no credible alternative thought. A return to Hegel, Marx, dialectical materialism? Althusser, no less?[17] If one is going to think seriously at the current time, one either has the mortalisms, or one struggles to maintain an event-based philosophy, whilst acknowledging the force of the mortalisms. McCarthy has no interest in the oblique line which abruptly transects the circle, the rare or occasional or sporadic event which is not a function of eternal recurrence, as in Badiou – Badiou (2001: 35) himself being correspondingly dismissive of a vision of the world in which (to repeat) the only thing that can really happen to one is death. It is thus no surprise that McCarthy's first novel should know nothing save the remainder, that *Remainder* should be the title of the whole text; the remainder being a world without events.[18] Badiou has been perhaps the only really significant critic of speculative realism so far. He says precisely of it what I have just said of McCarthy: its limit is that it contains no theory of the event, though the event is not just always possible, but logically possible. He is right about this: for Brassier, there are no events; for Meillassoux, all that can be said is that no law of necessity debars events. When Badiou criticizes the speculative realists for going no further than a 'detachment from the present', however, he seems to me to underrate exactly the power and value of their project. The speculative realists do not offer a 'stoicism' in the face of the present (Badiou, 2011a: 4). They think the present from its outside and think the outside within the present – as does McCarthy. That in itself is a significant endeavour at the current time, and is what McCarthy (1999) means when he writes of the necronautical task (admittedly reversing the vector) as 'bring[ing] death out into the world'.

Nonetheless: the manifesto of the necronautical society declares that the 'processes and avatars' of death are 'active' in formalisms, like radio, television, the internet (McCarthy, 1999). Up to this point, I subscribe to the necronauts and am McCarthy's confederate. Beyond it, I part company with him, as Badiou does with the speculative realists. One way of thinking of both them and McCarthy is as the intellectual vanguard of a disabused generation which, at its best, starkly acknowledges the – at the current time, seemingly definitive – collapse of politics and austerely refuses to think beyond it. At the same time, however, it rightly refuses to take refuge from the collapse in implausible and finally complicit contemporary ethics, whilst also turning in superb indifference from contemporary Panglossianisms and ostrich theologies. It prefers instead to institute a kind of minimalist play or trace of disparity at the edge of what, with Walter Benjamin in mind, Françoise Proust calls satanic modernity (Proust, 1994), if only *via* a mortalism which declares that modernity dead from the start. The project is serious and important. Finally: one way of putting my difference with McCarthy and the speculative realists alike is that, while the anthropocentric case has yet to be successfully made, there can be no absolute certainty that human beings will not at some point make it; which means of course that they would at that point have produced the hitherto inexistent centre itself. (This, I think, is the argument that Meillassoux should have put forward on the basis of his brilliant critique of correlationism, rather than his case for the possible future existence of a god in a thus far godless world).[19] To make the centre would also be to decree an end to satanic modernity, which is not a law of nature, 'bringing it to a halt, *now*', in Proust's (1994: 35) phrase. The humanist position in its largest scope – certainly not that of humanists thus far – is not categorically deniable. It is only deniable on the Humean basis, experience, the basis of what we have so far known the human thing to be, save when it is traversed by rare events. We might finally quote Beckett's endgamers (if also misrepresenting their concern), in tribute to a thought of the good. There was once something quite inadequately called man. But alas, in Hamm's words, as McCarthy suggests, 'Le salaud, il n'existe pas!', 'The bastard! He doesn't exist!'. Or rather, as Clov responds, 'Pas encore', 'Not yet' (Beckett, 1957: 74).

Notes

1 All references to 'the young McCarthy's' interests are to a series of conversations I had with him between 2002 and around 2007, in which almost all the literary names with which I connect him here arose.

2 For one account of the thought of the outside in Blanchot, Foucault and Deleuze, see Pebart (2001).

3 See for example some of the arguments in Rorty (1989, 1991).

4 On the Kantian concept of 'the ontological dignity of the positive', see Jambet (2002: 8). For the argument that it is presently a cultural dominant, see Gibson (2011: 278–80).

5 The period beginning at this 'moment' may already be passing; indeed, it may have died in 2008. If this is the case, however, it is, strangely, more obvious at the level of popular sensibility than academic discourse. Indeed, the academy may turn out to be one of the last refuges of contemporary Panglosses.

6 In Marx, the negation of the negation, the sudden reversal or turnaround in which a given barrier, identity or law of equivalence is negated and which is rife with political possibilities. See for example Marx (1993: 421).

7 The term 'reversal of the reversal' appeared in the original paper, and encouraged one or two of the audience to ask me why I wanted to 'go back'. I can see now that I did indeed imply that we were witnessing a 'return' to the inhumanisms. This was misleading, for reasons that should be clear here. In general, I take models of progress or regression to be by now irrelevant, and exactly coincide here with Tom McCarthy, who announced his own indifference to progressivisms at the conference. Any significant models that might replace progressive/regressive ones are structured around principles of the formalism and/or the event in my sense here, as for example in Benjamin. See also Gibson (2011).

8 The new inhumanisms are a significant occasion as, say, the Arab Spring, sympathetic though one might be, is not as yet (and may well not be). I see no extant or emergent politics anywhere at the present time that would qualify as such an occasion or promise one. Contrast however Badiou (2011a).

9 If any of the speculative realists concedes on this, it is Harman, chiefly in his populist style and points of reference, which can make him more pleasurable to read, but also tend to compromise the more radical aspects of his thought.

10 In Hamilton Grant's evocation of it (see Hamilton Grant, 2008: 204; Schelling, 1946: 11).

11 No politics seems emergent in *Nihil Unbound* – probably the most important 'speculative realist' text to date – nor should one necessarily be. But the fact seems strangely at odds with the major promise Brassier appears to think his 'new nihilism' offers. Such small flashes of a politics as one glimpses in his work are, disappointingly, banally postmodern-academic. He shows no interest in the aesthetic realm at all. In this respect, it may be revealing that, at moments, he appears hostile to expressive uses of language one might associate with the aesthetic domain.

12 See Sartre (2004: 256–70).

13 See Gillespie (2008).

14 The clinamen is the unpredictable event of the swerve of atoms Lucretius introduced into Epicurean theory in order to defend it.

15 The reading is not in fact from Faure's book on Velazquez, from but the pages devoted to the Spanish painter in the third volume of his *Histoire de l'art* (1914).

16 See for example the neo-Tolstoyan or neo-Jamesian conclusion to Chapter 8 of *Murphy*.

17 I am thinking particularly of the criticisms that come out of a second-wave, post-Althusserian, academic or 'theoreticist' Marxism which confidently lays claim to superior materialist credentials. See for example Toscano (2011), Johnston (2011). For a critique of (post-)Althusserian 'theoreticism', see Jambet (1991); cf. also Judith Balso's superb critique, on the basis, not least, of admirable, actual, inconspicuous political work in Paris over several decades, of the acutely problematic first Althusserian turn as inaugurating the conflation of theoretical with political work (Balso, 2010); and Rancière's, who indicts it as involving an excessive valuation of theoretical revolution (see Rancière, 1974: 239). Both critiques are exactly appropriate to second-wave theoreticism. Its self-evident limitation is its inability satisfactorily either to explain or to transcend the actual failure of classical Marxist historical and dialectical materialism as an explanatory system, patent from 1980 if not well before. Thereafter Marxism retreated into the academy, especially the American academy, which made it, however clever, increasingly open to question *as a materialism*. In order to convince as materialists, Toscano and above all Johnston and other North American Marxists would have to indicate the seriously visible, major political constituency to which they belong, on behalf of which they are working and on whose political future they can plausibly wager, as Marx did on the proletariat, if mistakenly. Otherwise

it is easy enough to turn the charge of pure mirage which they level at the materialism of the speculative realists on their own. Does not the significance of their own materialism have to do only with the political subject's (understandable) need for psychic reassurance? The necessary corrective to a delusional or, perhaps better, an academic-fantasy politics that does not sacrifice everything that that politics values is of course the lesson of the Frankfurt School.

18 For this concept and specific use of the term, see Gibson (2011: passim.).

19 For which see for example Meillassoux (2006b).

Works Cited

Austen, Jane (1882) *Emma*. London: Richard Bentley & Sons.

Badiou, Alain (2001) *Ethics: An Essay on the Understanding of Evil*, trans. Peter Hallward. London: Verso.

Badiou, Alain (2011a) *Circonstances, 6: Le réveil de l'histoire*. Paris: Lignes.

Balso, Judith (2010) 'To Present Oneself to the Present: Communism: A Possible Hypothesis for Philosophy, An Impossible Name for Politics?', in Slavoj Žižek and Costas Douzinas (eds) *The Idea of Communism*. London: Verso.

Baudrillard, Jean (1998), 'Simulacra and Simulation', *Selected Writings*, ed. Mark Poster, pp. 166–84. Stanford, CA: Stanford University Press.

Beckett, Samuel (1963) *Murphy*. London: John Calder.

Beckett, Samuel (1957) *Fin de Partie*. Paris: Minuit.

Brassier, Ray (2010) *Nihil Unbound: Enlightenment and Extinction*. London: Palgrave Macmillan.

Brassier, Ray (2011) 'Concepts and Objects', in Levi Bryant, Nick Srnicek and Graham Harman (eds) (2011) *The Speculative Turn: Continental Materialism and Realism*, pp. 47–65. Melbourne: re.press.

Bryant, Levi, Nick Srnicek, and Graham Harman (eds) (2011) *The Speculative Turn: Continental Materialism and Realism*. Melbourne: re.press.

Butor, Michel (1995) *La modification*. Paris: Gallimard.

Faure, Jacques Élie (1914) *Histoire de l'art, Vol. 3: L'art renaissant*. Paris: H. Floury.

Gibson, Andrew (2011) *Intermittency: The Concept of Historical Reason in Recent French Philosophy*. Edinburgh: Edinburgh University Press.

Gillespie, Sam (2008) *The Mathematics of Novelty: Badiou's Minimalist Metaphysics*. Melbourne: re.press.

Hamilton Grant, Iain (2008) *Philosophies of Nature After Schelling*. London: Continuum.

Harman, Graham (2009) *Towards a Speculative Realism.* Winchester: Zero.

Jambet, Christian (1991) 'Pour Louis Althusser', *Revue des deux mondes*: 103–10.

Jambet, Christian (2002) 'Preface', in Élodie Mailliet, *Kant entre désespoir et espérance.* Paris: Fayard.

Johnston, Adrian, 'Hume's Revenge: À Dieu, Meillassoux?', in Bryant et al. (eds.), pp. 92–113.

McCarthy, Tom (1999) 'INS Founding Manifesto', URL (consulted 18 January 2015): http://www.necronauts.org/manifesto1.htm

Marx, Karl (1993) *Grundrisse*, trans. with a foreword by Martin Nicolaus. London: Penguin.

Meillassoux, Quentin (2006a) *Après la finitude: Essai sur la nécessité de la contingence.* Paris: Seuil.

Meillassoux, Quentin (2006b) 'Deuil à venir, dieu à venir', *Critique* 704 & 705: 105–15.

Pebart, Peter Pál (2001) 'The Thought of the Outside, The Outside of Thought', *Angelaki* 5(5): 201–9.

Proust, Françoise (1994) *L'Histoire à contretemps: Le Temps historique chez Walter Benjamin.* Paris: Cerf.

Rancière, Jacques (1974) *La Leçon d'Althusser.* Paris: Gallimard.

Robbe-Grillet, Alain (1953) *Les gommes.* Paris : Minuit.

Rorty, Richard (1989) *Contingency, Irony and Solidarity.* Cambridge: Cambridge University Press.

Rorty, Richard (1991) *Philosophical Papers, Vol. 1: Objectivity, Relativism, and Truth.* Cambridge: Cambridge University Press.

Sartre, Jean-Paul (2004) *Critique of Dialectical Reason*, Vol I, *Theory of Practical Ensembles*, ed. by Jonathan Rée, trans. by Alan Sheridan-Smith. London: Verso.

Schelling, Friedrich (1946) *Die Weltalter: Fragmente, in den Urfassungen von 1811 und 1813*, ed. by Manfred Schröter. Munich: Beck.

Simon, Claude (1967) *L'histoire.* Paris: Minuit.

Toscano, Alberto (2011), 'Against Speculation, or a Critique of the Critique of the Critique: A Remark on Quentin Meillassoux's *After Finitude* (After Colletti)', in Levi Bryant, Nick Srnicek and Graham Harman (eds) (2011) *The Speculative Turn: Continental Materialism and Realism*, pp. 84–91. Melbourne: re.press.

Notes on Contributors

Mark Blacklock is Post-Doctoral Researcher on a collaborative project between Birkbeck College and The Arthur C. Clarke Award for Science Fiction Literature. He is the author of a novel, *I'm Jack* (Granta, 2015), while his monograph *The Emergence of the Fourth Dimension: Higher Spatial Thinking in the Fin-de-Siecle* will be appearing with Oxford University Press.

Arne De Boever teaches American Studies in the School of Critical Studies at the California Institute of the Arts, where he also directs the MA Aesthetics and Politics program. He is the author of *States of Exception in the Contemporary Novel* (2012) and *Narrative Care* (2013) and editor of *Gilbert Simondon: Being and Technology* (2012) and *The Psychopathologies of Cognitive Capitalism: Vol. 1* (2013). He also edits *Parrhesia: A Journal of Critical Philosophy* and the critical theory/philosophy section of the *Los Angeles Review of Books*.

Henderson Downing is researching psychogeography in literature and urbanism at Birkbeck, University of London. He is a visiting lecturer in the Department of Culture, Writing, and Performance at London South Bank University. He has taught at the Architectural Association School of Architecture and is a regular contributor to *AA Files*.

Dennis Duncan is a British Academy Postdoctoral Fellow at the Bodleian Centre for the Study of the Book, and a Junior Research Fellow at Jesus College, Oxford, where he is working on a history of the book index. He has published work on Italo Calvino, novels with indexes, and nuclear waste disposal, as well as a book-length translation of the Surrealist little magazine *Le Grand Jeu* (Atlas, 2015), along with other translations from French and Danish. He writes regularly on book history and the continental avant-garde for the *Times Literary Supplement* and the *London Review of Books* blog.

Martin Paul Eve is Professor of Literature, Technology and Publishing at Birkbeck, University of London. He specialises in post-War American fiction and primarily the works of Thomas Pynchon, Don DeLillo and David Foster Wallace, the former of whom he has written about in *Pynchon and Philosophy: Wittgenstein, Foucault and Adorno* (Palgrave Macmillan, 2014). In addition to his work on literature, Martin is well-known for his work on scholarly communication and open access and is the author of *Open Access and the Humanities: Contexts, Controversies and the Future* (Cambridge University Press, 2014).

Andrew Gibson is former Research Professor of Modern Literature and Theory at Royal Holloway College, University of London, now teaching part-time in the department. He is a former Carole and Gordon Segal Professor of Irish Literature at Northwestern University, Chicago, a member of the Conseil scientifique and the Comité de sélection at the Collège international de philosophie in Paris, and a permanent Associate Member of the International Beckett Foundation at the University of Reading. He has written, edited and co-edited more than twenty books. Among the most recent are: *Joyce's Revenge: History, Politics and Aesthetics in 'Ulysses'* (2002, 2005); *James Joyce: A Critical Life* (2006); *Badiou and Beckett: The Pathos of Intermittency* (2006); *Samuel Beckett: A Critical Life* (2010); *Intermittency: The Concept of Historical Reason in Contemporary French Philosophy* (2012); and *The Strong Spirit: History, Politics and Aesthetics in the Writings of James Joyce 1898-1915* (2013). His *Misanthropy: The Critique of Humanity* will be published by Bloomsbury in 2017. He is currently working on *Modernity and the Political Fix*, to appear from Bloomsbury in their *Political Theologies* series.

Sebastian Groes is a Senior Lecture in English Literature at the University of Roehampton. He is the Principal Investigator of the Memory Network, an AHRC and Wellcome Trust-funded Research Network bringing scientists, arts and humanities scholars, writers and artists together to think critically and creatively about memory in the twenty-first century. He is also Series Co-Editor of *Contemporary Critical Perspectives* (Bloomsbury), and wrote *The Making of London* (Palgrave, 2011), and *British Fiction in the Sixties* (Bloomsbury, 2015). In addition, he has edited volumes on Ian McEwan, Julian Barnes and two volumes on Kazuo Ishiguro's work: *Kazuo Ishiguro: Contemporary Critical Perspectives* (Bloomsbury, 2010) and *Kazuo Ishiguro: Critical Visions of the Novels* (Palgrave, 2011).

Nick Lavery is a PhD student in English Literature at the University of Roehampton. His thesis looks at representations of consciousness in the contemporary novel, with a focus on the extended mind and the influence of modernism. He has given papers on Tom McCarthy, Will Self, Zadie Smith and the neuro-novel.

Gill Partington is a Research Fellow at Birkbeck, University of London, working on theories of media, the history of reading and textual materiality. Her publications include *Book Destruction from the Medieval to the Contemporary* (Palgrave Macmillan, 2014) and a special edition of *Critical Quarterly* on 'Missing Texts' (2013). She is a regular contributor to the *London Review of Books*, and is currently completing a monograph on the misreading of fiction as fact.

Sam Slote is Associate Professor in the School of English at Trinity College Dublin and is the Co-Director of the Samuel Beckett Summer School. His most recent book is *Joyce's Nietzschean Ethics* (Palgrave, 2013). In addition to Joyce and Beckett, he has written on Virginia Woolf, Vladimir Nabokov, Raymond Queneau, Dante, Mallarmé and Elvis.

Milly Weaver is a doctoral candidate at the University of Warwick. The Wolfson Foundation funds her doctoral research. Her dissertation examines the visual potential of the contemporary novel, with an emphasis on British fiction. She has recently been working on mediality in the work of Ali Smith and Tom McCarthy.

INDEX

Index